Israel's Targeted Killing Policy

Boaz Ganor · Liram Koblentz-Stenzler

Israel's Targeted Killing Policy

Moral, Ethical & Operational Dilemmas

Boaz Ganor
International Institute for
Counter-Terrorism (ICT)
Reichman University
Herzliya, Israel

Liram Koblentz-Stenzler
International Institute for
Counter-Terrorism (ICT)
Reichman University
Herzliya, Israel

ISBN 978-3-031-13673-3   ISBN 978-3-031-13674-0   (eBook)
https://doi.org/10.1007/978-3-031-13674-0

© The Editor(s) (if applicable) and The Author(s), under exclusive license to Springer Nature Switzerland AG 2022
This work is subject to copyright. All rights are solely and exclusively licensed by the Publisher, whether the whole or part of the material is concerned, specifically the rights of translation, reprinting, reuse of illustrations, recitation, broadcasting, reproduction on microfilms or in any other physical way, and transmission or information storage and retrieval, electronic adaptation, computer software, or by similar or dissimilar methodology now known or hereafter developed.
The use of general descriptive names, registered names, trademarks, service marks, etc. in this publication does not imply, even in the absence of a specific statement, that such names are exempt from the relevant protective laws and regulations and therefore free for general use.
The publisher, the authors, and the editors are safe to assume that the advice and information in this book are believed to be true and accurate at the date of publication. Neither the publisher nor the authors or the editors give a warranty, expressed or implied, with respect to the material contained herein or for any errors or omissions that may have been made. The publisher remains neutral with regard to jurisdictional claims in published maps and institutional affiliations.

This Palgrave Macmillan imprint is published by the registered company Springer Nature Switzerland AG
The registered company address is: Gewerbestrasse 11, 6330 Cham, Switzerland

Acknowledgments

This book is dedicated to our families, for their patience and their support throughout the long period of preparations for the completion of this manuscript. For Boaz, to my dear wife and partner Amit Ganor, to my children Lee, Tom, and Dan, and to my grandchild Omer. Also to my dear parents of blessed memory, Shulamit and David Ganor, for inspiring me and nurturing my passion for research. For Liram, to my beloved husband Alex, who supported and assisted me in every way possible to allow me to devote myself to my writing. And to my children Harel, Ori, Ofek, and Lior, who encouraged and supported me, showed interest in the writing process, and didn't complain about having less "mother time" during the writing of this book. I also want to thank my parents, Efi and Dalia Stenzler, for helping me free up time to complete the book, and especially for instilling in me from a young age a love of reading, writing, and thorough research. I would like to thank my partner in the writing of this book, Prof. Boaz Ganor, for the day-to-day work of the International Institute for Counter-Terrorism (ICT) under your leadership. Being your co-author has been a source of learning and empowerment for me.

We are very grateful to Prof. Uriel Reichman, founding president and chairman of the Board of Directors of Reichman University, for giving us an academic home, for inspiring us through his academic vision, and for serving as a mentor to us and to many other faculty members and students

vi ACKNOWLEDGMENTS

at Reichman University. We are also thankful to Prof. Rafi Melnick, president of Reichman University, and to Prof. Assaf Moghadam, dean of the Lauder School of Government, Diplomacy & Strategy.

We are indebted to our wonderful colleagues at the International Institute for Counter-Terrorism (ICT) at Reichman University – particularly Shabtai Shavit, the chairman of our Board of Directors, and our deputy directors Dr. Eitan Azani and Stevie Weinberg. And special thanks to Ariel Rodal-Spieler who translated this book with exceptional professionalism and skill. All errors and mistakes are of course our own.

We are also grateful for the colleagues and friends who have inspired us over the years, and to the decision-makers and experts who have been interviewed for this book. They are (in alphabetical order): Former Chief Military Advocate General of the IDF Maj. Gen. (Res.) Sharon Afek, Former President of Israel's Supreme Court Prof. Aharon Barak, Former Head of the Jerusalem and West Bank Sector of the Shin Bet, Arik (Harris) Barbing, Former Deputy State Attorney Devorah Chen, Former Mossad Director Yossi Cohen, Former ISA Director and Former Minister Avi Dichter, Former IDF Chief of Staff Lt. Gen (Res) Gadi Eisenkot, Former IDF Intelligence Commander of the Southern District Col. (Res.) Avi Eliyahu, Former Mossad Deputy Director Naftali Granot, Former IDF Chief of Staff Lt. Gen. (Res.) Dan Halutz, Former senior ISA official Shalom Ben Hanan, Former 91st Division Commander of the IDF Brig. Gen. (Res.) Gal Hirsch, military ethics expert and author of the IDF Code of Ethics Prof. Asa Kasher, Former Prime Minister's Special Envoy for MIA and KIA Col. (Res.) Lior Lotan, Former Minister Dan Meridor, Former Defense Minister and IDF Chief of Staff Lt. Gen. (Res.) Shaul Mofaz, Former senior ISA official Oz Noy, Former Director of Israel's Counter-Terrorism Bureau Brig. Gen. (Res.) Nitzan Nuriel, Former Prime Minister Ehud Olmert, Former Head of the IDF International Law Department Col. (Res.) Adv. Daniel Reisner, Former Mossad Director Shabtai Shavit, Former Head of the Mossad's Intelligence Directorate Brig. Gen. (Res.) Dr. Amnon Sofrin, Former Defense Minister and Former IDF Chief of Staff Lt. Gen. (Res.) Moshe (Bogie) Ya'alon.

Finally, we would like to express our thanks, for their friendship and advice throughout the years, to Amb. Ronald Lauder, Daniel and Igal Jusidman, and Daphna Cramer and Gerry, who is dearly missed.

CONTENTS

1	**Introduction**	1
	References	12
2	**A Historical Survey of Israeli Targeted Killings**	13
	The Consolidation of the Method of Targeted Killings in Israeli Counter-Terrorism Strategy (1948–1972)	16
	Targeted Killings as a Means of Retaliation and Deterrence Following the Attack on the Israeli Athletes in the Munich Olympics (1972–1992)	17
	Targeted Killings as a Means of Preventing Suicide Bombings Against the Background of the Peace Process Between Israel and the PLO (1993–1999)	23
	The Use of Targeted Killings Following the Collapse of the Peace Process and the Events of the Al-Aqsa Intifada (the Second Intifada) (2000–2007)	32
	References	38
3	**Targeted Killings in Israel's Counter-Terrorism Strategy: Decision-Making Processes and the Intelligence Factor**	43
	The Importance of Targeted Killing as a Pillar of Israel's Counter-Terrorism Strategy	43
	The Decision-Making Process in the Execution of Targeted Killings	52

vii

viii CONTENTS

The Intelligence Component of the Targeted Killing
Operations 66
The "Operational Opportunity" Axis 74
Case Study—Salah Shehadeh 76
Case Study—Mohammed Deif 77
Case Study—Ali Hassan Salameh 79
References 81

4 The Legitimacy of Targeted Killings: A Death Penalty Under the Guise of Counter-Terrorism? 85
The Normative Foundation—The Right to Life 87
The Right to a Fair Trial 88
Death Penalty Without Trial? 91
Targeted Killing as a Means of Satisfying Public Opinion 101
Case Study—Ghassan Kanafani 108
References 109

5 The Principle of Distinction in Targeted Killing—Who Do You Target? 113
The Target Profile Axis 122
The Operational Need Model—Assessing the Need
for Targeted Killings 139
Case Study: The Targeted Killing of a Political
Leader—Sheikh Ahmed Yassin 140
References 142

6 The Principle of Proportionality: Are Targeted Killings Really Targeted? 145
Definition of the Principle of Proportionality 146
Assessing Military Effectiveness Versus Harm to Uninvolved
Civilians 153
The Proportionality Equation in Targeted Killings 159
Israeli Attempts to Minimize Collateral Damage 161
Case Study: Salah Shehadeh (2002) 165
Intelligence Information 166
The Weapon Selected for the Purpose of the Targeted Killing 168
The Result of the Operation 169
References 170

CONTENTS   ix

7	**The Boomerang Effect in Targeted Killings—Are Targeted Killings Effective?**	175
	Tactical Boomerang Effect—Revenge Attacks	176
	Operational Boomerang Effect—military and/or Diplomatic Imbroglios	183
	Strategic Boomerang Effect—long-Term Consequences	187
	Case Study of a Targeted Killing with an Operative Boomerang effect—the Attempt on Khaled Mashal	192
	References	195
8	**A Decision-Making Model for Targeted Killing Operations**	199
	Normative Considerations and Implications	199
	Assessing the Effectiveness of Targeted Killings	209
9	**Summary and Conclusions**	215
	Reference	221
	Appendices	223
	Index	225

LIST OF FIGURES

Fig. 3.1	Operational opportunity	75
Fig. 5.1	The target profile axis	123
Fig. 5.2	The target profile axis and the operational opportunity axis	139
Fig. 8.1	Targeted killing purposes index	200
Fig. 8.2	Identity of the target index	202
Fig. 8.3	Proportionality index	204
Fig. 8.4	Alternative action index	205
Fig. 8.5	Location of the operation index	206
Fig. 8.6	Intelligence operational opportunity index	207
Fig. 8.7	Inteligence realiability index	208
Fig. 8.8	Tacrical boomerang index	209
Fig. 8.9	Operational boomerang index	210
Fig. 8.10	Strategic boomerang index	211
Fig. 8.11	Disruption of the organization's activity index	211
Fig. 8.12	Deterrence index	212
Fig. 8.13	Morale—Psychological index	212
Fig. 8.14	Strategic impact index	213
Fig. 8.15	Targeted killing decision making tool model	214

CHAPTER 1

Introduction

The phenomenon of terrorism is a function of two variables—motivation to carry out attacks, and the capability to do so (Ganor, 2005). The fight against terrorism can be focused on one of these two variables; the underlying motives of terrorism can be dealt with through CVE (Countering Violent Extremism) efforts, and the capabilities of terrorist organizations and their operatives can be tackled by means of counterterrorism. Hence, the campaign against the phenomenon of terrorism is one that is long, complex, and full of contradictions. For example, the thwarting of terrorist attacks, as part of counter-terrorism efforts, requires a combination of offensive, defensive, deterrent, legal, punitive, and other measures, while CVE efforts entail the building of trust with the population producing the terrorist operatives, with the help of political, diplomatic, societal, and community processes. An effective fight against terrorism warrants parallel, integrated and synergetic activity between these two efforts; however, the actions taken to thwart terrorism and those taken to prevent it are often in conflict with each other (see, for

---

The introduction to this book and the model proposed at the end are based on Boaz Ganor. (2021). Targeted Killings: Ethical & Operational Dilemmas. *Terrorism and Political Violence*, 33:2, 353-366. https://www.tandfonline.com/doi/abs/10.1080/09546553.2021.1880234

© The Author(s), under exclusive license to Springer Nature Switzerland AG 2022
B. Ganor and L. Koblentz-Stenzler, *Israel's Targeted Killing Policy*, https://doi.org/10.1007/978-3-031-13674-0_1

example, the "boomerang effect," which occurs when counter-terrorism measures succeed in preventing certain attacks but increase motivation to carry out further attacks) (Ibid.).

The difficulty in combatting terrorism effectively stems from, inter alia, a lack of consensus on basic definitions and substantive professional disputes regarding the nature of the phenomenon and how to deal with it. The issues range from the question of how to define terrorism as a phenomenon, to classifying the subcategories of domestic and international terrorism and the various challenges arising from the ways in which they are confronted, to disagreement over who should be responsible for the campaign against terrorism—is terrorism a criminal act that should be countered through law enforcement, or is it an act of war that requires a military response? On top of all of this, there is the constant tension between the aspiration to achieve maximum effectiveness in counter-terrorism activities and the desire to minimize any possible harm to the country's liberal values in the context of these actions, hereinafter "the democratic dilemma in the war on terror" (Ibid.). Moreover, with regard to the effectiveness of counter-terrorism, there is not even a consensus among scholars of terrorism about which criteria to employ in order to assess and measure the effectiveness of various methods.

All of these fundamental dilemmas, and many more, are reflected in the examination of the operational, moral, and ethical aspects of targeted killings in the framework of the war on terror; they will be explored in this book against the backdrop of the case of Israel and the experience it has acquired.

Like many countries that have contended with the phenomenon of terrorism and sometimes used targeted killings as part of their arsenal of offensive actions, the State of Israel, which has had to cope with various types of large-scale terrorism since its establishment in 1948,[1] has carried out intensive offensive actions against terrorist organizations during various periods, including a number of targeted killings of operatives and leaders of the terrorist organizations who attacked it.[2] These

---

[1] Terrorist attacks were also carried out against the Jewish community in the Land of Israel, even before the establishment of the state.

[2] According to B'Tselem, Israel carried out 118 targeted killings in the Gaza Strip since its disengagement from Gaza in the summer of 2005 and until 2019. According to Asaf and Noam Zussman, between 2000 and 2004 (during the al-Aqsa Intifada), Israel made 159 targeted killing attempts against Palestinian terrorist organizations. According

personal offensive operations targeted the heads and senior commanders of active Palestinian and Shiite terrorist organizations, the organizers and dispatchers of the attacks, and the perpetrators themselves. The operations were carried out in various geographical areas, including the Gaza Strip (controlled by Hamas), Judea and Samaria (partly controlled by the Palestinian Authority), in the territory of the Arab countries bordering Israel, and in more remote countries with which Israel has no common border. Israel employed a variety of measures in these operations, such as firing missiles from the air, ground operations, ambushes, and explosive devices, as well as covert intelligence operations using undercover agents (Israeli soldiers disguised as Arabs and Mossad agents) and Palestinian collaborators. In a few cases, Israel has taken responsibility for carrying out targeted killings, and in many other cases it has chosen to maintain ambiguity regarding the identity of the operatives behind the operation.

The targeted killings carried out by Israel over the years raise many questions and dilemmas that can be divided into moral-ethical issues and dilemmas concerning the degree of the action's effectiveness. These issues will be discussed in detail throughout the chapters of this book.

The moral arguments against the use of this measure can be gleaned from the petition filed in the Israeli Supreme Court by Israeli human rights organizations against the Israeli government in 2002, which alleged that the "targeted killings policy is totally illegal and contradictory to international law, Israeli law, and basic principles of human morality. It violates the human rights recognized in Israeli and international law—both the rights of those targeted, and the rights of innocent passersby caught in the targeted killing zone" (HCJ 769/02, 2006).

This discussion in the Supreme Court and the ruling that followed shaped Israel's position on the subject of targeted killings within the framework of its counter-terrorism policy, and became a guideline for the execution of these operations over the years. In addition to responding to the petitioners' claims, the Supreme Court judges' ruling established a legal-moral basis for targeted killings in general, and for those carried out by the State of Israel in particular.

---

to them, the most frequently used method, employed in 47% of the cases, was shooting (light arms); in 34% of the cases missiles were fired from attack helicopters; and in 14% of the cases various explosive devices were used. Roughly 50% of the attempts were targeted at Hamas members, 31% at Fatah members, and 17% at Islamic Jihad members.

At the foundation of the ruling lay the question of whether targeted killings are a preventive military measure, or a punitive measure designed to respond to criminal activity. According to the petitioners, the legal system applicable to the armed conflict between Israel and the terrorist organizations is not the laws of war, but rather criminal law, laws of policing, and law enforcement. Their position was that "Since the State cannot claim self-defense against its own population, nor can it claim self-defense against persons under the occupation of its army." Thus, they argued, "suspects are not to be killed without due process, or without arrest or trial. The targeted killings violate the basic right to life, and no defense or justification is to be found for that violation." The petitioners cited the practice of other countries fighting terrorism, maintaining that it "unequivocally indicates international custom, according to which members of terrorist organizations are treated as criminals, and the penal law, supplemented at times with special additional emergency powers, is the law which controls the ways in which the struggle against terrorism is conducted" (Ibid.).

The Supreme Court ruled that the struggle between Israel and the Palestinian terrorist organizations is an armed conflict, and because of this, it is the laws of war that are applicable, and not Israeli criminal law. According to the judges:

> Our starting point is that the law that applies to the armed conflict between Israel and the terrorist organizations in the area is the international law dealing with armed conflicts...the fact that the terrorist organizations and their members do not act in the name of a state does not turn the struggle against them into a purely internal state conflict. Indeed, in today's reality, a terrorist organization is likely to have considerable military capabilities. At times they have military capabilities that exceed those of states. Confrontation with those dangers cannot be restricted within the state and its penal law. (Ibid.)

The petitioners also contended that "The targeted persons are not granted an opportunity to prove their innocence. The entire targeted killings policy operates in a secret world in which the public eye does not see the dossier of evidence on the basis of which the targets are determined. There is no judicial review: not before, nor after the targeted killing," despite the fact that there is sometimes a possibility that a target will be misidentified (Ibid.).

However, because targeted killings are not a punitive criminal measure, but essentially a military action subject to the laws of war, there is not a requirement for a judicial review prior to the carrying out of the operation.

Another argument made by the petitioners was that the policy of targeted killings violates the rules of international humanitarian law, which recognizes only two statuses of people—combatants and civilians: "Combatants are legitimate targets, but they also enjoy the rights granted in international law to combatants, including immunity from trial and the right to the status of prisoner of war. Civilians enjoy the protections and rights granted in international law to civilians during war. Inter alia, they are not a legitimate target for attack" (Ibid.) According to them, "Any person who is not a combatant, and any person about whom there is doubt, automatically has the status of civilian, and is entitled to the rights and protections granted to civilians at the time of war" (Ibid.). The petitioners added to this the claim that "The targeted killings are carried out under circumstances in which the conditions of immediacy and necessity – without which it is forbidden to harm civilians – are not fulfilled." They summed up by stating that "the State wishes to treat them [the terrorists] according to the worst of the two worlds: as combatants, regarding the justification for killing them, and as civilians, regarding the need to arrest them and try them" (Ibid.).

The Supreme Court judges adopted the interpretation that people who are considered to be combatants include those who collect intelligence about the army; those who transport unlawful combatants to or from the place where the hostilities are taking place; and those who operate weapons which unlawful combatants use, supervise their operation, or provide service to them. On the other hand, a person who sells food or medicine to an unlawful combatant; who aids the unlawful combatants by general strategic analysis, and grants them general-logistical support, including monetary aid; or who distributes propaganda supporting those unlawful combatants, are not taking a direct part in the hostilities, but rather an indirect part; therefore, any harm caused to them may be considered collateral or incidental damage of the military action. Justice Eliezer Rivlin added to this in his ruling, stating that "an analogy can be made between the means of combat permitted in a conflict between two armies and 'targeted killing' of terrorists. The attitude behind the 'targeted killing' policy is that the weapons should be directed exclusively toward those substantially involved in terrorist activity" (Ibid.).

President Beinisch added to these principles the need to ascertain that the information on which the classification between civilians, combatants, and unlawful combatants is based must be "well-founded, strong, and convincing regarding the risk the terrorist poses to human life – risk including continuous activity which is not merely sporadic or one-time concrete activity." In addition, "the level of probability of life-threatening hostilities is to be taken into account. On that point, a minor possibility is insufficient; a significant level of probability of the existence of such risk is required" (Ibid.).

Another contention of the petitioners to the Supreme Court was that targeted killings also violate the requirement of proportionality, which is a pillar of international humanitarian law and prohibits striking even legitimate targets if the attack is likely to result in excessive harm. In their words, the implementers of targeted killings "are aware that it may, at times nearly certainly, lead to the death and injury of innocent persons." They also claimed that the measure is used often, "including on occasions when there are other means for apprehending those suspected of terrorist activity" (Ibid.).

The ruling states that "in the context of the fight against terrorism, it is permissible to harm international-lawbreaking combatants, but harm to civilians should be avoided to the extent possible. The difficulty stems, of course, from the fact that the unlawful combatants, by definition, do not act according to the laws of war, often disguising themselves within the civilian population. They do so in order to gain an advantage from the fact that their opponent wishes to honor the rules of international law" (Ibid.).

Another directive emphasized by the judges with regard to the principle of proportionality is that "a civilian taking a direct part in hostilities cannot be attacked at such time as he is doing so, if a less harmful means can be employed…if a terrorist taking a direct part in hostilities can be arrested, interrogated, and tried, those are the means which should be employed. Trial is preferable to use of force." The judges also highlighted the need to ensure that "the benefit stemming from the attainment of the proper military objective is proportionate to the damage caused to innocent civilians harmed by it" (Ibid.).

It is interesting to note that while the petitioners' claims are derived from the axiom that human life is an inalienable right, and that there is never any justification to violate this right, many advocates of targeted killings base the moral justification for this measure on this very value—human life. In their view, the elimination of a terrorist involved in the preparation and execution of terrorist attacks is not only justified and moral, but essential in order to save lives (Ganor, 2005). As President Dorit Beinisch stated in the court's ruling, "It must be remembered that the purpose of 'targeted killing' is to prevent harm to human life as part of the State's duty to protect its soldiers and civilians…Ultimately, when an act of 'targeted killing' is carried out in accordance with the said qualifications and in the framework of the customary laws of international armed conflict as interpreted by this Court, it is not an arbitrary taking of life, rather a means intended to save human life" (HCJ 769/02, 2006).

Thus, the Supreme Court ruling's established, as stated, the basic moral principles and the normative standard for the use of the measure of targeted killing by the State of Israel in its fight against terrorism.

However, the discussion of the moral and legal issues surrounding the use of targeted killings is only one part of the equation. An additional, parallel discussion deals with the question of the measure's effectiveness. Bryan Price, who examined the subject of targeted killings with regard to 207 terrorist organizations between the years 1970 and 2008, concludes that targeted killings of the heads of terrorist organizations are an effective measure that helps bring an end to organization. Price argues that "leadership decapitation significantly increases the mortality rate of terrorist groups." Among Price's findings were that decapitated terrorist groups have a significantly higher mortality rate than non-decapitated groups. The earlier leadership decapitation occurs in a terrorist group's life cycle, the greater the effect it will have on the group's mortality rate. In addition, religious terrorist groups were found to be less resilient and easier to destroy than nationalist groups following leadership decapitation (Price, 2012).

Price explains the effectiveness of the measure by saying that it is difficult for the terrorist organization to find a replacement for its charismatic leadership. This difficulty stems in part from the paranoia of terrorist leaders, along with the decentralized structure of many organizations. Moreover, the change of leadership may lead to a shift in the organization's modus operandi and a different interpretation of the organizational ideology (Ibid.). Daniel Byman also emphasizes the difficulty terrorist organizations have in filling their ranks after targeted killings and the stress that such actions are likely to cause to terrorist operatives, not to mention the limits on the terrorist leaders' freedom of movement.

However, Byman, who examined Israel's use of targeted killings, also notes the prices a state may have to pay for such operations; these include international criticism, potential harm to innocent people, and the transformation of the deceased targets into "martyrs" in the eyes of many, resulting in their being touted as a role model in the terrorist organization's propaganda (Byman, 2006).

Steven David compared targeted killings to preventive offensive action designed to make it difficult for the enemy to act by reducing his freedom of movement and action. He finds a number of distinct advantages to targeted killings, among them an impact on the morale of the organization's senior officials; damage to the organization's operational capabilities; harm to the image of the organization and that of its leaders; and the bolstering of the morale of citizens affected by terrorism. On the other hand, David points out the shortcomings of this measure, pointing out that Israel's targeted killings during the al-Aqsa Intifada (from 2000–2002)[3] not only did not lead to the cessation of terrorist attacks, but on the contrary, seem to have led to an unprecedented number of terrorist attacks until mid-2002 (though he admits that the number of attacks may have been even greater without the targeted killing operations). David described the ineffectiveness of targeted killings in terrorist organizations with a decentralized structure, as well as the simplicity of carrying out attacks, which does not require any special training. He argues that these actions could lead to vengeance attacks, intensify international criticism against Israel, do not contribute to resolving the conflict peacefully, and sometimes even distract from more serious threats such as wars (David, 2003).

Ophir Falk, who examined the effectiveness of targeted killing in preventing suicide bombings, argues that although "targeted killing did not end the conflict or achieve peace ... it did have a clear effect on subsequent suicide bombing fatalities." He does, however, highlight the difficulties in attributing the reduction of suicide bombings entirely to the policy of targeted killing, but indicates that it played an important role. He also concludes that the targeting of ideological leaders had a more pronounced effect compared to the targeting of operational leaders (Falk, 2015).

---

[3] The wave of terrorism carried out against Israel in the early 2000s against the background of the failure of the Oslo process.

Asaf and Noam Zussman examined the effectiveness of Israeli targeted killings by analyzing their impact on Israeli stock market data between 2000 and 2004. In the study, they found that the market declines following the targeting of senior political leaders, but rises following the targeting of senior military leaders. Their conclusion was that to the extent that these reactions reflect expectations regarding future levels of terrorism, they imply that the market perceives the first type of killings as counterproductive, but the second as an effective measure in combating terrorism (Zussman & Zussman, 2006).

Avery Plaw provides an overview of the international legal debate on targeting terrorists, noting that there is a need to establish a compromise between the advocates and critics of the policy. Plaw identifies three categories of issues that critics usually raise: (1) the necessity of establishing targets as combatants; (2) the need for the decision on the targeted killing to comply with the laws of war; and (3) the imperative to avoid civilian casualties. He concludes that credible judicial oversight is key to resolving these issues, and that efforts should be focused on designing effective institutions able to ensure the legitimacy and effectiveness of targeted killings (Ganor, 2021).

Similarly, Asfandyar Mir, who attempts to explain counter-terrorism effectiveness using evidence from the US drone war in Pakistan, considers civilian protection to be essential for the effectiveness of targeted killings. He developed the "Legibility and Speed-of-Exploitation System" (L&S), suggesting that the level of effectiveness of the campaign can be determined by looking at two factors: (1) the state's "legibility" (clear identification) of the civilian population and (2) the "speed" or pace at which it uses legibility gains. Patrick B. Johnston and Anoop K. Sarbah also examine the impact of US drone strikes on terrorism in Pakistan. Their study reveals that the use of drone strikes against terrorist targets in Pakistan led to a decrease in the number and lethality of terrorist attacks, effectively bolstering US counter-terrorism efforts (Ibid.).

Finally, in a study conducted in 2019, Yasutaka Tominaga examined an area that is seldom discussed among scholars of terrorism, analyzing the effect of repeated leadership targeting on militant groups' durability. He concludes that while leadership targeting can initially increase a group's resilience, continued and successive targeted killings reduce militant organizations' survivability (Ibid.).

In light of the experience it has accumulated over the years dealing with the legal and ethical issues related to targeted killings, as well as their operational effectiveness, Israel is a test case for probing the moral and operational dilemmas related to the use of this measure.

Chapter 2 of this book surveys Israel's experience in carrying out targeted killings over the seven and a half decades that have passed since the establishment of the state in 1948, and the evolution of the use of this measure in the fight against terrorism in various areas (Judea, Samaria and the Gaza Strip, the states bordering Israel, and other countries) and against the various terrorist organizations. This historical review looks at different time periods with reference to the change in the characteristics of the terrorist challenge to Israel and regional geopolitical processes.

Like other terms in the field of terrorism and counter-terrorism that are politically charged, here too there is a need to first of all define "targeted killing." There are many books and articles that tackle the question of the definition of the term. This will also be discussed in the first chapter.

Chapter 3 of this book examines the decision-making process that takes place in Israel before a targeted killing operation is carried out, with an emphasis on the challenge of the need for precise and up-to-date intelligence for decision-making and the effective execution of the action. This chapter also discusses the translation of this intelligence into an operational opportunity to carry out the targeted killing.

Chapter 4 of this book focuses on the legitimacy and legality of carrying out targeted killings, posing the question of whether targeted killings are in effect a death penalty without a fair trial. Based on the ruling of the Israeli Supreme Court and on the accumulated Israeli experience, the chapter discusses this normative issue and the questions derived from it—whether, when and under what conditions a targeted killing may be considered legitimate.

Chapter 5, as a direct continuation of its predecessor, examines the question of the legitimacy of the identity of the target, distinguishing, inter alia, between different types of military-operational and political-ideological echelons of terrorist organizations.

Chapter 6 focuses on another major normative dilemma—the issue of proportionality in targeted killings. This dilemma is exacerbated when dealing with operatives belonging to a hybrid terrorist organization (a terrorist organization that controls territory and population and as such is assimilated into the civilian population and surrounds itself with "human shields."

Chapter 7 of this book moves from a discussion of normative questions to questions of the effectiveness of the measure of targeted killings, particularly in light of the fact that this method may increase terrorist organizations' motivation to seek revenge, possibly leading to a tactical "boomerang effect" (revenge attacks), an operational boomerang—military or diplomatic entanglements caused by the operation, or even a strategic boomerang—long-term strategic negative implications such as the intensification of hate, the development a new type of terrorist threat, the replacement of the deceased target with a figure that is more dangerous and effective than his predecessor, etc.

Chapter 8 summarizes and connects the book's insights into an operative model—the Decision-Making Model for Targeted Killings. This model is staged and integral, making it possible to weigh both the normative issues and the question of effectiveness in acts of targeted killings.

The nineth and final chapter summarizes the book and draws conclusions.

The various chapters of this book, which explore Israeli norms and practices in targeted killings, are based on an analysis of the changing Israeli experience over the years. This is accompanied by a survey of the attitudes of the Israeli public through opinion polls, as well as personal interviews with Israeli decision-makers and former heads of the defense and intelligence establishment on the key dilemmas involved in the execution of targeted killings. For the purpose of the book, the authors conducted in-person interviews with 23 interviewees, (see list in Appendix A) all former officials who were either involved in the carrying out of targeted killings or who escorted the decision-making processes. Among these interviewees are a prime minister; two defense ministers; a minister of justice; a minister of internal security; four chiefs of staff of the Israel Defense Forces (one of them also a former commander of the Air Force) and four former senior IDF officials; two former directors of Israel's Internal Security Agency (the ISA, also known as the "Shin Bet") and two former ISA officials; two Mossad chiefs and two other senior Mossad officials; the president of the Supreme Court, and five other legal and ethics experts. (Some of the interviewees held various positions throughout their professional careers.) On top of these interviews, the book includes excerpts from 15 additional personal interviews with former senior decision-makers, conducted by the authors in the 1990s and 2000s, that dealt, among other things, with the issue of targeted killing (see list in Appendix B). These interviewees include three other prime ministers, two defense ministers, two IDF chiefs of staff, two Mossad chiefs, three ISA directors, three heads of Military Intelligence (some of whom held other positions as well), and other senior officials. These interviews allowed the authors to analyze the goals underlying the decision to carry out targeted killings in the framework of Israel's war on terror, the development of the use of this measure by Israel over the years, the decision-making processes, the differences between various types of targeted killings, and the many dilemmas involved.

The book also offers two models for the classification and analysis of targeted killing operations—the **Operational Need Model** and the **Decision-Making Model for Targeted Killings**. These models may be used as a tool for retrospective analyses of targeted killings carried out against terrorist operatives by Israel and by other states, and as an aid to help make prospective decisions on targeted killings by decision-makers around the world.

REFERENCES

Byman, D. (2006). Do targeted killings work? *Foreign Affairs, 85*(2), 95–112.

David, S. (2003). Fatal choices: Israel's policy of targeted killing. *Review of International Affairs, 2*(3), 138.

Falk, O. (2015). Measuring the effectiveness of Israel's 'targeted killing' campaign. *Perspectives on Terrorism, 9*(1).

Ganor, B. (2021). Targeted killings: Ethical & operational dilemmas. *Terrorism & Political Violence, 33*(2), 353.

Ganor, B. (2005). *The counter-terrorism puzzle—A guide for decision makers*. Routledge.

HCJ 769/02. (2006). *The Public Committee Against Torture in Israel v. The Government of Israel, 62*(1) 507.

Price, B. (2012). Targeting top terrorists: How leadership decapitation contributes to counterterrorism. *International Security, 36*(4), 43–44.

Statistics: Palestinians who were the object of a targeted killing in the Gaza Strip, before Operation Cast Lead. B'Tselem. https://www.btselem.org/heb rew/statistics/fatalities/before-cast-lead/by-date-of-event/gaza/palestinians-who-were-the-object-of-a-targeted-killing

Statistics: Palestinians who were the object of a targeted killing in the Gaza Strip, since Operation Cast Lead. B'Tselem. https://www.btselem.org/heb rew/statistics/fatalities/after-cast-lead/by-date-of-event/gaza/palestinians-who-were-the-object-of-a-targeted-killing

Zussman, A., & Zussman, N. (2006). Assassinations: Evaluating the effectiveness of an Israeli counterterrorism policy using stock market data. *Journal of Economic Perspectives, 20*(2), 195–196.

CHAPTER 2

A Historical Survey of Israeli Targeted Killings

Targeted killings are a counter-terrorism measure that has been employed by the State of Israel ever since it has been forced to deal with the phenomenon of terrorism, i.e., since the establishment of the state in 1948 (in fact, it was used even prior to this, during the British Mandate era in the 1940s, which saw violent clashes between Arab gangs and the Jewish underground). In retrospect, it can be said that this type of activity was carried out during various periods for the purpose of achieving different goals and against various enemies of Israel (mainly terrorist operatives and those who assisted them). Generally speaking, this measure was intended to neutralize adversaries who carried a very high threat level and whom it was very difficult to stop any other way.[1] Over the years, this method has been dubbed various things, including assassinations, killings, and eliminations. However, the concept of "targeted killings" was actually coined only after the year 2000, when the Israeli-Palestinian peace process hit a wall and an unprecedented and prolonged wave of severe violence and terrorist attacks, known as the "Second Intifada" began. During this time, this counter-terrorism measure became particularly common, with various experts in Israel claiming that the term used to describe it—"targeted assassination"—was problematic and unfair to Israel (Kremnitzer, 2006, p. 5), because it raised connotations of organized crime, and was

---

[1] Personal interview with Arik "Harris" Barbing, February 21, 2022.

© The Author(s), under exclusive license to Springer Nature Switzerland AG 2022
B. Ganor and L. Koblentz-Stenzler, *Israel's Targeted Killing Policy*, https://doi.org/10.1007/978-3-031-13674-0_2

13

perceived by some of the public as a form of reverse terrorism (Yaffe, 2006). On the other hand, the Hebrew term "*sikul memukad*" ("targeted prevention") is perceived as "sterile" and bears a defensive connotation that better describes the reality.[2] For the purpose of this book, however, we will use the commonly accepted term "targeted killing."

In order to explain and concretize the concept of targeted killings, in 2001 then-Attorney General Elyakim Rubinstein stated that "this is an action against someone whom, due to their active involvement in the planning and execution of terrorist attacks, every effort must be made to arrest, in order to prevent the continuation of their fatal activities and save human lives. In the absence of any possibility of doing so, and relying on well-founded information regarding the person's ongoing activities and the imminent threat they pose, and given the duty to protect the citizens of the country, there are cases where terror attacks must be thwarted through a targeted hit on such an enemy, assuming of course that it is carried out according to the legal guidelines of the Military Advocate General" (Alon, 2001). Prof. Mordechai Kremnitzer went on to state that a targeted killing is "a tool used to assassinate a specific individual: a political or military leader, commander or activist in a terrorist organization, or an individual responsible (according to intelligence information) for terrorist activity" (Kremnitzer, 2006, p. 5). The working definition of targeted killings we use in this book is: "An offensive operation in which a state entity fighting terrorism attacks a specific individual terrorist or a group of terrorists who are engaged in initiating, directing, planning or preparing (recruiting, training or providing operational aid to terrorists) terrorist attacks, for the purpose of killing or at least neutralizing them" (Ganor, 2021).

The objectives underlying the targeted killings carried out by Israel over the years have changed, as have the methods employed. For example, in the 1930s, even before the establishment of the state, the Jewish underground and especially the Irgun ("Etzel") and Lehi (the "Stern Gang") sometimes carried out retaliatory actions against Arab targets for terrorist

---

[2] It is interesting to note in this context that in the series of interviews conducted with senior Israeli officials for the purpose of research for this book, former senior ISA official Oz Noy argued that the term "targeted prevention" does not accurately describe the situation and misleads public opinion. A more appropriate term to describe the phenomenon should be, he claims, "preventive strikes" (Oz Noy, personal communication and interview, February 16, 2022).

attacks committed by Arab gangs, as well as hits against British Mandate targets. These "offensive retaliatory actions" were initially directed against known targets—bases and villages from which members of Arab gangs would carry out attacks against Jews. The identity of the individuals targeted in these actions was not important, so long as they belonged to these gangs; in this way, these retaliatory actions differed from the targeted killings of specific figures. In this context, we can mention the example of the offensive retributions carried out by the Irgun led by David Raziel as revenge for the murder of three Jews in September 1937, in which ten Arabs were killed and others wounded. (Bowyer Bell, 1977). Actions carried out by these organizations against British targets were more targeted, such as the explosion of a landmine planted by the Irgun in August 1939, which resulted in the death of Ralph Cairns, commander of the Jewish Section of the Criminal Investigation Department, who was accused of torturing Irgun prisoners, as well as that of another British officer (Ibid.). In 1944, the Lehi killed Lord Moyne, the British Resident Minister whom the group considered to be one of the key figures in the British immigration policy that prevented Jews from fleeing Nazi-occupied Europe to Palestine. (Byman, 2011).

The targeted killings carried out by Israel since its establishment in 1948 can be classified into four main periods: The period that saw the consolidation of the method of targeted killings in the state's early decades (1948–1972), the period during which targeted killings abroad were employed as a means of retaliation and deterrence (1972–1992), the period of the Oslo Accords, during which targeted killings were used to prevent suicide bombings against the backdrop of the peace process between Israel and the PLO (1993–1999), and the period of the "Al-Aqsa Intifada" (the Second Intifada), during which targeted killings were a key counter-terrorism tool following the collapse of the peace process (2000–2007). The strategy of targeted killings developed over the years in accordance with changes in the scope and nature of the terrorist challenge that Israel had to deal with in different periods and arenas, as well as the formation of normative rules and unique practices that arose from the experience accumulated by Israel in employing the method of targeted killings.

The Consolidation of the Method of Targeted Killings in Israeli Counter-Terrorism Strategy (1948–1972)

Following the War of Independence and the establishment of Israel in 1948, the Israel Defense Forces was charged with carrying out retaliatory actions in the territories of the Arab countries bordering Israel as a result of the infiltration of Palestinian *fedayeen* from these areas into Israel, particularly after terrorist attacks carried out by these *fedayeen*. The reprisal operations were not targeted but were rather directed against the villages near the border that served as the exit points for the *fedayeen*. These Israeli actions sometimes caused significant collateral damage, for example in an operation carried out in the Jordanian village of Qibya following an attack on the Israeli town of Yehud in 1953 (Byman, 2011). More than fifty civilians living in the village were killed in the operation, which led to much domestic and international criticism of Israel and brought about a change in the Israeli reprisals policy and a decision to be more targeted in further operations beginning in the mid-1950s. Despite the criticism Israel faced in the state's early years, it seems that the reprisal operations achieved their goal by motivating the Arab states to impose their authority on the Palestinian fedayeen and prevent them from continuing to infiltrate Israel. In the years that followed, Israeli intelligence agencies carried out targeted killings using letter bombs. This is how, in July 1956, Mustafa Hafez, the commander of Egypt's military intelligence in the Gaza Strip who was responsible for sending the *fedayeen* from the Gaza Strip to Israel, was killed (Melman, 2004). Former Director of the Mossad Shabtai Shavit explains that in the first decade following the establishment of the state, the targeted killings were conducted by a military unit and carried out by Arab agents recruited for intelligence purposes.[3] During these years, Israel was also engaged in the elimination of German scientists, some of whom had previously served in the Nazi regime and who were involved in the production of advanced weapons in Egypt in the 1960s. The Mossad, headed by Isser Harel, was responsible for these operations, however, because the organization did not have a suitable operational framework at the time, the Mossad carried out these actions via a small operational unit led by Yitzhak Shamir in cooperation with

---

[3] Personal interview with Shabtai Shavit, February 17, 2022.

the ISA's Operations Unit led by Zvi Malchin and Rafi Eitan. In 1962, in Operation Damocles, Dr. Heinz Krug, who was involved in a missile construction project in Egypt, was killed by Israeli intelligence. Another attempt, on Dr. Hans Kleinwachter, failed. These Israeli actions ceased with the change of the head of the Mossad in the mid-1960s, when Meir Amit was appointed in place of Isser Harel. Following this, Israeli intelligence did not carry out targeted killings until the murder of the Israeli athletes at the Munich Olympics in September 1972. On the whole, it can be stated that in the first two decades of Israel's existence, targeted killing was considered a last resort to be used sparingly and prudently, mainly because Israeli decision-makers feared that this policy could be a double-edged sword; that is, what you do to your enemies may also be done to you. The cases in which Israeli intelligence and the political echelon did not hesitate to carry out killings were usually when the targets were considered "valuable"—people whose elimination would severely impair the adversary's operational capability.

Targeted Killings as a Means of Retaliation and Deterrence Following the Attack on the Israeli Athletes in the Munich Olympics (1972–1992)

The murder of 11 Israeli athletes at the Munich Olympics was a watershed in the history of Israeli targeted killings. During the twentieth Olympics Games in Munich in September 1972, a terrorist cell called "Black September" (likely a mixed cell of Popular Front for the Liberation of Palestine and Fatah terrorists) infiltrated the Olympic Village and took over the living quarters of the Israeli athletes. Two of the athletes were murdered at the outset of the attack and nine others were held hostage for about 19 h before being killed during a failed rescue attempt at a nearby airport. The attack, which is considered a significant event in the phenomenon of modern terrorism due to the extensive media exposure it received, shook the Israeli public. Aharon Yariv, Golda Meir's counter-terrorism adviser at that time, claimed that following the terrorist attack in Munich, Israel became a "nation in shock. Israelis were murdered in Germany and all the horrific memories of the Holocaust came back" (Zonder, 2001). The public outcry compelled decision-makers to demonstrate resolve by taking particularly harsh measures in the wake of the attack. Then-Israeli Prime Minister Golda Meir instructed the head of the Mossad, Zvi Zamir, to pursue PLO operatives, first and foremost the eleven Black September terrorists who were responsible for the massacre, and eliminate them. This directive led to a global operation dubbed "Operation Wrath of God," whose mission was to eliminate all those involved in the initiation, planning, preparation, management, and execution of the attack. To this end, the Mossad employed various methods, including letter bombs and explosives placed in the homes of the terrorists and activated from a distance (among other things by the ringing of a telephone, as was the case in the killings of Mahmoud Hamshari and Basil Al-Kubaisi.)

It was the first time in history that Israeli intelligence was tasked with the elimination of terrorist operatives as part of a systematic campaign against a group of terrorists, and not as a one-time operation against a single terrorist. Each of the individuals in this group of targets were approved by a special committee—"Committee X"—that included three ministers. Committee X was appointed by the Ministerial Committee on Security Affairs, and acted as a court of law of sorts to approve death sentences (Melman, 2004). This "quasi-judicial" procedure was intended to address the difficulty arising from the policy of targeted killings and attempt to resolve the moral dilemma of taking a person's life without a trial (Meisels, 2004). The Mossad would prepare a list of possible targets and then, prior to the operation, present each plan to the Committee of Secret Service Chiefs and submit it to Committee X for approval. One of the ministers served as the "prosecutor" and brought as witnesses the heads of Military Intelligence, the Mossad, and the ISA. The minister of justice served as the terrorist's defense, presenting arguments as to why he should not be assassinated, and the prime minister, minister of defense, and leader of the opposition served as judges (Ganor, 2005).

On the face of it, the wave of targeted killing operations carried out in the early 1970s following the Munich attack was characterized by motives of revenge and the sowing of fear of "Israel's long arm." Although in some cases the declared motive was "deterrence" or "the prevention of future acts of terror," it seems that the main motivation was the desire to avenge the blood of the Israeli athletes murdered in Munich. The task was assigned to the Mossad's special operations unit, "Caesarea," and according to one of its operatives, "We wanted to create a noisy effect... A genuine killing, from close range, that would evoke fear and trembling, a deed that, even if Israel denied having anything to do with, it would be clear that an Israeli finger squeezed the trigger" (Bergman, 2018). Aharon Yariv, on the other hand, explained that the basis for these actions was the desire to eliminate terrorism. According to him, the targeted killings "created a dilemma for Golda, for whom deliberately killing people wasn't easy. But there was no other way to eliminate terrorism. It wasn't just about revenge for Munich. The idea was to eliminate terrorism because it was not possible to continue living with it" (Zonder, 2001). Even if this was indeed the objective behind Israel's decision-making at the time, it was a goal of a strategic nature with long-term consequences—destroying Black September—and not a tactical goal of thwarting a concrete attack, as would be the case in the years to come.[4]

In any case, while the operation was taking place, Prime Minister Golda Meir stated, "Our war against the Arab terrorists...cannot be limited to defensive means, to safeguarding and self-defense, but must be active in all that has to do with the detection of murderers, of their bases, their actions and operations, to foil their designs and, in particular, to stamp out the terrorist organizations" (Melman, 2004; Yaffe, 2006, p. 56). Indeed, according to Yariv, the impact of these targeted killings on PLO terrorists was significant, given that these were senior officials in sensitive positions who now felt unsafe even in their homes (Zonder, 2001).

The targeted killings that were carried out in the framework of Operation Wrath of God took place in various European countries over the course of about a year. Among the actions attributed to the operation during this period were the elimination of senior members of Black September Abdel Wael Zwaiter on October 16, 1972 in Rome (Goldblum, 2020); Dr. Mahmoud Hamshari, a PLO representative killed on December 8, 1972 via a remote-controlled telephone explosion in his hotel room in Paris (Israel Defense, 2012); Hussein Abu-Khair, the PLO representative in Cyprus, who was killed on January 24, 1973 in Nicosia by an explosive device planted in his home (Ibid.); Basil Al-Kubaisi, who was killed on April 6, 1973 in Paris (Ibid.); Mussa Abu Zayd, killed in a bomb blast in his hotel room in Athens in April 1973 ("Jordanian killed in Athens hotel explosion," 1973); Zaid Muchassi, killed on January 25 in Athens (Israel Defense, 2012); Mohamed Boudia, one of the leaders of Black September who was responsible for the operational links with European terrorist organizations (Baader–Meinhof and The Red Brigades),

---

[4] Personal interview with Oz Noy, February 16, 2022.

who was killed on June 28, 1973 when his car exploded in Paris ("The Mossad agent was hysterically attacked," 1990); and Ghassan Kanafani of the Popular Front for the Liberation of Palestine, who was killed in an explosion in July 1972 (Peleg, 2018).

The operation came to an end in July 1973 due to a severe mishap that occurred when a Mossad hit team attempted to kill senior Black September member Ali Hassan Salameh, the organization's chief of operations and planner of the Munich attack, in Lillehammer, Norway. Due to a mistaken identity, instead of Salameh, the Mossad agents killed a young Moroccan man named Ahmed Bouchikhi. Some of the members of the Mossad team that carried out the operation were caught and sentenced to prison terms, and the revelation of the affair caused significant embarrassment and criticism of Israel and essentially led to the conclusion of Operation Wrath of God.

The pinnacle of the targeted killings during this period was Operation Spring of Youth in the Lebanese capital of Beirut in April 1973. The operation was carried out by IDF special forces in cooperation with Mossad and the Israeli Navy (Israeli Air Force, Operation Spring of Youth) following an attempt by Palestinian terrorists to strike Israeli targets in Cyprus—an Israeli Arkia aircraft parked at the Nicosia airport and the home of Chaim Timor, Israel's ambassador to Cyprus at the time (Ibid.). In the framework of the operation, the Israeli forces raided a number of Beirut neighborhoods and hit various infrastructure targets and the headquarters of the Fatah and PFLP terrorist organizations. Among the targets were three senior officials who were killed in their homes—Kamal Adwan, head of Fatah's "Western Sector," the wing responsible for organizing terrorist attacks in Israel and the Palestinian Territories; Kamal Nasser, Fatah's spokesman, and Muhammad Youssef al-Najjar, a Black September operative, Arafat's deputy, and head of Fatah's operational intelligence apparatus.

In the two decades that passed following the wave of targeted killings of the 1970s, several members of Palestinian terrorist organizations were killed, some of whose deaths were attributed to Israel in the international media; in the majority of cases, Israel did not take responsibility for the killings.[5] The targets included Said Hammami, the PLO's representative

---

[5] It should be borne in mind that at that time there were also competing Palestinian organizations hostile toward the PLO that had set themselves the goal of harming its operatives, such as Fatah—The Revolutionary Council headed by Sabri al-Banna (a.k.a Abu

to Great Britain, who was shot and killed in London on January 4, 1978 (Ronel, 2010); Ali Yassin, director of the PLO's office in Kuwait, who was killed in his office on June 15, 1978 ("PLO leaders eliminated over the past 15 years," 1998a); Izz al-Din al-Kalak, the PLO representative in France, who was killed in Paris along with his deputy on August 3 of that year (Ibid.); Zuheir Mohsen, the military operations chief of PLO, who was shot and killed in Cannes, France on July 25, 1979 (Ibid.); Samir Tuqan, the second secretary of the PLO office in Nicosia, who was killed on December 15 of that year (Ibid.); Naim Khader, the PLO representative in Belgium, who was shot and killed in Brussels on June 1, 1981 (Ibid.); Kamal Husain, deputy director of the PLO office in Italy, who was killed by an explosion in Rome on June 17, 1982 (Ibid.); Fadl Dani, the deputy director of the PLO office in France, who was killed in Paris by a bomb that had been placed in his car on July 23 of that year (Ibid.); Mamoun Meraish, one of Abu Jihad's top aides, who was killed in Athens on August 20, 1983 (Ibid.); Ismail Darwish, head of the PLO's operations department in Italy, who was gunned down in Rome on December 15, 1984 (Hoffman, 1985); Khaled Nazal, a senior member of the Democratic Front for the Liberation of Palestine who was responsible for terrorist attacks in the Palestinian Territories, who was killed in Athens on June 10, 1986 (Ibid.); and Munzer Abu Ghazala, a senior Fatah official and commander of the organization's naval units, who was killed a car bomb in Athens on October 21, 1986 (Ibid.). His commander, Abu Jihad, accused the Israeli Mossad of assassinating him ("And who is blamed? Usually, the Mossad," 1991).

Abu Jihad (Khalil al-Wazir), Yasser Arafat's deputy and head of Fatah's military wing, who was responsible for carrying out the most severe attacks by Fatah in Israel in the two decades preceding his killing, was himself eliminated in Tunis on April 16, 1988, in one of the key targeted killing operations carried out by Israel. This operation, which took place during the "First Intifada" in the Palestinian territories (the popular Palestinian uprising that took place in Judea, Samaria, and Gaza and was characterized by acts of political violence and terrorism that caused many casualties on both sides) effectively sealed this period of targeted killings. During the operation, IDF special forces broke into Abu Jihad's home and shot him, gathering documents from his house before leaving. The

Nidal) and the Popular Front for the Liberation of Palestine's armed wing, led by Wadie Haddad.

PLO noted that those who killed Abu Jihad intentionally spared the lives of his wife and two daughters, who were standing at the doorway of the bedroom watching what was happening ("The work of professionals," 1988b).

The Israeli media reported that the killing of Abu Jihad was brought before the cabinet for discussion several days before the operation and that Ezer Weizmann, who was serving as a minister in the Israeli government at the time, opposed the operation. Responding to a report on the subject published in the foreign media, Weizmann said:

> If I had to make a decision about the killing of Abu Jihad, I would have made a different one. His elimination will only increase terrorism and may harm the peace process...Those who made this decision were wrong. Killing people has an impact but not a big enough impact. Arik Sharon rushed to praise the move and declared that it is an excellent thing. I declare that this action was a mistake and I am of course not addressing the question of who carried it out...There are those who say that the operation was carried out in order to strengthen the IDF's deterrent capability. So, if that is the reason, why don't all the 'heroes' stand up and announce who did it? If they decided not to talk, to neither confirm nor deny, why give out compliments and congratulations to the IDF?...NBC reported that Peres and I objected in the cabinet. This morning a Reuters reporter called me and asked if this was true. I do not lie, so I didn't deny it. (Bachar et al., 1988; *Yediot Aharonot*, April 20, 1988)

At the cabinet meeting following the operation in Tunis, Minister Shimon Peres asked, "Will we hear the report on the killing of Abu Jihad?" Prime Minister Yitzhak Shamir replied, "I myself heard about it on the radio" (Ibid). In an interview published in the Israeli media with the prime minister's counter-terrorism adviser Rafi Eitan after the operation, Eitan said:

> We can presume that the killing of Abu Jihad will cause internal upheaval in the terrorist organizations. He was a man with a lot of experience....The action taken against Abu Jihad is a blow to the residents of the territories (West Bank and Gaza strip). We can assess that in the short term it will cause an escalation in the riots and there will be unrest for a few more days, but then they will diminish, because Abu Jihad as you recall was the person directing the civil uprising in the territories. This is despite the fact that the uprising did not begin at his order – after the riots started, he made an effort to coordinate them remotely. (Tal, 1988)

When asked who he thought carried out the killing, Eitan replied, "I have no data on this and therefore I will not answer the question. But regardless, my position has always been that we should pursue the elimination of all leaders of terrorist organizations. Their political leaders are also involved in terrorism…" (Ibid.).

Targeted Killings as a Means of Preventing Suicide Bombings Against the Background of the Peace Process Between Israel and the PLO (1993–1999)

The next wave of targeted killings carried out by Israel commenced in the early 1990s. The beginning of this wave was marked by the strategically targeted killing by Israel in February 1992 of the leader of the terrorist organization Hezbollah in Lebanon, Abbas al-Musawi. Based on intelligence received in Israel which identified the exact location of the Hezbollah secretary-general, Israel carried out an airstrike using Apache helicopters on the motorcade that accompanied al-Musawi. The Hezbollah leader was killed in the strike, along with his wife and five-year-old son, as well as four other operatives who were nearby (Klein, 1992). Following the operation, the Israeli media reported that al-Musawi's killing had not been discussed in an official political forum in the government or in the security cabinet. According to one Israeli minister quoted in the media at the time, he was "not at all certain that there was room to bring such an action before the cabinet's approval. It's possible that this was a routine action in the ongoing activity against terrorist organizations operating in Lebanon, and not an advance plan to strike the senior Shiite leader" (*Ha'aretz*, February 17, 1992). The former head of Israeli Military Intelligence Maj. Gen. Shlomo Gazit also spoke out after the targeted killing, saying, "The timing was undoubtedly coincidental. The information that was obtained and which enabled the attack on the vehicle of the Hezbollah leader is the kind that is incidental and not easily attainable. This is extremely rare information that accurately and reliably specifies when and where the target will be, on a schedule that allows for the preparation of a strike in operational conditions that will enable a 'clean' operation with minimal risk to those in the area of the target" (Gazit, 1992).

Gazit assessed the considerations underlying the decision to carry out the targeted killing, saying:

> Three considerations were taken into account, or so I hope, in making the decision: The first consideration was the response of Hezbollah fighters, which was not long in coming. We have learned from experience. It would be inconceivable that an important leader could be eliminated without a painful response. The massive firing of Katyushas on the northern towns is the first reaction to al-Musawi's killing, and it presumably will not be the last…The second consideration was the delicate negotiations for the release of navigator Ron Arad (an Israeli pilot who was captured in Lebanon after his plane was shot down). We know that he had been held by an extremist Shiite organization, hence his captives may tie his fate into the killing of al-Musawi…The third consideration was the impact on the peace process. (Ibid.)

Two former defense ministers, Moshe Arens and Yitzhak Rabin, assessed after the operation that al-Musawi's killing would cause significant damage to Hezbollah (*Ha'aretz*, February 17, 1992). According to Arens, "Al-Musawi's killing caused serious damage to the organization. This is a message to all terrorist organizations that whoever opens an account with us – the account will be closed by us" (Shtull-Trauring, 2012). Rabin said that the elimination was "a serious blow to Hezbollah. But anyone who thinks that this is the end of Hezbollah's activity is simply wrong" (Ibid).

Hezbollah's response was not long in coming. About a month after al-Musawi's elimination, a Hezbollah suicide bomber blew up a car near the Israeli embassy in Buenos Aires, destroying a part of the embassy building, killing 29 people, and injuring many others ("Attack in the heart of the community," 2014).

Following the signing of the mutual recognition agreement between Israel and the PLO—the Oslo Accords—on August 20, 1993, and in the years that followed, with the Israeli-Palestinian negotiations and the aspiration of Islamist Palestinian terrorist organizations, Palestinian Islamic Jihad and Hamas, to sabotage the peace process, the security situation in Israel dramatically deteriorated. Numerous terrorist attacks were carried out against civilian targets and an unprecedented wave of suicide bombings began among crowds in large cities and the Israeli home front, causing many Israeli casualties.

The terrorist organizations found themselves easily able to recruit for, plan and organize terrorist attacks within the territories that were transferred to Palestinian control in Judea, Samaria, and Gaza in accordance with the agreements signed between the parties in 1993. The West Bank was divided into three areas: Area A was an autonomous Palestinian region, which included the major Palestinian cities and in which Israeli civilian, military, and police control were banned (this was carried out instead by the Palestinian Authority). Area B comprised the Palestinian rural areas in which a Palestinian civilian administration was established and Israeli security activity was permitted in coordination with the Palestinian Authority. Area C was defined as being under full Israeli control.[6]

Then-IDF Chief of Staff Ehud Barak said in September 1994 that "It was clear in advance that the IDF would not carry out any elimination, prevention, or retaliatory activities within the autonomous areas. This has been passed into the hands of a clear address, and this address is being tested in Gaza and Jericho." The address was the Palestinian Authority, and the decision was to leave the responsibility for counter-terrorism in its hands. This decision was due in part to the fact that activity in these areas, where there was a hostile and armed population, was extremely complex, but also due to the Israeli government's desire not to infringe on the sovereignty of the Palestinian Authority or jeopardize the peace process (Ganor, 2005, p. 117).

However, the wave of suicide bombings that swept Israel and led to an unprecedented number of casualties soon proved to Israel that the Palestinian Authority was either incapable or unwilling to play its part in thwarting terrorism.

Against this backdrop, Israel launched a wave of targeted killings in the territories not under its control, with the intention of disrupting the terrorist operatives' planning of terrorist attacks and deterring them from continuing to attack Israel. On November 24, 1993, Emed Akel, commander of Hamas's military wing, responsible for numerous attacks on Israel, was killed by Israeli undercover operatives in the Gaza neighborhood of Shuja'iyya (Aviad, 2008). On February 3, 1994, Israeli undercover forces in Rafah eliminated Salim Moafi, commander of the "Fatah Hawks," who had carried out attacks against the IDF (Bohbot,

---

[6] Personal interview with Arik "Harris" Barbing, February 21, 2022.

2021). Following the operation, Chief of Staff Ehud Barak said that it was "a very important achievement by the special forces and the ISA…It is very important for them to know that alongside the diplomatic talks and the preparations for the possibility of an agreement being signed, the pursuit of the terrorists will continue." (*Ma'ariv*, February 2, 1994, p. 2). About three weeks later, on February 25, 1994, Abd al-Rahman Hamdan of Khan Yunis was killed after he carried out shooting attacks on IDF soldiers and was involved in the murder of an ISA official (*Ma'ariv*, February 25, 1994, p. 3) On March 23, 1994, three members of Hamas's military wing—Marwan Abu Ramila, Eyad Abu Hadid, and Muhammad Atrash—were killed in Hebron on the basis of intelligence that they intended to carry out a major terrorist attack. According to the commander of the IDF forces in the West Bank at the time, Maj. Gen. Shaul Mofaz, "There is no doubt that they were on the verge of an attack. It was enough to see the weapons they had in their possession…" (*Ma'ariv*, March 24, 1994, p. 2). On May 30 of that year, the murderer of ISA agent Noam Cohen, (*Ma'ariv*, June 1, 1994, p. 7) Abd al-Manam Muhammad Yusuf Naj, was killed in Kfar Ar-Ram along with another Hamas operative, and on July 12, 1994, Ali Othman Muhammad Atzi, one of the most-wanted Hamas operatives in the West Bank at the time, was killed in Nablus. (*Ma'ariv*, July 12, 1994).

Following the suicide bombing on a bus on the main street of Tel Aviv on October 19, 1994, which resulted in the deaths of 22 civilians and the injury of 46, Prime Minister Yitzhak Rabin instructed the heads of the ISA, Mossad, and Military Intelligence in a security cabinet meeting, "We must search for, find, and arrest or eliminate those who organized this terrorist act" (Ganor, 2005, p. 117). On November 2, 1994, one senior member of Palestinian Islamic Jihad in the Gaza Strip, Hani al-Abed, was killed by an explosive device attached to his vehicle in Gaza. Following the operation, three Palestinians living in the Gaza Strip were arrested by the Palestinian police on suspicion of collaborating with the ISA in carrying out the killing (*Yediot Aharonot*, December 13, 1994). In the wake of Abed's killing, two revenge attacks were carried out; eight days later, three IDF officers were killed in a suicide bombing at an IDF post in the settlement of Netzarim in the Gaza Strip by a terrorist riding an explosive-laden bicycle, and on April 3, 1995, two suicide bombers blew themselves up at a bus stop at the Beit Lid junction in the center of the country, killing 22 soldiers and injuring many others (*Ma'ariv*, June 23, 1995) On April 2, 1995, an explosion in a building in the Sheikh Radwan neighborhood of

Gaza killed Kamal Kahil, Israel's most-wanted terrorist in Gaza, and his deputy Hatam Hassan. Israeli spokespeople claimed that it was a "work accident"—the two were involved in the preparation of explosives when they detonated, but Hamas maintained that it was an Israeli assassination (*Ma'ariv*, April 7, 1995; *Yediot Aharonot*, April 4, 1995). On April 16, 1995, a vehicle of people dressed in civilian clothes (who, according to various media sources, were members of the Israel Border Police's national counter-terrorism unit) ambushed a car in the Hebron suburbs carrying members of a Hamas terrorist cell—Jihad Faiz Ghulmeh, Adel Falah, and Tarek Natche—who were responsible for numerous shooting attacks. The three were killed during a shootout that took place at the scene. According to an Israeli spokesman, "We worked hard to track down the members of this Hebron cell, to whom a series of terrorist attacks has been attributed" (*Ha'aretz*, April 17, 1995; *Ma'ariv*, April 17, 1995, p. 3, 5). On June 3, 1995, a senior Hamas operative wanted by Israel, Hamed Yamur, who had been involved in an attempt to kidnap Israelis, was killed in Hebron. Neighbors said that around 2 o'clock at night, army helicopters landed soldiers on the roofs of the houses and courtyards nearby. The soldiers called on all the residents to go outside, and when Yamur did not come out, they opened fire on the house and eliminated him (*Ma'ariv*, June 5, 1995, p. 7). On June 22, 1995, three masked men shot Mahmoud al-Hawajah, a senior member of Islamic Jihad's military wing. Palestinian police chief Nasser Yusuf blamed Israel for the act (*Ma'ariv*, June 25, 1995; *Ma'ariv*, June 23, 1995).

At the time, there were reports in the Palestinian and foreign media that Israel had compiled a list of targets for killings, mainly Islamist extremists who belonged to the Palestinian Islamic Jihad organization (*Yediot Aharonot*, October 29, 1995, p. 7). Taher Kafisha, a senior member of Hamas's military wing who had escaped from Dahariya Prison two years earlier, was killed on June 29, 1995, in an operation in the Hebron area (*Ha'aretz*, June 30, 1995). On August 21, 1995, a Palestinian terrorist from Hamas carried out a suicide bombing on Bus No. 26 in the Ramat Eshkol neighborhood of Jerusalem, leaving four civilians dead and wounding 106 (Huberman, 2009). Three days later, based on new and accurate intelligence obtained by the ISA shortly before the operation, Israeli special forces from the undercover unit "Duvdevan" shot dead in Hebron Nader Shehadeh, and Ibrahim Qawasmi—members of Hamas's military wing. Regarding this operation, Chief of Central Command Ilan Biran said it was "A clean action by the Duvdevan unit, which engages in this type of activity all year round." He added, "This was a very important operation that prevented murderous terrorism against Jews and soldiers in the Hebron area, all on the basis of high-quality surgical intelligence from the ISA... in this way we must continue to pursue them and damage every mechanism and every leader in every place, and demonstrate unwavering perseverance" (*Ha'aretz*, August 27, 1995).

One of the strategic targeted killing operations attributed to Israel during this period was the killing of the leader of the Islamic Jihad terrorist organization who was responsible for carrying out numerous terrorist attacks in Israel, Fathi Shaqaqi, on October 26, 1995, in Malta. Shaqaqi was shot in the head as he was leaving his hotel by two motorcyclists who had been following him (Ifergan, 2013). According to foreign media reports, Prime Minister Yitzhak Rabin was the one who ordered Shaqaqi's killing as early as January 1995, after his organization, Islamic Jihad, carried out a double suicide bombing at the Beit Lid junction ("Death Blow," 2012). The international media also reported that the assassins belonged to the Mossad's "Kidon" unit (Ifergan, 2013). After the operation, Prime Minister Rabin said that "If he is the man who was killed, I am not sorry about it" (*Ha'aretz*, October 29, 1995). Rabin's deputy and foreign minister, Shimon Peres, declared in the Knesset's Foreign Affairs and Defense Committee that "Islamic Jihad is a murderous organization, and its leader was Shaqaqi. Anyone who engages in murder risks murder himself" *Ma'ariv*, October 10, 1995. A few days after Shaqaqi's death, Islamic Jihad issued a proclamation announcing "We pledge to Allah and the Palestinian people and the Arab and Islamic nation that we will continue on the path that our great deceased leader began. We will shake the earth beneath the terrorist entity whose commanders rely on cowardly assassinations and murders" (*Ha'aretz*, October 30, 1995). In fact, the organization did not carry out a retaliatory attack in the weeks following Shaqaqi's death.

A few months later, in January 1996, one of the most significant targeted killings in Israel's history was carried out—the killing of the "Engineer" Yahya Ayyash, who topped Israel's most-wanted list for his responsibility for the deaths of 48 Israelis and the injuries of more than 300 in a series of suicide bombings carried out in various cities in Israel, including Afula, Hadera, Tel Aviv, Bet Lid, Ramat Gan, Jerusalem, Mehola, and more (Intelligence and Terrorism Information Center, 2010; Mitchnik, 2016;). Ayyash was killed via a mobile phone that was given to him in the Beit Lahia neighborhood of Gaza (Intelligence and Terrorism Information Center, 2010). Ayyash was the force behind the wave of suicide bombings in Israel—it was he who "imported" this method from Hezbollah and turned it into the preferred modus operandi of the Palestinian terrorist organizations in the years following the signing of the Oslo Accords. At the order of Prime Minister Peres, government ministers refused to comment publicly on the Ayyash's killing. Opposition leader Benjamin Netanyahu, on the other hand, declared that "The only way to fight terrorism is for its perpetrators to know they have no refuge. We all hope that the Ayyash's comrades in murder will meet the same end. I applaud the fact that this despicable person got what he deserved. The men who eliminated him did important work for the people of Israel." (*Ma'ariv*, January 7, 1996, p. 7) After Ayyash's death, the Hamas leader in the Gaza Strip, Mahmoud al-Zahar, declared that "there will certainly be retaliation against Israel. The principles of the Hamas movement require that Palestinian blood will not be lost without revenge." And indeed, over the next few weeks, Hamas carried out a number of severe retaliatory attacks that killed dozens of Israelis and injured hundreds—two suicide bombings on buses in Jerusalem and a suicide bombing in Dizengoff Center in Tel Aviv, as well as a car-ramming attack in Ashkelon (Zonder, 2001).

About a year and a half later, one of the resounding failures in the history of Israeli targeted killings operations occurred, in the Jordanian capital of Amman. On September 25, 1997, Mossad agents attempted to eliminate the head of Hamas's political bureau, Khaled Mashal, by injecting him with poison in the middle of a busy street. The poison was injected into Mashal's body, but the agents were caught, and under pressure from Jordan's King Hussein, Israel was forced to deliver the antidote needed to save his life to the Jordanians (Gal, 2013). According to the Israeli media, the head of Military Intelligence, the head of the ISA, and the IDF chief of staff were not in on the plan, which was carried out under the direction of Prime Minister Netanyahu and Mossad chief Danny Yatom (*Ma'ariv*, October 8, 1997, p. 4; *Ha'aretz*, October 5, 1997, p. 3A) At a press conference after the operation, the prime minister said:

> In the war on terror there are successes and there are failures. Ten times an operation will succeed and one time it won't. There is no insurance policy on this issue....I bear the overall responsibility in the war on terror.

When there are successes and when there are failures, the responsibility for this war is ultimately mine... I hear the frightened voices rising from certain circles telling us why we should remain idle in the face of these murderous leaders. But the government is determined to continue to strike against terrorism. If you capitulate to terrorism and avoid taking courageous decisions, terrorism will hit you even more powerfully...Khaled Mashal was a person who directed Hamas's terrorist activities and had ties with other terrorist organizations and with Iran. He applied constant pressure to carry out attacks against Israel and was a man of major importance in Hamas...Terrorism cannot enjoy immunity in any country, including Jordan. We expect every country that wants peace to fight terrorism. I believe that Jordan wants peace and we look forward to cooperating in the fight against terrorism. (*Ma'ariv*, October 7, 1997, p. 2, 3)

A few days after the failed attempt, Mashal recounted the incident, saying:

They looked foreign, not Arab. From our experience, they looked like Israelis, Jews. They used an innovative device that I did not see, but which my attendant noticed. I was hit in the left ear, and that second I understood that this was an assassination attempt on my life, with the attackers trying to avoid shooting me. I felt a ringing in my left ear and suddenly I was shivering and something that felt like an electric shock passed through my body. Two hours later I felt new symptoms and was immediately transferred to the hospital. I was vomiting relentlessly and lost my sense of balance. (*Ha'aretz*, October 5, 1997, p. 4)

In a speech delivered by King Hussein a few days after the attempted killing, he said:

48 hours before the incident, I sent a letter to the Israeli prime minister saying that there was a possibility of establishing a dialogue between Hamas and Israel in order to stop the violence and discuss all of the matters...I can tell you that the prime minister of Israel himself, the minister of defense and the minister of infrastructure came here on the night between September 28 and 29, and I instructed my brother to meet with them. They were full of pain and remorse for Jordan being treated like this and promised that it would never happen again. The minister of infrastructure came again on the night of October 3-4, and we finally achieved the release of 23 Palestinian detainees...50 detainees from the West Bank and Gaza will be released within two weeks... In addition, Israel undertook to honor

the peace agreement as it is written. I said that for me, the life of the peace process depends on the life of this Jordanian (Mashal). Praise be to God who has healed him. (*Ha'aretz*, October 9, 1997, p. 3A)

Indeed, the botched operation caused Israel severe damage—it undermined the bilateral relationship with Jordan and King Hussein, marred Israel's diplomatic relations with Canada (when it emerged that the Israeli agents were holding Canadian passports), exposed the technical means Israel used in the operation, tarnished the reputation of the Mossad, and led to the release of Hamas leader Sheikh Yassin from prison, in accordance with King Hussein's demands (*Ma'ariv*, October 8, 1997, p. 4).

Following the failed operation in Jordan, Israel established a commission of inquiry, the Ciechanover Commission, which was tasked with examining the decision-making process and execution of the targeted killing attempt. Among the questions the committee addressed were: Did Prime Minister Netanyahu force the Mossad chief to carry out the operation in Jordan? Were the consequences of the possibility of failure considered? Why was there no formal discussion in the IDF, Military Intelligence and the Mossad about the operation? Was the operation well-planned? Was a simulation carried out beforehand? Were the appropriate people for this type of operation selected? Why was the operation carried out on a crowded street? Why did the agents use an Israeli embassy vehicle? (*Ha'aretz*, October 7, 1997) The commission held 47 closed-door meetings, heard from 35 witnesses, and reviewed hundreds of documents. Upon the completion of its work in February 1998, its members produced a report concluding that:

> In examining the conduct of the Prime Minister…with our own criteria…we reached the conclusion that he had dealt with the case in a responsible manner, having considered and examined the plans presented to him from every possible aspect…He inquired about details of the plans…he repeatedly asked that the operation be coordinated with the other heads of the intelligence community, and we are aware of the fact that a number of discussions were held in the Prime Minister's Office before the plan was approved and executed. We reached the conclusion that the Prime Minister's conduct in no way deviated from the norms and procedures customary in similar cases in the past. The Commission also examined the question of whether the Prime Minister had exerted any unreasonable pressure to carry out the operation "quickly and at any cost," so that it might

serve as an immediate response to the terrorist attacks. We reached the conclusion that no unreasonable pressure had been exerted by the Prime Minister in this matter.

Regarding the head of the Mossad, the commission noted that in his appearance before it, he addressed the question of the extent to which the head of the Mossad must delve into details of the plans of Mossad units before giving his approval.

We did not wish to answer this question in a general manner, but we are certain that before approving a plan of the type in question, the head of the Mossad must indeed study it in detail. We believe that the head of the Mossad erred in his handling of the operation and in approval of the plan. This should not have been structured as a 'silent operation,' without providing for contingency measures should it become a 'noisy' one. The Commission believes that the Head of the Mossad had enough time at his disposal to convene an additional orderly discussion with the heads of the intelligence services, prior to the operation.

In its conclusions, the committee determined that the operation revealed a "conceptual fixation prevailing in the Mossad, at the various levels involved in planning, approving and carrying out the operation," who "hardly took into account the possibility that it could fail for any reason, and the planning...did not seriously consider such a possibility, nor was this aspect sufficiently emphasized when the plan was presented to the Prime Minister" (Marom, 1998).

The Use of Targeted Killings Following the Collapse of the Peace Process and the Events of the Al-Aqsa Intifada (the Second Intifada) (2000–2007)

The fourth period in the development of the Israeli measure of targeted killings began with the events of the "al-Aqsa" or "Second" Intifada. In September 2000, against the backdrop of the collapse of the peace process between Israel and the Palestinians (the Oslo Process), a wave of violent incidents and terrorist attacks of an unprecedented magnitude and nature erupted. The Palestinian Islamist organizations Hamas and Palestinian Islamic Jihad, who had been carrying out non-stop terrorist attacks in an attempt to sabotage the peace process since the signing of the Oslo Accords in 1993, were now joined by Fatah operatives and other Palestinian terrorist organizations, which in the years that followed led to an unparalleled number of terrorist attacks and casualties in Israel.

During this Intifada, a second wave of suicide bombings erupted (following the wave of attacks that took place between 1993 and 1996), which lasted until 2004 but reached its peak in early 2001, and especially in March of that year, which witnessed several suicide bombings each week. That month, about 135 Israeli civilians were killed in attacks and approximately 1,400 people were injured. These attacks severely intensified the anxiety of the Israeli public and caused significant damage to morale. Israel's vulnerability increased the Palestinian terrorists' sense of achievement (Pedhazur, 2004). According to then-Israeli Minister of Defense, Shaul Mofaz, these attacks and the understanding that Israel was facing the reality of suicide bombers "who had no intention of returning home, made us realize that we needed to create a richer toolbox than we had previously had."[7] Thus, during this period, a doctrine of targeted killings was formulated and in November 2000, an intense wave of killings began (David, 2003).

During the Second Intifada, in light of the large number of terrorist attacks and deaths, Israel began to wonder whether these reflected an existential threat to the state and its citizens. The fundamental question was not only whether an existential threat existed from a security perspective, but also what was the quality of Israelis' existence? The events of the Intifada and the suicide bombings damaged Israel's ability to carry on with routine activities in industry, the economy, and tourism. There was a sense of terror in Israeli cities, with buses exploding frequently and hundreds of Israeli citizens being killed.[8]

Given this reality, Israel decided to move from defense to attack, once again making massive use of the method of targeted killings; most of these were carried out in the West Bank and the Gaza Strip. A record of the targeted killings during this period shows that Israel carried out more targeted killings during these years than in its entire history (David, 2003). Along with the elimination of terrorists from Hamas and PIJ, Israel also began to target operatives from the Fatah organization

---

[7] Personal interview with Shaul Mofaz, February 22, 2022.

[8] Personal interview with Gal Hirsch, February 20, 2022.

who were involved in terrorist attacks. According to the Association for Civil Rights in Israel, until the Second Intifada, the Israeli government tended not to take responsibility for targeted killings; during this period, however, Israel began to acknowledge them, even identifying who its next targets would be ((HCJ 769/02, 2006). During these years, Israel also began to use sophisticated weaponry in its execution of targeted killings, such as attack helicopters and fighter jets (David, 2003).

In the legal arena, then-Defense Minister Shaul Mofaz came to the conclusion that it was necessary to create a new legal toolbox to help the security forces in dealing with terrorism. In order to give this toolbox a legal seal of approval, Mofaz decided to make the military advocate general a member of the general staff for the first time in Israel's history.[9] Former IDF Chief of Staff Gadi Eisenkot, who was a senior IDF officer at the time, says that he decided to learn from Israel's experience in the 1970s during Golda Meir's term as prime minister. "I saw a pattern there in which Golda decided, together with Dayan, Yigal Alon and Galili, to establish 'Committee X', the four of them. And they would make a decision that was in practice a combination of revenge and prevention of harm to Israel by launching Operation 'Wrath of God.' So we decided to set up a small committee made up of a few ministers before whom would be brought the decision to carry out targeted killings."[10]

Yuval Diskin, who was the deputy head of the ISA at that time, was appointed to establish a joint operations room for the security agencies to carry out the targeted killings (Ashkenazi, 2019). This model was unique in the world, and facilitated cooperation between ISA and IDF intelligence personnel, and, if necessary, representatives from the Navy, Air Force, or special forces. Intelligence materials would flow into this room, and the people in it would be responsible for delivering instructions for the execution of the targeted killing in real time, with the variety of tools available to them.[11]

This period of targeted killings began with the November 9, 2000 elimination of Hussein Abayat, a senior commander of Fatah's Tanzim wing, in Beit Sahur. It was the first time that an IDF spokesman issued an announcement about a targeted killing carried out by Israel. Prime

---

[9] Personal interview with Shaul Mofaz, February 22, 2022.

[10] Personal interview with Gadi Eisenkot, February 28, 2022.

[11] Personal interview with Shaul Mofaz, February 22, 2022.

Minister Ehud Barak said that this elimination was "not an operation but a trend, which sets a new standard – whoever hits us will be hit." Chief of Staff Shaul Mofaz said in this context, "I believe that the hit on Abayat sends everyone the message that we will strike anyone who harms IDF soldiers and residents of the State of Israel" (). Indeed, shortly after that operation on December 31, 2000, the head of Fatah in Tulkarem, Thabet Thabet, was killed. It was the first time a member of the organization's political wing had been targeted, but Israeli sources at the time claimed that "Thabet was a senior terrorist operative and the force behind the shooting incidents in the Tulkarem area" (Ibid.).

Among the targeted killing operations carried out in 2001 were the those of Massoud Ayyad, a senior officer in Fatah's Force 17, on February 13, 2001; Jamal Salim, the head of Hamas's political wing, in Nablus on July 31, 2001 ("Eight killed in IDF bombing of Hamas headquarters in Nablus," 2001) and Mahmoud Abu Hanoud, commander of Hamas's military wing in the West Bank, who was killed by a missile fired at his car in the Nablus area on November 22 (Harel, 2001). The most noteworthy targeted killing that year, however, was that of the leader of the Popular Front for the Liberation of Palestine, Abu Ali Mustafa, via a missile fired at his office in Ramallah on August 27, 2001. This was the first attack on the leader of a terrorist organization during this period. After the operation, a senior Israeli official explained the decision, saying, "We are aware that Mustafa was a Palestinian political leader and we took this fact into account. The attack does not indicate that Israel has decided to target political actors. The strike on Mustafa was carried out despite his being on the political level and not because of it. Because the Popular Front is a small organization, Mustafa was also a military leader and personally organized terrorist attacks against Israel" ("Secretary General of the PFLP killed in Ramallah," 2001). Abu Ali Mustafa's death was followed by a grave revenge attack—the assassination of the Israeli Minister of Tourism Rehavam Ze'evi ("Gandhi") in a Jerusalem hotel on October 17, 2001 by PFLP operatives. With the increase in terrorist attacks in Israel in the years 2002–2004, Israeli targeted killings also grew in number. Among the most notable killings carried out during this period were that of the Tanzim commander in Tulkarem, Raed Karmi, on January 14, 2002 (Frisch & Waked, 2000a, 2000b); the founder and head of Hamas's military wing in Gaza, Ibrahim Makdama, on March 8, 2003 (Yitzhak, 2003); and Ismail Abu Shanab, one of the top Hamas officials in the Gaza Strip, on August 21 (Frisch & Waked, 2003).

In March 2002, in the wake of a severe wave of suicide bombings in Israel, Operation Defensive Shield was launched by the IDF, who regained control of the territories of Judea and Samaria that had been controlled by the Palestinian Authority until then. These areas included cities that offered refuge and bases for terrorists. Israel gradually took control of these territories in Area A, which enabled it to reduce its targeted killing operations in favor of a strategy of thwarting terrorist attacks by arresting and prosecuting the perpetrators. In the Gaza Strip, the policy of targeted killings continued, and even intensified at times. In the following years, a long list of operatives, commanders, and senior members of Palestinian terrorist organizations in the Gaza Strip were eliminated.

One of the most significant operations during this period, and one that impacted Israel's policy of targeted killings, was that of senior Hamas official and one of the founders of its military wing, Salah Shehadeh, in Gaza on July 22, 2002. Shehadeh and his aide were killed by a missile fired from a fighter jet carrying a 1000 kg warhead; along with them, 15 uninvolved civilians were killed (Waked et al., 2002). Former IDF Chief of Staff Dan Halutz, who was serving as commander of the Air Force at the time, explained that the significant collateral damage from this operation stemmed from an intelligence error. "It was an intelligence failure par excellence," he said.[12] The failure stemmed from the fact that Israel was not aware that there were people in the tin shacks next to the building that was demolished. "Had we known about the presence of 14 people in the shacks, the attack would not have taken place. Unequivocally. It's black and white."

In 2004, Israel carried out two strategic targeted killings, one after the other. The founder and leader of the Hamas movement, Ahmed Yassin, was killed on March 22 as he was leaving morning prayers at a mosque, and his replacement as Hamas's new leader, Abdel Aziz al-Rantissi, was killed on April 17. After Yassin's death, IDF Spokeswoman Ruth Yaron issued an official statement, saying: "It should be remembered that this is the man who sent terrorists to the carry out the largest attacks – the Dolphinarium, the Park Hotel in Netanya, Cafe Moment – and the list goes on. This is a man who preached death. He did so actively and now he will not be able to do it anymore" (Waked & Greenberg, 2004). At

---

[12] Personal interview with Dan Halutz, March 4, 2022.

a cabinet meeting, Prime Minister Ariel Sharon said, "This morning, the State of Israel hit the first and foremost perpetrator of murderous Palestinian terrorism. The essence of this man's ideology was the murder and killing of Jews wherever they are, and the destruction of the State of Israel." He added, "The war on terror is not over, and it will continue every day and everywhere. It is a difficult battle, one that all of the nations of the free world understand that they must take part in. It is the natural right of the Jewish people, like any other life-loving nation, to pursue those who want to annihilate it." Defense Minister Shaul Mofaz added, "Hamas has carried out 52 suicide bombings that have left 288 dead and 1,646 wounded. Hamas is on the list of terrorist organizations, including in Europe, with no distinction between its political and military wings. Yassin sent hundreds of terrorists and suicide bombers to kill civilians. He is a Palestinian bin Laden – his hands are covered in blood" ("Sharon: We struck an enemy of Israel," 2004).

In the years following 2007, after the suppression of the al-Aqsa Intifada and the phenomenon of suicide bombers, Israel used the method of targeted killing sparingly. The terrorist organizations in the Gaza Strip began firing rockets and missiles against civilians in Israel as revenge for targeted killings against their men, which added to the difficulty and complexity of carrying out such operations.[13] This is how a kind of 'mutual deterrence' developed between Israel and the Palestinian terrorist organizations in the Gaza Strip.

Among the prominent targeted killings carried out over the last decade was that of Mahmoud al-Mabhouh, a senior Hamas figure who was killed in Dubai in 2010. The Dubai police chief attributed the killing to Israeli Mossad agents who allegedly arrived in Dubai using foreign passports (Lachter, 2020). On November 14, 2012, the head of Hamas' military wing, Ahmad Jabari, was killed in Gaza. Jabari was responsible, among other things, for the abduction of soldier Gilad Shalit and for conducting negotiations for the release of terrorists imprisoned in Israel in exchange for Shalit's release (Zeitun, 2012). Jabari's death signaled the launch of Operation Pillar of Defense in the Gaza Strip, which lasted about a week and involved heavy barrages of about 1,700 rockets fired at the Israeli home front by Hamas ("Operation Pillar of Defense," 2012).

---

[13] Personal interview with Gadi Eisenkot, February 28, 2022.

In 2019, Israel killed Baha Abu al-Ata, commander of the northern brigade of Islamic Jihad's military wing. It was the first targeted strike against a senior member of the military wing of a terrorist organization in the Gaza Strip, and the first firing from the air since 2014. Al-Ata was considered a ticking time bomb, and according to an IDF spokesperson he had planned to carry out sniper, drone, and rocket attacks against Israel. Israel had previously tried and failed to kill al-Ata during Operation Pillar of Defense. In a statement issued by Prime Minister Benjamin Netanyahu, he said, "The operation was recommended by the IDF chief of staff and the head of the ISA, and signed off by the prime minister and defense minister after being presented and approved by the cabinet" (*Hadashot*, December 2019).

Thus, over the years, targeted killings became an effective and accessible measure in the Israeli security community's toolbox in the war against terrorism. It has been carried out using various means (air strikes, shootings during ground operations, letter bombs, etc.), and in various areas (the Gaza Strip, the West Bank, on the territory of enemy countries, and even in friendly countries.) The scope and nature of the employment of this method varied over different time periods, in accordance with the development of the phenomenon of Palestinian and Shiite terrorism that has been perpetrated against Israel since its establishment.

REFERENCES

Alon, G. (2001, December 1). The Attorney General supports the "elimination policy." *Ha'aretz*. https://www.haaretz.co.il/misc/1.752992

And who is blamed? Usually, the Mossad. (1991, August 5). *Hadashot*.

Ashkenazi, E. (2019, November 13). *From "Spring of Youth" to Yassin: A history of targeted killings*. Walla! News. https://news.walla.co.il/item/3323605

Attack in the heart of the community. (2014). *Israel Hayom*. https://www.israel hayom.co.il/article/200711

Aviad, G. (2008). *Lexicon of the Hamas movement*. Tel Aviv: Ministry of Defense.

Bachar, I., Amir, G., Menachem, R. & Shefi, G. (1988, April 20). Ma'arach and Likud accuse each other of leaks about the assassination of Abu Jihad. *Ma'ariv*.

Bergman, R. (2018). *Rise and kill first: The secret history of Israel's targeted assassinations*. Random House.

Bohbot, A. (2021, September 18). *The attacks, the eliminations, the rockets and the escape from prison: The long account between Israel and Islamic Jihad*. Walla! News. https://news.walla.co.il/item/3459249

Bowyer Bell, J. (1977). *Terror out of Zion: Irgun Zvai Leumi, Lehi, and the Palestine underground, 1929–1949*. St. Martin's Press.

Byman, D. (2011). *A high price: The triumphs and failures of Israeli counterterrorism*. Oxford University Press.

David, S. (2003). Israel's policy of targeted killing. *Ethics & International Affairs, 17*(1), 122.

Death blow. (2012, February 6). *Israel Hayom*. https://www.israelhayom.co.il/article/33655

Eight killed in IDF bombing of Hamas headquarters in Nablus, including a key operative. (2001, July 31). *Globes*. https://www.globes.co.il/news/article.aspx?did=510310

Frisch, F., & Waked, A. (2000a, November 11). *Barak: Whoever hurts us will be hurt in return*. Ynet. https://www.ynet.co.il/articles/0,7340,L-244129,00.html

Frisch, F., & Waked, A. (2000b, December 31). *The Palestinians: Fatah Secretary eliminated in Tulkarem*. Ynet. https://www.ynet.co.il/articles/0,7340,L-388008,00.html

Frisch, F., & Waked, A. (2002, January 14). *The Palestinians: IDF assassinates senior Tanzim leader Raed al-Karmi*. Ynet. https://www.ynet.co.il/articles/0,7340,L-1539788,00.html

Frisch, F., & Waked, A. (2003, August 21). *IDF assassinates a senior Hamas figure in Gaza*. Ynet. https://www.ynet.co.il/articles/0,7340,L-2732642,00.html

Gal, S. (2013, October 4). *Sixteen years later: Mashal file opened*. N12. https://www.mako.co.il/news-military/security/Article-449a98746848141004.htm

Ganor, B. (2021). Targeted killings: Ethical & operational dilemmas. *Terrorism & Political Violence, 33*(2), 353.

Ganor, B. (2005). *The counter-terrorism puzzle—A guide for decision makers*. Routledge.

Gazit, S. (1992, February 23). War but also peace. *Yediot Aharonot*.

Goldblum, A. (2020, January 27). Why was the revenge against the Nazis directed at the Palestinians? *Ha'aretz*. https://www.haaretz.co.il/blogs/amiramgoldblum/2020-01-27/ty-article/0000017f-f8c3-d47e-a37f-f9ffaa8d0000

Harel, A. (2001, November 24). Apache helicopters fired at the car; Abu Hanoud was identified only by his scar. *Ha'aretz*. https://www.haaretz.co.il/misc/1.751239

HCJ 769, 02. (2006). The public committee against torture in Israel v. *The Government of Israel, 62*(1), 507.

Hoffman, B. (1985). *Recent trends in Palestinian terrorism II*. Rand Corporation.

Huberman, H. (2009, May 31). The eliminated terrorist was planning an attack on a train to Be'er Sheva. *Arutz Sheva*. https://www.inn.co.il/news/189895

Ifergan, S. (2013, October 9). Elimination games. *Mako*. https://www.mako.co.il/pzm-weekend/Article-855501957cc9141006.htm

Intelligence and Terrorism Information Center. (2010). *The Palestinian Authority continues to allow, and even encourage, turning shahidim into role models*. https://www.terrorism-info.org.il/Data/pdf/PDF_10_081_1.pdf

Israel Defense. (2012, June 12). *The terrorist attack that led to the establishment of "Kidon."* Israel Defense. https://www.israeldefense.co.il/content/%D7%9E%D7%AA%D7%A7%D7%A4%D7%AA-%D7%94%D7%98%D7%A8%D7%95%D7%A8-%D7%A9%D7%94%D7% 91%D7%99%D7%90%D7%94-%D7%9C%D7%94%D7%A7%D7%9E%D7%AAE2%80%9C%D7%9B%D7%99%D7%93%D7%95%D7%9F.

Israeli Air Force. Operation "Spring of Youth."http://www.iaf.co.il/Templates/FlightLog/FlightLog.aspx?lang=HE&lobbyID=40&folderID=48&subfolderID=322&docfolderID=842&docID=7220d&docType=EVENT

Jordanian Killed in Athens Hotel Explosion. (1973, April 13). *Davar*.

Klein, A. (1992, February 17). Musawi's killing was planned in advance; high alert on the northern border. *Hadashot*.

Kremnitzer, M. (2006). *Is everything kosher when dealing with terrorism?* The Israel Democracy Institute.

Lachter, E. (2020, January 17). A decade since the al-Mabhouh elimination: This is how a senior Hamas official was killed in Dubai. *N12*. https://www.mako.co.il/news-military/2020_q1/Article-6548484fea4bf61027.htm

Marom, D. (1998, February 17). The Ciechanover Commission report. *Globes*. https://www.globes.co.il/news/article.aspx?did=113946

Mitchnik, G. (2016, March 15). This is how Israel eliminated the "engineer" of Hamas, Yahya Ayyash. *Nrg*. https://www.makorrishon.co.il/nrg/online/1/ART2/761/301.html

Meisels, T. (2004). Targeting terror. *Social Theory and Practice, 30*(3), 297–326.

Melman, Y. (2004, March 23). Assassinations were once a last resort today, today they are carried out wholesale. *Ha'aretz*. https://www.haaretz.co.il/misc/1.954331

Operation Pillar of Defense. (2012). Israeli Security Agency: https://www.shabak.gov.il/publications/Pages/study/OperationPillarofDefense.aspx

Pedhazur, A. (2004). The new terrorism and the Palestinian arena. In Ministry of Defense (Ed.), *Aspects of terrorism and counter-terrorism* (pp. 1–183). Tel Aviv: Ministry of Defense.

Peleg, M. (2018, December 27). Why was Kanafani's monument taken down? *Ha'aretz*. https://www.haaretz.co.il/opinions/2018-12-27/ty-article-opinion/.premium/0000017f-f2cd-d487-abff-f3ff50030000

PLO leaders eliminated over the past 15 years. (1988a, April 17). *Hadashot*.

Ronel, A. (2010, January 4). 32 years ago today: PLO representative in London murdered by Palestinians. *Ha'aretz.* https://www.haaretz.co.il/news/educat ion/2010-01-04/ty-article/0000017f-e6a1-df5f-a17f- ffffc11f0000

Secretary General of the PFLP killed in Ramallah; Hamas: A declaration of war. (2001, August 27). *Globes.* https://www.globes.co.il/news/article.aspx?did= 517271

Sharon: We struck an enemy of Israel; US: We didn't know in advance. (2004, March 22). *Ynet.* https://www.ynet.co.il/articles/0,7340,L-289256 7,00.html

Shtull-Trauring, A. (2012, February 16). February 16, 1992: IDF eliminates Hezbollah leader. *Ha'aretz.* https://www.haaretz.co.il/opinions/today-bef ore/2012-02-16/ty-article/0000017f-e5b5-dc7e-adff- f5bd6cb40000

Tal, S. (1988, April 17). We must aim to eliminate all the military and political leaders. *Hadashot.*

The Mossad agent was hysterically attacked. Carlos murdered his man. (1990, September 17). *Ma'ariv.*

The work of professionals. (1988b, April 17). *Hadashot.*

This is the senior Islamic Jihad leader who was killed. *N12.* https://www.mako. co.il/news-military/2019_q4/Article-63877c7e9ed5e61027.htm

Waked, A., & Greenberg, H. (2004, March 22). Israel eliminated Hamas leader Sheikh Yassin in Gaza. *Ynet.* https://www.ynet.co.il/articles/0,7340,L-289 2347,00.html

Waked, Bachor & Somfalvi. (2002, July 23). *Salah Shehadeh killed along with 15 other civilians.* Ynet. https://www.ynet.co.il/articles/0,7340,L-2015833,00. html

Yaffe, A. (2006). Targeted killing: Prospect and risk. *Nativ, 19*(2), 109.

Yitzhak, Y. (2003, March 8). Police and Shin Bet increase leaders' security. *News1.*https://www.news1.co.il/MemberLogin.aspx?ContentType= 1&docid=20948&subjectid=1

Zeitun, Y. & Levy, E. (2012, November 14). Hamas chief of staff Ahmad Jabari killed in Gaza alongside his son. *Ynet.* https://www.ynet.co.il/articles/0,734 0,L-4305340,00.html

Zonder, M. (2001, July 27). Shooting and not crying. *Nrg.* http://www.nrg. co.il/online/archive/ART/169/638.html

CHAPTER 3

Targeted Killings in Israel's Counter-Terrorism Strategy: Decision-Making Processes and the Intelligence Factor

Targeted killing as a modus operandi is not a new phenomenon, but rather one that has changed and developed over the years. Some see this method as a direct continuation of the assassinations that have been recounted beginning in Biblical times—Ehud ben Gera's assassination of the Moabite King Eglon, or the killing of Julius Caesar, the leader of the Roman Republic—as well as the many political assassinations that have been carried out against heads of state and other political and military figures over the years.[1] In any event, targeted killing has taken root over the years as a key tool in Israel's counter-terrorism strategy.

THE IMPORTANCE OF TARGETED KILLING AS A PILLAR OF ISRAEL'S COUNTER-TERRORISM STRATEGY

The centrality and importance of targeted killings in the context of Israel's fight against terrorism can be learned from interviews conducted with key Israeli decision-makers and former heads of the defense establishment who have grappled with this issue. The vast majority of the interviewees

---

[1] These examples were taken from interviews conducted for this book with senior Israeli decision-makers.

© The Author(s), under exclusive license to Springer Nature Switzerland AG 2022
B. Ganor and L. Koblentz-Stenzler, *Israel's Targeted Killing Policy*,
https://doi.org/10.1007/978-3-031-13674-0_3

emphasized that targeted killings are one of the most effective means of dealing with the phenomenon of terrorism in general, and in preventing terrorist attacks in particular. Others, on the other hand, expressed various reservations regarding the use of this method.

Former Prime Minister **Ehud Olmert** believes that Israel is no different from other countries in the use it makes of this measure. He says, "I have ordered targeted killings, so I will not take a position that is contradictory to what I did…There are many pretenses with regard to this matter. There is no country in the world that does not employ the measure of targeted killings of terrorists. The world is divided between those who do it and do not apologize for it, and those who do it and do apologize for it."[2] Another prime minister, **Shimon Peres**, declared that "In principle I am against targeted killing, unless this person is a 'ticking bomb.' I was told that Abu Jihad [Arafat's deputy in the Fatah organization], for example, was one of their most moderate men, and we eliminated him. What did that give us?"[3]

Former Defense Minister and IDF Chief of Staff **Shaul Mofaz** believes that the importance of targeted killings lies mainly in the deterrent effect it has on terrorist organizations and their leaders and operatives. In his words, "The decision on targeted killings was part of the policy we adopted in the armed conflict with the Palestinians, but in order to succeed, we had to be determined to implement and adhere to the policy over time." He explains that the targeted killings have focused on two types of targets—heads of terrorist organizations and "ticking bombs." "Our deterrence stemmed from their sense of being hunted. Once they realized that we were able to get to them wherever they are, their desire to save their own lives outweighed their aspirations to dispatch others. So they went underground and we searched them out everywhere…they went underground and some of their activities were stopped."[4]

Discussing the importance of targeted killings in the prevention of terrorist attacks, Mofaz recounted a meeting held while he was minister of defense during the Second Intifada in 2004 with Omar Suleiman, director of Egypt's General Intelligence Directorate and President Mubarak's special envoy for Palestinian affairs, who came to Israel with the request

[2] Personal interview with Ehud Olmert, February 5, 2014.

[3] Personal interview with Shimon Peres, December 7, 1999.

[4] Personal interview with Shaul Mofaz, February 17, 2014.

that Israel cease carrying out targeted killings against Hamas and Islamic Jihad in the Gaza Strip. According to Mofaz, he responded to Suleiman's request by saying, "'Listen, we will not stop until we are sure they have stopped.' So he asks me, 'How will you know they have stopped?' I said, 'When the suicide bombings stop.'" Mofaz went on to say, "He left the meeting quite angry (and said) 'You don't know what you're doing. So we told him, 'Listen, we've paid a terrible price in blood here, and we will not stop the killings because they are under pressure, on the contrary, we will only increase them." Suleiman, who did not like this answer, asked to meet with Prime Minister Sharon to discuss the issue. The meeting did indeed take place; it lasted only ten minutes and ended in crisis. Mofaz said, "Sharon told him that this was the policy of the Ministry of Defense, the IDF chief of staff, and the head of the ISA, and he could not change that. He supported them." Mofaz said that after two or three weeks, Suleiman came to Israel again and told him, "Look, they stopped." I told him, "It's true that they stopped. We will give it another certain period of time, and if it seems that they have indeed stopped, we will also stop." According to Mofaz, the fact that Suleiman was sent by the terrorist organizations time and time again to meet with the chief of staff and the heads of the Israeli defense establishment in an attempt to stop the targeted killing operations proves that this measure was indeed "very, very effective" and that it ultimately led to a halt to the wave of suicide attacks during that period.[5]

Another IDF chief of staff, **Gadi Eisenkot**, explains why he believes that targeted killings are an effective course of action. In his words, "The most important thing is the cognizance that you are willing to sacrifice and defeat them and make them understand that the use of force is pointless for them. Targeted killings made an important contribution to achieving this...In 2001 to 2004, the insane phenomenon of suicide terrorism ceased, and we were able to say that we defeated terrorism." However, Eisenkot emphasizes that targeted killings are not the only means of countering terrorism, and not even the main one: "Which measure had the greatest effectiveness in the victory over terrorism?... For 98 percent, it's arresting those involved in terrorism in their beds and putting them in jail or administrative detention, and for the remaining two to three percent, it's the targeted killing that stops them." Another

---

[5] Personal interview with Shaul Mofaz, February 17, 2014.

former defense minister and IDF chief of staff, **Moshe (Bogie) Ya'alon**, says, "I think targeted killings are one of the most effective tools in the war on terror, if not the most effective... it is the most effective tool in the war on terror, the most precise, with the least collateral damage and with the greatest amount of good results – both for deterrence and for impairing the capability of the terrorists."

Several senior ISA officials who were in charge of carrying out targeted killings emphasize the effectiveness of this measure, despite the dilemmas involved in their implementation. Former ISA Director **Avi Dichter** expresses unreserved support for the use of targeted killings. Dichter, however, emphasizes that it is but one of a variety of possible measures and that from an intelligence point of view, arrests can actually carry more importance than eliminating terrorist operatives. He says, "Contrary to what people think, a targeted killing is the second option, not the first. The first option is always to arrest and interrogate...Targeted killing is the course of action when there is no capability of making an arrest, or when doing so is too dangerous for our forces. Or when there is not a good chance of making the arrest and taking the person while he is still alive." Dichter explains the effectiveness of targeted killing by the fact that this measure requires the terrorist adversary to worry about protecting himself. "When you carry out a targeted killing, you change his [the terrorist's] balance. He can no longer plan attacks 90 percent of the time. He needs more time to think about hiding." Dichter illustrates his point with the following example: "They realized that we carry out a lot of targeted killings using helicopters, so every day that a helicopter was in the air, the wanted persons would hide. A hiding wanted person does not generate terrorism." Dichter adds that targeted killings also achieve a deterrent effect due to the intelligence superiority involved in this modus operandi:

> When you target someone, whether it is with a missile or a sniper or something else, the first thing he realizes is that we have received reports about his whereabouts. They don't know how we know that at that moment he is in a black car, near Abu Ali's grocery store, and that he is alone. And then we act. This, of course, puts butterflies in the stomach of anyone dealing with terrorism and knows that we know about it, either because

he knows that he has become a wanted person or because he believes that he may become one soon. Therefore, this measure creates deterrence.[6]

Former senior ISA official **Oz Noy** stresses that "There is no doubt that this tool is exceptional on every scale." According to Noy, at the basis of an understanding of the need to use targeted killings lies the perception that "this tool is not a punitive tool but a preventative one, and is used against those who are intending to carry out an attack and only against those whose elimination we believe will prevent the attack...this means that two basic key conditions must exist: One, that there is no other way that the attack can be avoided. Because everything that can be done has already been done – we have exhausted all other options. And two, that the elimination of that operative will prevent the attack. If these conditions are not met, there is no operation."[7]

Another former ISA official, **Arik "Harris" Barbing**, continues this argument, saying that targeted killings are about the "targeting of adversaries whom it is very difficult to get to by other means and arrest them. Those who represent a level of threat that is very high due to their experience, their leadership, and their ability to motivate suicide bombers and lead complex attacks in which innocent people are murdered." Barbing concludes by saying that "Targeted killings are an effective tool, but do not constitute a capability or tool for constant security. It is not a tool to be used on a daily basis and should be regarded as a unique capability, to be used when there is no other operational option to thwart a ticking bomb; every such operation should be treated as if it were the first, and its approval should be approached with great reverence."[8]

Shalom Ben Hanan, another former ISA official, expands on this, saying, "The idea behind 'targeted' action is a precise, planned and surgical strike. A lot of effort is put into preventing collateral damage. The plan is to hit a target that poses a significant future threat only when there is no other way to stop this threat, such as an arrest."[9] According to Ben Hanan, targeted killings should be classified into several types based on the degree of publicity and exposure of the body behind the operation:

[6] Personal interview with Avi Dichter, March 11, 2022.

[7] Personal interview with Oz Noy, February 16, 2022.

[8] Personal interview with Arik "Harris" Barbing, February 21, 2022.

[9] Personal interview with Shalom Ben Hanan, February 21, 2022.

Targeted killings are divided into different levels, based on the extent of the 'signature' of the operation, which is the degree of suspicion or knowledge with regards to who carried out the action. The scale ranges from targeted killings for which responsibility is taken publicly, to killings for which no responsibility is taken, even though the culprit or suspect or is quite clear, to killings with a very low signature, to the point of lack of awareness of it being a killing at all; for example, deaths that are attributed to natural or 'normal' causes, in which the targeted killing operation is not revealed. There are, of course, various methods of targeted killings, and various tools employed that need not be expanded upon; these range from 'noisy' and visible military tools to quieter ones. There are targeted killings that are carried out in the framework of a military campaign or a round of combat, such as dropping a bomb on a target's home or launching a precision missile. In these cases, the action is defined as a targeted killing, although it is debatable whether such an action carried out as part of a broad campaign and during battle does indeed meet this definition.[10]

Ben Hanan presents another type of action that is liable to be considered a targeted killing (though he claims that it is not at all)—cases in which Israeli security forces apprehend armed terrorists in order to arrest them, but they resist arrest and open fire and are eventually killed in action. He says, "In a case in which, after the hiding place of the person you want to arrest is exposed, he chooses to fight against the forces, the 'pressure cooker' protocol is applied – the target is eliminated after refusing to surrender. The first choice is to allow the person to surrender, which also sometimes gives him time to prepare for combat. It is a decision that endangers the lives of soldiers, but it is not a targeted killing because there was no advance decision to eliminate the target, but rather to arrest him."[11]

The heads of the Mossad who were interviewed on the subject also express great support for the measure of targeted killings in Israel's fight against terrorism. **Shabtai Shavit** says in this context, "In my view, targeted killings are one of the most important tools in the state's arsenal of weapons in dealing with terrorist organizations."[12] In another interview, Shavit explained that the effectiveness of targeted killings is due to the fact that "the effect is immediate – neutralizing a person who has

[10] Ibid.

[11] Ibid.

[12] Personal interview with Shabtai Shavit, February 17, 2022.

enormous potential for harm. However, there is another advantage in that the entire circle around him, activated by the power of his leadership, becomes completely paralyzed for a defined period of time, that is, until the power is rebuilt. There is also a deterrent effect in broader circles, far beyond that of the specific organization, and there is a moral contribution to your own forces." At the same time, Shavit points out that "The effectiveness of this measure is derived directly from the selectivity of its use. If you use it against any problematic person then you will lose the effectiveness and pay a price in public opinion...The more selective you are, targeting only those who represent the greatest threat, the higher the effectiveness and the more it will be accepted by the public."[13]

Another former Mossad chief, **Meir Dagan**, also a supporter of the use of targeted killings, preferred to place a restriction on the use of this measure:

> One should always examine this measure in terms of its benefit and what it serves. It should serve purposes. One goal is prevention. If eliminating a person prevents an attack, then he is definitely a legitimate target. A second goal is deterrence. The third is, I think such actions should also be used as punishment. That is, there are three goals: prevention, deterrence, and punishment, which to me certainly seem to be legitimate goals. Within these goals, the cost versus the benefit must be weighed. Would I target a religious figure who is not involved in terrorism but only constitutes authority? The answer is no. Because it is counterproductive...[14]

From the various positions presented above, and especially from comparing the approaches of former ISA directors and Mossad chiefs, it can be understood that there is a fundamental difference between targeted killings that Israel carries out in its war against terrorist organizations, operatives and their leaders located in the West Bank and the Gaza Strip—actions carried out mainly by the ISA and the IDF—and those against other terrorist operatives located in the neighboring countries bordering Israel or in far-away countries—operations carried out mainly by the Mossad. The targeted killings belonging to the first group are carried out very selectively during routine times, but during military operations and severe waves of terrorism, their number rises, possibly

---

[13] Ibid.

[14] Personal interview with Meir Dagan, December 2, 1999.

reaching dozens a year. In contrast, the second group involves a very limited number of isolated actions executed over the years. Whereas the first group has consisted mainly of operations with a loud and clear Israeli "signature," (along with those that were more low-profile), most of the operations in the second group were almost always carried out covertly, and usually without Israel taking responsibility publicly.

Regarding targeted killings from the first group, it is interesting to note the words of **Avi Eliyahu**, a former senior Military Intelligence official, who said:

> I think this is a significant, powerful and effective tool in the toolbox that Israel has in combatting terrorism, and I say this from an analysis of the dramatic impact that it has, in my opinion, on the enemy. The enemy's constant fear of being eliminated, living with a sense of insecurity, the change in his patterns of behavior, the fact that he has to remain hidden all the time, the fact that he understands that he may pay a price at any time, the element of surprise in targeted killings – all of these things greatly strengthened the balance of deterrence in Israel's favor. Beyond the physical harm to major operatives, and beyond the damage caused to the organization's morale, this tool has a significant impact on the enemy's military and organizational capabilities.[15]

In contrast to the previous interviewees, Eliyahu claims that this measure has not been used sufficiently in routine times and laments the fact that it is put into practice mainly during military campaigns.

> Unfortunately, this tool has been eroded and we use it today only in battle or in response to a really significant event. For example, in the Gaza Strip, or in Lebanon, they feel safe. They are sure they are protected, because in routine times we don't touch them. That is, bottom line, it is a very significant tool that we stopped using because the enemy dictated to us that if we want quiet then there cannot be any killings...Israel has slowly come to terms with this and chosen quiet over targeted killings.[16]

On the other hand, **Shlomo Gazit**, who served as the IDF intelligence chief in the 1970s, suggests examining the effectiveness of targeted killings with a different classification lens—those targeting senior terrorist

---

[15] Personal interview with Avi Eliyahu, April 6, 2022.

[16] Ibid.

operatives from small and underground organizations and those targeting senior members of popular and large terrorist organizations. According to Gazit:

> If someone tells me I can eliminate the leader of a small terrorist gang, Shaqaqi [former head of Palestinian Islamic Jihad] or Abu Nidal [former head of Fatah – The Revolutionary Council], it is worth doing. But when you operate in Beirut and do "Spring of Youth" [the name of the 1973 operation in which Israeli special forces killed senior members of Fatah and Popular Front for the Liberation of Palestine in Beirut], it is meaningless. When you kill Abu Jihad [Arafat's deputy, who was eliminated in Tunisia in 1988] it is meaningless, because an organization like Fatah or the PLO is a large, political popular movement, not built on one man. And such an action will not have an impact and will only have negative implications.[17]

Despite the few reservations and various limitations raised by the interviewees in the context of the use of targeted killings in the framework of the Israeli counter-terrorism policy, most of them support the use of this measure for the purpose of preventing terrorist attacks and deterring terrorists. The stances adopted by Israeli decision-makers and former heads of the security establishment faithfully reflect the sentiment and attitude of the Israeli public towards targeted killings. A national opinion poll conducted by the International Institute for Counter-Terrorism (ICT) at Reichman University in early 2022 to assess the Israeli public's positions on the targeted killings in Israel's counter-terrorism activity shows that the vast majority of the Israeli public believes that targeted killings are the most effective method in the fight against Palestinian terrorism. 78% of the respondents, representing all sectors of Israeli society, answered that this method is very effective (62%) or effective (16%), while only 7% saw this method is ineffective (3% stated that targeted killings are ineffective and 4% stated that it is not effective at all). It is interesting in this context to note that about a third—31%—of the respondents who identified themselves as Arab Israeli citizens believed that targeted killings are effective. Moreover, according to this public opinion poll, 74% of the entire Israeli public believes that targeted killings are a moral and legitimate course of action, with only 14% responding that this method is immoral (here too, 31% of the respondents who identified as members

---

[17] Personal interview with Shlomo Gazit, November 7, 1999.

of the Arab minority answered that in their view, targeted killings are a moral course of action, while 48% believed it is immoral).[18]

THE DECISION-MAKING PROCESS IN THE EXECUTION OF TARGETED KILLINGS

The decision to carry out a targeted killing is one of the most difficult and problematic in the field of counter-terrorism. The reasons for this include the fact that targeted killings are deadly and therefore one of the most severe tools in the arsenal of counter-terrorism measures; the serious consequences a targeted killing can lead to (if it is successful and certainly if it fails), both due to the domestic and international criticism that the use of this measure may bring about, and because of the normative issues involved in making such a decision (which will be further detailed below), and especially the fear of accidentally causing collateral damage (which can result both from the need to make decisions within a short period of time and sometimes under heavy pressure and operational considerations) and from the possibility of the operation deteriorating from a targeted offensive strike into an all-out military campaign. As a result, in Israel, the decision to carry out a counter-terrorism operation in general and targeted killing, in particular, is usually made by the highest echelons of decision-makers, namely, the Security Cabinet—a group of Israeli government ministers who, due to their previous military and security experience or their political status, have been appointed as members of the Security Cabinet. It is headed by the minister of defense and the prime minister.

Former Prime Minister Ehud Olmert says in this context:

> The prime minister must approve everything. In order to do so, he must know everything, and in order to know everything he must be involved at such a level that he cannot retrospectively say, 'I knew, I approved, but I did not know *that*.' He's in charge, so he needs to know all the relevant things...I demanded that before any action was taken by an operational unit of the Mossad, that I be brought the personal biographies of each of the participants, and I wanted to know exactly what each one's role would be in the operation. It happened more than once that I came across people whose parents I knew. I also had a custom where after covert operations,

---

[18] National Public Opinion Poll on Targeted Killings, conducted for the International Institute for Counter-Terrorism (ICT) by *Ma'agar Mochot*, February 21, 2022.

I would come and say thank you. They don't get any recognition. Even their wives don't know what these officers did. Their family members don't know. So I said, at least they should know that the prime minister knows what they did, so I personally came to say a big thank you to them. So they would know that the people of Israel are behind them.[19]

The decision to carry out targeted killings, then, may be made for the purpose of thwarting one terrorist organization or another in order to prevent a future attack, or following a major terrorist attack in an attempt to deter terrorist organizations from continuing to carry out attacks, and when other alternatives (such as the bombing of the organization's military installations) have been considered and found to be less effective or relevant. The decision to carry out targeted killings may also be made in the framework of an ongoing military campaign or a targeted operation in the context of a round of violence and exchanges of fire between Israel and terrorist organizations (especially in the Gaza Strip, which is a Hamas-controlled territory). Therefore, the decision-making process for carrying out a targeted killing operation may be bottom-up, beginning with the operational ranks on the ground, as a result of "intelligence and operational maturity or opportunity" and in light of the arrival or accumulation of operational intelligence by one of Israel's intelligence agencies (the ISA, Mossad, or Military Intelligence), or information conveyed to Israel by a friendly intelligence source, indicating the intention of an attack by one terrorist operative or another. Then, the military or security echelons will turn to the political decision-makers for approval to carry out the operation. Alternatively, the decision to carry out targeted killings may be the result of the political echelon identifying a need and then instructing the operational echelon to carry out an action. In these cases, where the decision-making process is top-down, the request will come from the political leader, and the intelligence agencies will then examine the current "target bank" and select the most appropriate target for elimination and for achieving the goal set before them. (For example, after the Hamas suicide bombing at an Israeli discotheque in 2001, in which 21 people, including many teenagers, were killed, the Security Cabinet took a decision to authorize the prime minister and defense minister to pursue a policy of targeted killings of terrorist leaders and "ticking bombs".) To this end, Israel established a special committee composed

---

[19] Personal interview with Ehud Olmert, March 3, 2022.

of senior members of the Israeli defense establishment—the "Committee of Two" (one of whose members is a military official and the other a senior member of the ISA), who put together the list of "candidates" for targeted killings, from which the targets were ultimately selected. This list was modified from time to time in accordance with the intelligence information accumulated about the targets, with the addition of new candidates based on fixed criteria, such as the terrorist operative's past, the potential danger he represents, and information about his future plans, and more. The decision-making process in these cases was based on the Committee of Two's recommendation regarding the most relevant candidate for elimination. Their recommendation went to the IDF chief of staff for approval; following his approval, it was then passed on for the approval of the minister of defense and, if he approved it, the recommendation was presented for the decision and approval of the prime minister (Benziman, 2011b).

This process is fundamentally different in cases of targeted killings carried out against terrorists defined as "ticking bombs." In these cases, the operational intelligence echelon recognizes the urgent need to carry out the operation. It is this echelon that initiates the action and passes on its recommendation to the political echelon. Naturally, the process in these cases must be faster, due to the clear and imminent danger they pose. Former IDF Chief of Staff **Dan Halutz** points out that in cases of ticking bombs, the approval procedures are shortened. "A ticking time bomb means that someone is on his way, he's on the move. And when someone is on the move you have to shorten [the process] a bit because you want to end up hitting the target and not to deal with other things. You obtain approvals ahead of time. There are sweeping approvals given in advance for ticking bombings..."[20] Former Chief of Staff **Gadi Eisenkot** adds to this, explaining that in cases of ticking bombs, the decision-making circles were "very fast, because suddenly an opportunity arises for an hour or two...the opportunity is taken advantage of very quickly with small circles...If we know that X is a suicide bomber and he is about to carry out an attack, there is no time, and very quickly the circles become very small."[21]

---

[20] Personal interview with Dan Halutz, March 4, 2022.

[21] Personal interview with Gadi Eisenkot, March 2, 2022.

Brig. Gen. (Res.) **Gal Hirsch** offers an example of the dilemmas involved in making a decision to carry out a targeted killing against a ticking bomb:

> There is a taxi leaving Tulkarem – I will remind you that there is no 'seam line' so there is no separation, nothing. Inside the taxi sits a suicide bomber. There are ten people with him, and they have nothing to do with the attack. Now, I have to stop the attack and he is going to Netanya (a nearby Israeli city). I need to target only the terrorist. How? Take out the whole cab? Eliminate them all? The answer was no. But then will thirty people be killed in Netanya? We have to find another solution. What a difficult dilemma. This is not a discussion that can last for days. This is a decision where I go into the command room and we have to deal with something that is going to happen in a matter of minutes ... and then we succeed, with the wonderful creativity of our units, to somehow stop [the taxi] and separate the people and kill those who we need to and not the others.[22]

In analyzing the Israeli decision-making process in carrying out targeted killings, a distinction must be made between the processes carried out within the Israeli security agencies—in the ISA, the IDF, and in the joint war rooms, and processes carried out at the political level—the Israeli government. Former ISA official **Oz Noy** describes the tension that exists between these two levels in the process of approving targeted killing operations: "In these situations, the debates are between the operational echelon, which always has a tendency to carry out the operation and expand the circles, and the decision makers, who see the other side and exercise restraint and put restrictions in place."[23]

Regarding the internal processes that take place within a particular security agency, former head of the Mossad's Intelligence Directorate **Amnon Sofrin** explains that first, the agency agrees that a certain person is an appropriate target, and then he must be "matured" from an intelligence point of view. This means employing various intelligence gathering and operational measures to collect and understand the information about his daily routine, schedule, and the way in which he conducts himself.

---

[22] Personal interview with Gal Hirsch, February 20, 2022.

[23] Personal interview with Oz Noy, February 2, 2022.

According to Sofrin, the intelligence gathering efforts seek out the potential target's patterns of behavior; from these, one can find his weak points, on which the further intelligence gathering is then focused. When the stage of gathering and processing the intelligence has been completed, the plan of action is brought for approval to the relevant most senior rank, be it the IDF chief of staff, the head of the Mossad, or the head of the ISA. Once they approve the plan, it is brought before the political echelon and the prime minister for approval. The prime minister may or may not approve, depending on various strategic and geopolitical considerations, or alternatively may impose conditions, stipulations, and restrictions on the action.[24]

Referring to internal processes, former ISA official **Arik "Harris" Barbing** says that "In the preliminary stage of any such operation, in order to approve the targets of the strike, you first carry out a very long period of risk management and try to stop him [the terrorist] or deter him or intimidate him without harming him. You have to really and truly prove to yourself, first of all, and then to the establishment, that professionally every effort has been made to thwart him without causing him harm." In the next stage, he said, the intelligence regarding his involvement in terrorism must be examined. Here, **Barbing** emphasizes, it must be determined whether the target is a ticking bomb—is he planning an attack that is difficult to prevent in other ways? This process is accompanied by intelligence and operational processes as well as legal counsel that also examines the facts and the broad implications of striking the target. At this stage, additional operational considerations come into play, such as whether the targeted killing could jeopardize and reveal the source of the intelligence. "In addition it must also be ensured that this is a targeted strike, without collateral damage, without causing harm to innocent people," he says. All of these considerations should be examined every few hours in order to see that there is no change in the situation during the process of obtaining all of the required approvals at the various levels, up to the deputy director of the ISA and the director himself and from there to the political level.[25] Regarding the need for regular updating of the information throughout the decision-making process and the issuing of approvals, Oz Noy notes: "What is important is to ensure

---

[24] Personal interview with Amnon Sofrin, February 22, 2022.
[25] Personal interview with Arik "Harris" Barbing, February 21, 2022.

that during this time, the intelligence does not change, because sometimes the intelligence changes. And you automatically continue. You have to make sure that the person still poses at least the same level of threat. That his elimination will really thwart the attack and that you're not continuing automatically because you have invested a lot of resources and you are already on it and there are all the usual biases we have as human beings, determination and sense of mission..."[26]

Defense Minister and former IDF Chief of Staff **Shaul Mofaz** explains the decision-making process by saying, "There is a process and method by which all of the ranks approve, the ISA chief approves, the chief of staff approves, and then it goes up for approval by the political echelon, and after the political echelon approves, it goes down again to the operational level, where we decide who will carry it out, based on each body's advantages and disadvantages, whether it is the ISA or the army. Then it goes down to the operations room."[27] Mofaz highlights the fact that operations from the air were considered more complex, because in ground operations, the operational unit has the ability to see the target, identify him, and survey his surroundings, whereas in an aerial operation the pilot in the plane or helicopter can usually see the target, but it is hard for them to survey the environment and even more difficult to know in real time what the situation is on the ground with regard to civilians and children in the target's vicinity.[28]

Dan Halutz, who served as IDF chief of staff and before that as commander of the Air Force, describes the particular difficulty resulting from the lack of eye contact between the pilot and the target of the strike in a densely populated area. "They do not see with their eyes and they have to rely on the whole chain of command until they press the button. The responsibility ultimately lies with the headquarters that gave the order to open fire. The one who told the pilots 'Launch.' You tell him to launch and he presses the button." Halutz adds, "This trust must not be broken...this is the method. You need the ISA, you need Military Intelligence, you need the Air Force's operational headquarters – they are sitting next to you."[29] According to him, the pilot knows that "the motorcycle

---

[26] Personal interview with Oz Noy, February 16, 2022.

[27] Personal interview with Shaul Mofaz, February 23, 2022.

[28] Ibid.

[29] Personal interview with Dan Halutz, March 4, 2022.

now on the road is about to launch a rocket. This is a ticking time bomb for us... Someone knows the name of the biker – the Air Force usually doesn't know, the ISA knows, but the pilots do not know names. We also don't want them to know, except for in very rare circumstances. This is not a personal matter and they don't need the names of the targets... they need to know to trust the intelligence provided to them with their eyes shut, and this trust must not be broken." Halutz draws attention to the fact that although the decision-making process for carrying out targeted killings may be complex and lengthy and require many approvals, the decision to stop the targeted killing is likely to be much shorter and simpler. "The operational staff that is monitoring and commanding the mission can stop it at any given moment, until the weapon is dropped. It at their sole discretion; they don't need anyone's permission to stop it. Not the prime minister's, not the defense minister's. They can stop it. The ISA can stop [the targeted killing] by telling us, the Air Force, 'Guys, there is new data, stop'. So we stop."[30]

At a certain stage, a joint war room was opened for the ISA and the IDF, which remains active throughout the entire operation. In this room, the ISA and Military Intelligence officials who have dealt with the intelligence sit side by side, next to the Air Force officers responsible for the firing of the weapons. This way, when the approval is obtained for the targeted killing from the political echelon, this situation room manages the planning and execution of the strike on a short timeline (Levy, 2012). In addition to the intelligence officers present in the war room, various operational officials are also present, as needed, from representatives of relevant military forces, to the police, the national counter-terrorism unit, the coordinator of activities in the territories, the Mossad, and more. "In the war room, you see the whole intelligence picture. There are the intelligence disciplines, commanders and professionals and officials from the operating unit...All the intelligence agents sit in the room and see one intelligence image on the huge screens and everyone can put their insights onto the screen and receive feedback... At the main table sit the commanders of the operational unit managing the operation (ISA, the national counter-terrorism unit, or the IDF)."[31] The modus operandi of joint war rooms between the various relevant security agencies developed mainly

---

[30] Ibid.
[31] Personal interview with Arik "Harris" Barbing, February 21, 2022.

during and after the period of the Second Intifada. Before that, "there was a lot of hesitation and fear of exposing sources between the IDF and the ISA."[32]

The activity in the situation room allows the intelligence personnel to be in direct contact with the person who is about to carry out the strike (for example, the UAV operator). In order to reduce the possibility of an intelligence error, from the moment the green light for the strike is given and until the operation is carried out, the target is monitored using technological means. These means are locked onto the defined target and allow for direct communication with those firing the weapons.

With regard to the legal considerations involved in the process of approving targeted killings, Adv. **Daniel Reisner**, who served as head of the IDF's International Law Department, notes that military legal counsel has established five tests, or conditions, for targeted killings:

> First of all, the target must be an active security threat at the level of a commander or terrorist operative. Not a supporter, not a financer, not someone in the intermediate circles. He must constitute a real threat. Today, not in the past; a real, tangible threat. Two: There must be no alternative of arrest. If you have the alternative to arrest, you are not allowed to carry out the killing. The third test is derived from the second test: You cannot operate in an area in which the IDF is responsible for security – in Israeli territory or in Area C in Judea and Samaria [areas under Israeli military control in Judea and Samaria in accordance with the Oslo Accords – BG]... Four: When you strike, adhere to the rule of proportionality. And five: In order for the process not to become automatic, any strike requires the approval of the political echelon; the military and the ISA are not enough. You need the personal approval of the prime minister or defense minister.[33]

Reisner adds that these five conditions were later presented as an opinion in a petition submitted to the Supreme Court on the subject, and the court did indeed adopt these principles in its ruling in the petition (except for the fifth condition, the rank approving the operation, which was not a matter for the Supreme Court). Reisner talks about a dilemma he faced—should the legal advisor take part in the discussions

---

[32] Ibid.

[33] Personal interview with Daniel Reisner, April 8, 2022.

prior to the decision to carry out the targeted killing, or should he simply pass on his opinion to the decision-makers' forum?

> I debated. If a military lawyer is sitting in the discussion, there is a danger that if he says it's okay, they won't think about it at all. The whole discussion becomes one in which the lawyer decides. On the other hand, the military asked me for help interpreting what I devised. So I went to the Attorney General, Elyakim Rubinstein, and I told him, 'The army wants me to sit in the room. He said to me 'I wouldn't go. Tell them to do what they want and that you will do the analysis in retrospect.' I told him that that didn't make sense. If I can prevent them from making a mistake before the decision then that is my job. I can't tell them 'You work it out.' We therefore agreed that the military attorneys would sit in on the approval processes before the decision takes place and that the civilian attorneys would participate afterwards and do the retrospective analysis. And that was the division we agreed on.

Former IDF Chief Military Advocate General **Sharon Afek** explains the Military Advocate General's policy on this issue by saying that military lawyers do not sit in the war room during targeted killings. "It is the commander's responsibility. He shouldn't need to consult a jurist in real time." According to Afek, "Once the operation is approved and there is real-time identification of the target, we have no relative advantage over the commander, neither with regards to the question of proportionality nor with regards to the identification of the target."[34]

Reisner illustrates the dilemma of legal counsel by relaying the following instance:

> Once, I was urgently called in for a discussion with the head of the Operations Directorate and it turns out that it was in the middle of a targeted killing. They were confronted with the question of whether it was permissible to fire the missile or not, and they wanted me to decide...I was called into the room and I saw the drones in the air on the picture, showing Gaza from above, and they told me that there is a terrorist cell there who caught someone suspected of collaborating with us, and they are now violently interrogating him in this room. They were talking on the phone with their handler about the fact that they would be finishing the interrogation in half an hour and were then planning on leaving.

---

[34] Personal interview with Sharon Ofek, March 13, 2022.

Reisner told those present that they knew it was legal to fire a missile that will kill everyone in the room, including the interrogee himself, because it was clear that he was going to die anyway. He asked: "'So why am I here?' They said that the operations research concluded that the only missile we have would cause the 85 percent destruction of the adjoining apartment. 'What's in the apartment next door?' I asked. They said, 'That's it, we don't know. I said, 'Well, it could be Hamas headquarters and it could be a kindergarten. They said, 'It could be anything.'"

Reisner says:

> I started activating everyone there. Through the ISA I spoke with the agent on the ground and asked what he could see about the building next door. At my request, the drone was flown above the roof...I asked the agent if there was any laundry hanging from the window. He said no...so I said, most likely there is no family living there then... and then I understood what was happening. They couldn't decide, so they said, 'Let's call Daniel.' If the lawyer says yes, then yes. If he says no, then we can blame the lawyers.' I exploded and told them they were pathetic cowards and that's not how the army should conduct itself, hiding behind its lawyers. But I added that if it had been up to me, I would have fired.[35]

Reisner notes that he was eventually told by military officials that the defense minister did not approve the strike.[36]

Former President of the Supreme Court **Aharon Barak** presents a different position regarding the need to integrate legal counsel in the decision-making processes in targeted killing operations. According to him, "There is justification for the decision about whether to use targeted killings to be made not only by military personnel but also by jurists sitting in the room where the decision is made, because they [the jurists] find this balance, and can do [this] is in the most objective manner, detached from the desire to postpone the operation and to look good in the eyes of the public."[37] Barak said that in a meeting with the General Counsel of the U.S. Army, he was told that when the Americans were fighting in Vietnam, he had about 100 lawyers there to advise the forces. He also heard a similar story from the General Counsel of the U.S.

---

[35] Ibid.

[36] Ibid.

[37] Personal interview with Aharon Barak, February 20, 2022.

Air Force, who told him that his legal advisers sit in the Pentagon and approve every decision to carry out a targeted killing.[38] Indeed, **Shalom Ben Hanan** emphasizes the involvement and centrality of legal counsel in each of the decision-making stages and at all different levels, from the field levels, through the command ranks, to the decision of the ISA chief:

> It is important to emphasize the central and committed involvement of legal entities in the process of approving a target for killing. Legal advisers from the ISA and the army are involved in the approval process from the beginning, in writing, and in an orderly and integrated process. A legal advisor must address all aspects of the operation, including the possible implications for innocent people. In the ISA, there is a lengthy bureaucratic process that begins with an employee who suggests the target for killing and ends with the head of the agency, through the entire relevant chain of command, which includes legal advisers at various levels, up to the ISA's legal advisor and the head of the ISA. The system has developed the ability to approve targeted killings, even in a very short period of time, and therefore legal counsel is present in every targeted killing or combat operations room.[39]

At the end of the decision-making processes carried out by the relevant security and intelligence agencies, approval for targeted killings is required by the Committee of Israel's Secret Service Chiefs. They discuss the case and formulate a recommendation for the cabinet and the prime minister. In these operations, a decision by the minister of defense alone is not sufficient; the approval of a ministerial committee (the Security Cabinet) and the prime minister is required. The approval by highest level of decision-making in Israel is not only given in regard to the identity and target of the strike, but also to the most appropriate course of action given the characteristics of the target and the possible risk of collateral damage.[40] Former IDF Chief of Staff **Gadi Eisenkot** notes in this context that the purpose of the discussion in the ministerial committee is for the decision not to be ultimately made by a single individual.[41]

[38] Ibid.

[39] Personal interview with Shalom Ben Hanan, February 21, 2022.

[40] Personal interview with Arik "Harris" Barbing, February 21, 2022.

[41] Personal interview with Gadi Eisenkot, March 2, 2022.

Former Mossad Chief **Shabtai Shavit** explains the decision-making process in the chain of command in cases of targeted killings in the territory of a foreign country:

> In most cases, it starts from the bottom. And work is underway to prepare an 'indictment' against the target. This is done within the Mossad. The Mossad's intelligence officers, the ISA, and Military Intelligence look for material on the target. The intelligence officers bring the subject up for discussion with the head of the division, who then raises it with the head of the Mossad for his decision. The head of the Mossad presents this to the Committee of Secret Service Chiefs – the director of the ISA, the head of the Mossad, the chief of Military Intelligence, and the prime minister's military secretary. In the next stage, the head of the Mossad invites himself to a small committee headed by the prime minister and including the defense and foreign ministers. And he tells them, 'Listen, we think that X is a target that needs to be dealt with," shows them the 'indictment,' tells them that his recommendation also includes the recommendation of the ISA and the Military Intelligence chiefs, and asks them to decide. This trio is the one who decides, and only after that is the operation carried out.[42]

According to Shavit, this complex and lengthy decision-making process illustrates how seriously and sensitively the Israeli defense establishment and decision-makers take such a difficult decision. The process is based on three main considerations, according to Shavit. "One: Is the damage the target has already caused and the potential future threat he represents of such a magnitude that he needs to be dealt with? Two: The political consideration – any such operation conducted in foreign territory should take into account the political considerations if it does succeed and in the case that it doesn't. It affects the relations between Israel and the country in which it takes place. And three, a set of moral-ethical [considerations]."[43]

Another former Mossad Chief, **Yossi Cohen**, emphasizes that the decision to carry out a targeted killing first requires a definition of the purpose of the operation and of what needs to be achieved; secondly, an assessment of whether the goal and achievement can be attained (and if the answer is positive, whether the mission can be carried out by

---

[42] Personal interview with Shabtai Shavit, February 17, 2022.

[43] Ibid.

Mossad agents or by a proxy); and finally, an assessment of the possible boomerang effects and strategic implications of the action.[44]

Avi Dichter expands on this, explaining that the decision to carry out a targeted killing "goes up for approval by the minister of defense and the prime minister. In some circumstances it also goes to the Cabinet. For example, [the targeted killing] of Sheikh Yassin, which went to the Cabinet. Then, you define the target of the action and start doing the operational planning. Operational planning can take days or weeks. If a lot of time passes you have to revalidate the approval. It is not 'fire and forget' – you can't get an approval in January and carry out the strike in December."[45]

Once the main decision to carry out the targeted killing has been made, the exact date of the operation must also be considered. This date may be derived from the operational need arising from the planning of the operation itself (a date when there is access to the target, or when he will be in a place where there is no risk of collateral damage, etc.). Alternatively, the date may be derived from international or regional geopolitical events or processes within the country itself that may delay or expedite the implementation of the operation (such as a high-level visit to Israel or the region, the signing of a diplomatic agreement, etc.). Dichter elucidates the considerations involved in scheduling such an operation by saying, "You don't want to carry out a targeted killing when there is suddenly some important meeting or visit, or the prime minister is going abroad, or something like that. That's why these things require approvals from above, and it's not a field commander who says, 'Okay, the conditions are present for a targeted killing so I'm going ahead. It doesn't work that way."[46]

Former Director of the Counter-Terrorism Bureau at the Prime Minister's office **Nitzan Nuriel** also discusses to the considerations involved in determining the timing of the targeted killing operation. According to him, there are many factors that need to be taken into account in this context, such as holidays and festivals, school vacations, visits by heads of state to Israel, and so on. As an example, Nuriel cites the decision to refrain from killing Imad Mughniyeh on the eve of the IDF's withdrawal

---

[44] Personal interview with Yossi Cohen, May 1, 2022.

[45] Personal interview with Avi Dichter, March 11, 2002.

[46] Ibid.

from Lebanon. The desire to carry out the withdrawal from Lebanon on time, without any mishaps and delays, Nuriel said, took precedence over the intelligence opportunity that arose to target Mughniyeh.[47]

The process of decision-making in targeted killings, is, therefore, a dynamic process that may change from time to time depending on the circumstances. In this regard, Dichter describes a targeted killing operation that took many weeks to prepare:

> It was impossible to stop him. So there was no choice, we needed a targeted killing. So we sent helicopters, I think for over two weeks. For more than two weeks the helicopters hovered at a safe distance, but he did not leave the house. They already understand that the noise of a helicopter does not bode well for them. By the way, there could be a helicopter that came to spray the orchards or the cotton. For him, it doesn't matter – there's a helicopter in the air, he does not leave the house. Then, after two weeks or so, we had to change the operation and work with snipers, which requires preparing for another operation.[48]

Sometimes, even after the targeted killing itself takes place, the operation is still not over. According to **Barbing**, "At the end of such operations, we disseminate all sorts of disinformation in all sorts of places in order to hide how we reached our target."[49]

In conclusion, in examining the decision-making process in targeted killings, a distinction must be made between different modi operandi taken in this type of operation—air strikes (precision missiles fired at the target) or ground operations (sniper fire); between public and covert operations; between operations led by the ISA, Mossad, or the IDF through various operational units; and finally between operations carried out in the Gaza Strip, West Bank, in the territory of neighboring countries, or in the territory of far-away countries (either hostile or friendly toward Israel).

---

[47] Personal interview with Nitzan Nuriel, February 14, 2022.

[48] Personal interview with Avi Dichter, March 11, 2022.

[49] Personal interview with Arik "Harris" Barbing, February 21, 2022.

The Intelligence Component of the Targeted Killing Operations

Intelligence is a necessary element of any counter-terrorism action, but its importance is especially significant in offensive counter-terrorism and, first and foremost, in targeted killings. According to former Defense Minister and IDF Chief of Staff **Moshe (Bogie) Ya'alon**, "When I look at the tool of targeted killings over the years, it really is a tool that has been developed. It relies on very accurate intelligence, intelligence capabilities, a fusion of intelligence, a combination of all sources of intelligence, and ultimately, the ability to say that the man/terrorist/commander of the organization is really in a certain place. This is a very high intelligence capability."[50]

Obtaining accurate, verified, and up-to-date intelligence information is already an essential need at the stage of determining the targets of the strike—defining the "target bank" and selecting the concrete target from it. Once the target has been established, specific information must be obtained regarding the target's location, habits, plans, and any other details required for the precise planning of the operation. Intelligence is also required to ascertain who is in the vicinity of the target to ensure that the strike does not cause collateral damage, and before carrying out the operation it must be established that there has not been any last-minute change that could jeopardize the entire operation or necessitate an adaptation. Any mistake in the process of intelligence gathering, analysis of the information, its verification and its conversion into the operational plan could result in the failure of the operation, and, in more serious cases, in harm caused to innocent people.

In answer to the question of whether he remembers any intelligence errors in targeted killing operations, **Avi Eliyahu**, a former senior Military Intelligence officer replied:

> It's incredible that in the many attacks we have carried out, the entire defense establishment, I don't think we have ever made a mistake. This is thanks to accurate and high-quality intelligence and our extreme care in verifying information. We may have erred in estimating the number of people in the place or the collateral damage. But we were never wrong about the person who was defined as a target. It shows the quality of

---

[50] Personal interview with Moshe (Bogie) Ya'alon, February 17, 2022.

the intelligence and extreme meticulousness in the incrimination process. The tremendous rigor in this process is a strength of the Israeli security establishment and instills confidence in the decision-makers in the people dealing with these matters.[51]

The intelligence activity in a targeted killing operation can be divided into three stages:

The first and ongoing phase is carried out over time, during which the "target bank" is built and updated. At this stage, details are gathered about the target's daily routine, place of work, hobbies, friends, family, and more. This intelligence allows an understanding of the patterns and routines of his life and activity. However, this "infrastructural" intelligence is not enough to make a decision to carry out a targeted killing. **Arik "Harris" Barbing** says that "The intelligence information gathered about the target is called 'negative security material' and is intended to prove that he [the wanted person] really does pose a security threat. It is necessary to explain what threat exactly (shooting, explosives …), what the latest information is about him, and how many times we have prevented his attacks. Is he a ticking bomb…and is he intending on carrying out an attack or is he organizing an attack that is difficult to prevent in other ways?"[52]

Former Deputy Head of the Mossad **Naftali Granot** explains that this intelligence activity is preliminary and ongoing, and becomes concrete prior to the decision.[53]

In the second stage, after the decision to carry out the killing of a specific target has been made, "pre-operation intelligence" is gathered— this should verify the existing information to date and add the concrete and updated information required for the detailed planning of the operation. At this stage, the intelligence gathered includes accurate information about the whereabouts of the target, who is in his immediate vicinity, and the like. The intelligence picture built from all relevant intelligence sources allows for an understanding of the target's routine, location, and activities, as well as his future plans. From this, an operational plan will be derived relevant to the target. The plan will include, inter alia, the modus operandi, necessary weapons and forces, and the timing of the strike, as

[51] Personal interview with Avi Eliyahu, April 6, 2022.

[52] Personal interview with Arik "Harris" Barbing, February 21, 2022.

[53] Personal interview with Naftali Granot, February 17, 2022.

well as the means of approach and withdrawal from the attack (Pinko, 2020). One of the main problems at this stage is the difficulty in obtaining quality and up-to-date intelligence information because the terrorist operatives often know or presume that they are wanted and therefore try to remain under the intelligence radar, hide in different places and change these hiding places frequently, "break" their normal routine of activities, avoid using means of identification and communication, avoid personal contact with friends and relatives, and rely on a very small number of aides and other operatives. All of this makes it difficult to monitor them and plan the targeted killing operation (Levy, 2012; Reich, 2004, p. 81).

Former IDF Chief of Staff **Gadi Eisenkot** says in this regard that he interviewed an apprehended terrorist who was responsible for a series of attacks in Jerusalem, who told him that he did not understand how he had been caught even after taking every precaution and disconnecting himself not only from every means of communication, but also from almost all electronic devices. He said that the only exception was a lamp; he ensured that there was no radio, no cell phone, and no computer around him."[54]

Shalom Ben Hanan describes a situation in which the wanted persons assume that they might be targeted and therefore "hide in various, bizarre hiding places. For example, inside double walls, in caves, under the foundations of houses, and more. These wanted people surround themselves with a very limited circle of aides and do not use digital devices at all in order to avoid getting caught. These circumstances make it extremely difficult to locate someone, and can sometimes expedite a decision on targeted killing when there is window of opportunity and an indirect course of action available to strike the target and thus prevent future attacks."[55]

Avi Dichter notes that whereas in the first stage, "the target for the operation should be defined, and the approval from the prime minister and minister of defense should be obtained, following the approval by the IDF chief of staff and the director of the ISA. After that [in the second stage—BG], information on the target is gathered and you have to ensure that the information is current and up-to-date, not as of the day of the operation, but up the minute."

---

[54] Personal interview with Gadi Eisenkot, March 2, 2022.

[55] Personal interview with Shalom Ben Hanan, February 21, 2022.

The third stage of intelligence is the execution phase. It begins with the intelligence assessments for the operation—the opening of the war room, regular updating of the information on the whereabouts of the wanted person, the identity and number of the people in the vicinity, etc. According to Dichter, "You have to assemble a lot of means of intelligence-gathering in order to decide that the conditions [for carrying out the targeted killing] are present. To give the green light to a pilot or a sniper or an ISA operative to press the button, to release the missile, bullet or bomb. It requires a lot of tools, a lot of people, a lot of skills."[56]

Dan Halutz explains that with the growing sophistication of technological capabilities, it has become possible to improve upon the updated intelligence on the wanted person. "We work alongside the technology. The amount of unmanned aerial vehicles that can give us real-time intelligence and can observe the situation on the ground, scan 24/7 ... the video centers we set up for intelligence gathering..., for example UAVs, they constantly see the picture in real time. Even at headquarters you see the picture all the time... if you suddenly see that there is a crowd, then you stop. Moreover, the directive is that if you see a change like this on the ground you deflect the bomb."[57]

In deliberating the decision to carry out a targeted killing operation, particular weight is given at this stage to the protection of the source of intelligence, to the point that sometimes the ISA officials on the ground are given the right to veto the operation if they assess that there is a risk to the source. At this stage, as in the previous stages, it must be constantly ensured that the intelligence continues to be up-to-date and relevant not only for the purpose of carrying out the operation, but also for the purpose of making the possible decision to abort it. In this context, Oz Noy says that when "we understand that the intelligence has changed and the person's elimination will not thwart the attack, the targeted killing must be avoided."[58]

Former Chief Military Advocate General Sharon Afek explains that in targeted killing operations, there is usually a great deal of reliable intelligence information "regarding the military or terrorist activity in which the target was involved and on the basis of which it is decided to carry out

---

[56] Personal interview with Avi Dichter, March 11, 2022.

[57] Personal interview with Dan Halutz, March 4, 2022.

[58] Personal interview with Oz Noy, February 16, 2022.

a targeted killing. There are operational rules determining the manner in which the identification of the target is to be done in real time."[59]

In general, intelligence gathering, including counter-terrorism intelligence, is based on two main sources of information: HUMINT—human intelligence—agents acting as moles in the terrorist organization, defectors from the organization, arrested terrorist operatives, and any other human source who has information about terrorist activities, intentions, and capabilities; and COMINT—communications intelligence—intelligence gathered electronically, mainly by listening in on telephone calls, monitoring online interactions, etc. In targeted killing operations, each of these two sources of intelligence gathering may serve as important and even critical sources of information for locating the target and learning about his lifestyle and plans; they may support and verify each other's information or refute it.

Because terrorist organizations in general and operatives, in particular, are aware of the possibility that their phone calls will be intercepted, many of them are wary of using electronic means in general and telephones in particular, in order to make it more difficult to locate them. For example, a proclamation distributed by Hamas reads: "The Zionist enemy has succeeded in assassinating many of our fighting brothers ... All the fighters must consider themselves a target for assassination... brothers should not reveal their travel times and location using any kind of phone, as all signals from the phones are intercepted...You are wanted and bring tracked..." (Ben-Israel, 2006). In these cases, the importance of HUMINT increases, with an emphasis on recruiting and activating intelligence sources that are close to the target—personal assistants, family members, friends, and others whom he trusts and shares important operational details with (Levy, 2012).

Indeed, the use of human intelligence resources is an important component of intelligence gathered for targeted killing operations. For example, according to the Palestinians, without the help of collaborators, the elimination of Hamas leader Abdel Aziz al-Rantissi on April 17, 2004 (about a month after the killing of the previous leader and founder of Hamas, Ahmed Yassin), would not have taken place. After Yassin's death and his appointment as Hamas leader, Rantissi went underground for fear of his life and led the life of a fugitive. He turned off

---

[59] Personal interview with Sharon Afek, March 13, 2022.

his cell phone and was in always on the move, wearing an elderly man's get-up with a keffiyeh, continuously breaking his routine and changing vehicles frequently. Rantissi also refrained from moving around during the day and surrounded himself with members of the Izz ad-Din al-Qassam Brigades' personal security unit. It is against this background that the Palestinians claimed that the elimination of Abdel Aziz al-Rantissi was made possible only by collaborators who followed his bodyguard, Akram Nassar. According to them, while he was being followed, Nassar came to Rantissi's hiding place, from where they both drove a short distance with another bodyguard and then transferred to another vehicle, the bombing of which was approved (Berger, 2004).

Another killing carried out in 1996—that of the "Engineer" Yahya Ayyash, one of the founders of Hamas' Izz ad-Din al-Qassam Brigades and the brains behind the method of suicide bombings by Palestinian terrorists in Israel in the 1990s—was also apparently carried out with the help of a collaborator working with the ISA. He succeeded in transferring a booby-trapped cell phone to Ayyash, which was then detonated remotely, killing him (Levy, 2012). On the other hand, intelligence agencies generally have great difficulty in recruiting and operating sources in terrorist organizations, because these organizations are aware of their efforts and therefore take measures to uncover collaborators and agents, such as background checks prior to their joining the organization, periodic security checks, loyalty tests, etc. (Reich, 2004, p. 81). Criticism has sometimes been voiced with regard to recruiting moles among terrorist organizations, calling such activity as "immoral" as it endangers the life of the collaborator. When terrorist organizations discover such a collaborator, they arrest him and often even execute him, sometimes following severe torture. For example, in 2001, following a wave of targeted killings carried out by Israel, then-Commander of the Palestinian General Intelligence Service in Gaza, Amin al-Hindi, called on "Palestinian collaborators with Israel" to surrender themselves and report to the Palestinian security forces any information they had on any planned eliminations. He further said that their cooperation with the Palestinian Authority would help ease the legal action taken against them. In order to intimidate them, he added that "In recent days, the PA has arrested dozens of suspected collaborators, and four of them have been sentenced to death" (Reuters, 2001). According to official Palestinian data, from September 2000 to 2004 (during the events of the Second Intifada), 114 Palestinian collaborators were apprehended in the territories, 83 of whom were killed by

Palestinian lynching, and 23 of whom were shot to death by Palestinian security forces (Berger, 2004).

It should be noted that this was a period in which many targeted killings were carried out, against the backdrop of an unprecedented scale of terrorist attacks in Israel during the Second Intifada. These Israeli actions were accompanied by the decision to create an orderly doctrine to carry out targeted killings, involving all the relevant arms of the Israeli defense establishment in order to "close the circle" on the wanted person before he succeeded in carrying out an attack. This move was led by the then-Deputy Director of the ISA Yuval Diskin and then-Deputy IDF Chief of Staff Moshe (Bogie) Ya'alon. Diskin was tasked with formulating the military doctrine, which included, inter alia, deepening the intelligence infiltration into Palestinian-controlled territory while bolstering and increasing the use of technological means of intelligence gathering (Ashkenazi, 2019; Levy, 2012).

Another argument made against the use of collaborators is that their recruitment by Israel undermines the stability of the local Palestinian community, as Israel encourages them to act against their people in exchange for money (Gross, 2003). Similar contentions accuse Israeli security officials of using problematic means in recruiting agents, such as torture, extortion, or bribery (Stein, 2003, p. 127). Yusuf Issa, former commander of the anti-espionage department in the Palestinian Preventive Security Service in the Gaza Strip, claimed that between 1999 and 2004, about 300 cases were opened against suspected collaborators with Israel and that since the outbreak of the Intifada there seemed to be an increase in the number of Palestinians cooperating with Israel, likely because Israel was taking advantage of the difficult economic situation in the Gaza Strip and the financial temptation had become greater (Berger, 2004).

On the other hand, the attempt to preserve the intelligence source in the terrorist organization's life (especially when he is suspected of being an Israeli agent) or the desire to strengthen the source's status within the organization, may put his handlers in various moral dilemmas. Here, for example, the question arises as to whether agents can be allowed to be involved in illegal activity? In terrorist activities or actions that endanger human life? An Israeli committee appointed to investigate the events that led to the assassination of Israeli Prime Minister Yitzhak Rabin in 1995 determined that one of the ISA agents, who headed an extremist right-wing movement, was in contact with the prime minister's killer before the assassination and acted believing that his being an ISA agent provided him immunity from the law. The answer to this dilemma is therefore that from a moral-ethical point of view, a collaborator whose activity requires illegal activity and actions that may harm others should not be used, unless these actions are essential to saving lives and are controlled, and that all precautions have been made to ensure that these actions do endanger human lives (Ganor, 2015).

Despite the great importance of human intelligence in counter-terrorism activity in general and targeted killing operations in particular, technological means of tracking, such as locating the target using his cell phone and listening in on his phone calls (COMINT) cannot be underestimated. This information, arising from listening or from detecting electronic signals received from cellular phones may be cross-checked with visual intelligence derived from observations, aerial photographs, drones, and other visual means (VISINT) as well as from open intelligence sources such as websites or social networks (OSINT) (Berger, 2004; Ganor, 2015).

When gathering intelligence information prior to carrying out a targeted killing operation, one should therefore strive to formulate an intelligence picture that is as complete, comprehensive, and up-to-date as possible, in order to be able to plan a precise operation and to reach the target at the most appropriate time and in the most ideal circumstances. This intelligence picture is essential to preventing misidentification and minimizing collateral damage during the operation.

To conclude, Avi Eliyahu, a former senior Military Intelligence officer, states that although the targeted killing relies on accurate and high-quality intelligence, at the same time the operation also makes it possible to develop intelligence capabilities over time. In his words, "When you use them [targeted killings] frequently, you greatly develop your intelligence and operational capabilities. When you do them less often, you lose a very significant layer...Usually specific capabilities that serve targeted killings can be used for a lot of other things. The targeted killings made us much sharper. Because we had to pinpoint. We had to deal with a very complex incrimination process. And it requires you to be very sharp."[60]

---

[60] Personal interview with Avi Eliyahu, April 6, 2022.

The "Operational Opportunity" Axis

The intelligence component plays a key role in the decision-making process prior to carrying out a targeted killing. However, the operational information gathered is not only essential for the meticulous planning of the operation, it also influences the decision itself—whether to carry out the operation or to refrain. Moreover, intelligence considerations may also affect the degree of collateral damage that the planners of the operation are willing to accept. In other words, the more often a terrorist operative who is a target appears on the "intelligence radar," the less willing the planners will be to take operational risks and pay a higher price in collateral damage (that is, more civilian casualties, though still proportionate to the operational goal). Similarly, the quality of the intelligence may have an impact on the operational risks taken in the operation. According to **Gadi Eisenkot**, "The problem is when you are told, 'Listen, our information about this building is weak, it is not clear whether he [the target] is there or not, whether he has been evacuated or not. So are you going to kill 60 people now based on this information? Therefore, the strength of the intelligence and the extent to which it is up-to-date is a critical component of decision making."[61]

However, if the target is an elusive terrorist operative who strictly maintains secrecy and therefore appears on the intelligence radar very rarely, the operational practicability at some point, based on the arrival of rare intelligence, will increase decision-makers' willingness to take operational risks and perhaps even to pay a greater price in collateral damage. This is reflected in the "Operational Opportunity Axis" below.

On the Operational Opportunity Axis, reflecting the degree of intelligence available on the target, four generic situations can be identified (Fig. 3.1):

- **Frequent operational opportunity**—In this situation, a terrorist operative who is a target for elimination appears on the intelligence radar very often. The intelligence agencies have a good and ongoing understanding of the target's movements and they can locate him at almost any given moment. This makes it possible to carry out the targeted killing in the most favorable conditions and circumstances— at a time when the attack on the target is expected to cause minimal

---

[61] Personal interview with Gadi Eisenkot, March 2, 2022.

Rare operational opportunity
Infrequent operational opportunity
Periodic operational opportunity
Frequent operational opportunity

Fig. 3.1 Operational opportunity

collateral damage. (The operational restrictions required in this state of affairs are reflected in the orange area of the axis.)

- **Periodic operational opportunity**—In this situation, the terrorist operative appears on the intelligence radar from time to time, and when he does, it is possible to examine whether the conditions and circumstances are suitable for carrying out the targeted killing in a way that minimizes collateral damage. (The limitations on the targeted killing in these cases are reflected in the yellow area of the axis.)
- **Infrequent operational opportunity**—In this situation, the terrorist operative adheres to strict procedures in order to maintain his personal safety. He does not live in one place but rather moves from one place to another, avoids communications via telephones or computers that may reveal his whereabouts, and surrounds himself with a very small number of loyal aides. Because of this, the terrorist operative's appearance on the intelligence radar is infrequent and distorted, so when an operational opportunity arises to carry out the targeted killing, it is likely that the decision-makers will be willing to take greater risks and perhaps also approve a higher rate of collateral damage, albeit still proportionate. (This willingness is reflected by the color green on the Axis of Opportunity.)
- **Rare operational opportunity**—In this situation, the terrorist operative believes that he is likely a target for elimination, and he, therefore, takes all the precautions described above, surrounds himself with human shields everywhere he goes, and tries to spend most of his time in underground facilities. The window of opportunity for

the targeted killing in these cases, should it exist, is very narrow and rare; therefore, in these cases, it is likely that decision-makers will tend to approve targeted killing operations that involve a high level of risk, both with regard to the operation itself and with regard to uninvolved people who are in the target's vicinity. (In these cases, too, the willingness to carry out the targeted killing, even at a very high cost, is reflected by the color green on the axis.)

Case Study—Salah Shehadeh

One of the clearest examples of the serious consequences of an intelligence failure was in the case of the targeted killing of Salah Shehadeh, commander of Hamas's Izz ad-Din al-Qassam Brigades, carried out by Israel in July 2002. The operation caused extensive collateral damage, more than any of Israel's previous targeted killings, and was widely condemned both in Israel and around the world. Along with Shehadeh, another Hamas operative was killed, as well as Shehadeh's wife and daughter who were with him and 13 innocent civilians, including children; dozens of others were wounded (Sofer, 2011). The reason for this large extent of collateral damage was an intelligence failure and a flawed assessment of the presence of people in the buildings adjacent to Shehadeh's home, where most of those who died had been living (ibid.). In a Special Investigatory Commission that was set up to investigate the targeted killing, Israeli security sources claimed that the intelligence information was collected in real time through a collaborator—an ISA source. An interrogation of the collaborator following the incident revealed that he was not up-to-date with the details of the immediate vicinity as he did not live nearby. Although the source had reported that there were tin shacks near Shehadeh's house, he did not say that they were inhabited, likely due to the fact that he had visited the place about a month before the operation and found the shacks empty (Special Investigatory Commission, 2011). In addition to reports from the human source, prior to the operation, intelligence gathering was also carried out by technological means on the surroundings of Shehadeh's home. In this framework, many photographs were taken. In retrospect, these aerial photographs showed solar water heaters and satellite dishes on the roofs of the shacks—something that should have indicated that they were inhabited—but an error was made in the intelligence assessment that led to the mistaken assumption that the shacks were vacant (Special Investigatory Commission, 2011). **Daniel Reisner** notes that in the case of the Shehadeh killing it is not clear whether the mistake was in intelligence or in assessing the damage that the bomb would cause. In any case, he says, "If we had known that 17 people were going to die, we probably would not have approved the strike on Salah Shehadeh. In terms of the balance between the need and the damage caused, he would not have been worth the number of civilians killed."[62] **Dan Halutz**, who was serving as commander of the Air Force at the time, maintains that it was an intelligence failure. "It was not known that there were people living in the tin shacks. There was a clear indication, however, given that there was laundry hanging there. If they had researched the intelligence to the end, it would have been possible to understand that a full clothesline hanging outside indicates that people live there."[63] Halutz notes that Israel had twice called off targeted killing operations against Shehadeh due to intelligence received testifying to the presence of innocents in his vicinity.

Case Study—Mohammed Deif

Mohammed Deif has been considered the head of Hamas's military wing in the Gaza Strip since the 1990s. He has become Israel's most wanted person in the Gaza Strip, due to his responsibility for dozens of terrorist attacks. The Israeli defense establishment claims that all of Hamas' operational plans, including how and when to attack, go through Deif. He is the one who determines when to begin escalations and when to launch rockets at Israel and in which areas. Over the course of two decades, he has survived five targeted killing attempts, despite having been injured and having lost limbs. This has led to his turning into a sort of mythical figure in the eyes of young Palestinians and Hamas operatives (Shaul & Golan, 2004; Levy, 2021; Waked & Greenberg, 2006). They refer to him as a "cat with nine lives" (Heller, 2014).

It seems that from an intelligence point of view, Deif is difficult for Israel to locate (Levy, 2021). During fighting, for example, like other leaders, Deif remains hidden in bunkers located in sensitive places, for

---

[62] Personal interview with Daniel Reisner, April 8, 2022.

[63] Personal interview with Dan Halutz, March 4, 2022.

example under Shifa Hospital. It is from this bunker that the terrorist organizations conduct hostilities, with some of the senior officials hiding in it. There is likely also a tunnel or bunker under the UN facilities in Gaza, where Deif and other officials may sometimes hide (Levy, 2021). Moreover, Deif is known as a man of few words, who maintains a low profile, lives within the Gazan population, and changes identities constantly. The circle of people around him is very small, and because he moves around in a wheelchair, he likely does not change locations very often, which adds to the difficulty in targeting him (Rubina, 2014). In contrast to some other senior members of terrorist organizations, it has been said that Deif behaves like a fugitive even during periods when tensions with Israel are low (Levy, 2021). Israel, therefore, has tried to target Deif on the rare occasions that he rises to the surface. For example, in August 2001, the IDF tried to kill Deif and his deputy, Adnan al-Ghoul, but the attempt failed (Bohbot, 2014). Then, in 2002, Israel launched two Hellfire missiles at the vehicle in which he was traveling. One missile hit the front part of his car, killing the two people sitting in the front seats. Deif was seriously injured, losing an eye and sustaining an injury in his arm, but was not killed (Bohbot, 2014; Frisch & Waked, 2002). Another elimination attempt was made in 2003, while Muhammad Deif was in a third-floor apartment in a building in the Gaza Strip with a small group of Hamas leaders. Israel launched a quarter-ton bomb on the building using an F16 aircraft. Due to the use of a relatively small bomb, the operation failed (Harel, 2011). In July 2006, Israel once again attempted to target him, bombing the house in which he was staying. He lost his hands and feet, but once again survived the attacks (Bohbot, 2014). During Operation Protective Edge in 2014, Israel launched an air strike on Deif's home in the Gaza neighborhood of Sheikh Radwan. Deif managed to escape, but his wife and two children were killed (Hemo & Lachter, 2021). In 2021, during Operation Guardian of the Walls, he again survived an attempted elimination by Israel, which had stated at the beginning of the operation that if it succeeded in killing him, it would be one of the most significant achievements of the operation (Levy, 2021). Thus, it tried to attack the underground secret location where it knew that Deif was hiding from a number of firing angles and with different types of weapons from the air (Zeitun & Levy, 2021).

Case Study—Ali Hassan Salameh

Background: The murder of 11 Israeli athletes in Munich in 1972 and the launch of Operation Wrath of God, in which it was decided by the order of then-Prime Minister of Israel Golda Meir to eliminate all those who were involved in the planning and execution of the murder, led to the decision to establish the Kidon unit—the Mossad's special operations unit. Among other things, the unit was tasked with locating Black September members who were responsible for the murder of the athletes at the Olympics and with carrying out the eliminations in various European countries (Israel Defense, 2012).

Salameh was the son of Hassan Salameh, one of the leaders of the Arab revolt against the British Mandate and the Jews of Israel. He was later nicknamed the "Red Prince," being the son of the leader of the Arab uprising and due to his affinity to blood. Salameh emigrated with his family from Israel to Lebanon when he was eight years old. When he grew up, he joined the Fatah organization, where he developed a close relationship with the organization's leader, Yasser Arafat. Due to his skills, he was sent for guerrilla and intelligence training and was considered by many to be Arafat's future successor. He rose through the ranks of Fatah, until he decided to form the Black September organization. Among the terrorist acts carried out by the organization was the abduction of the Sabena plane on May 9, 1972, and the murder of 11 Israeli athletes in the Olympic Village in Munich in September 1972 (Ofek & Bachar, 2007). Salameh was one of the main targets for elimination on the list of 11 terrorists who were involved in the Munich attack in the framework of Operation Wrath of God (Druckman, 2014).

Preparations for the operation: The intelligence gathering conducted by the Mossad continued on and off for about seven years. From intelligence information received in Israel, it emerged that Salameh would regularly work out in a hotel gym. A Mossad agent was planted as a fellow trainer at the gym, and over time he gained Salameh's confidence. The acquaintance became a close friendship. The Mossad agent provided information about the street and the apartment where Salameh lived. In the end, due to the unrest in Beirut at the time, it was decided not to carry out the killing at that time (Ben David, 2019).

Flawed intelligence information: In 1973, the Mossad attempted to eliminate Salameh in the Norwegian town of Lillehammer. After the operation, it turned out that the victim was not Salameh but Ahmed

Bouchikhi, a Norwegian citizen of Moroccan descent who worked as a waiter and lived in the town with his wife. The incorrect intelligence information was obtained from a Mossad agent who had claimed that Salameh was planning to fly from Geneva to Oslo. Doubts and suspicions about Salameh's identity had already surfaced among agents of the Mossad's Special Operations Division, Caesarea, who had boarded the flight on which Salameh was supposed to be, but could not find him on the plane. Mossad agents then thought they identified Salameh in Lillehammer. The final identification was determined by Mike Harari, who was serving as Caesarea's commander at the time, and who left town before the operation. The operation proceeded as planned, and Ahmed Bouchikhi was inadvertently killed. Following the operation, six Mossad agents who had taken part in it were apprehended and arrested. They served prison sentences in Norway and were released after varying periods of time that lasted up to about two years (Ben David, 2019).

Another attempt: After the failed operation, the intelligence gathering on Salameh continued. In January 1979, based on the intelligence gathered, it was decided to try to target him once again. The operation was carried out by an agent who had been stationed in Lebanon years earlier and became a close friend of Salameh, and another agent, a British Jew. An explosive device was planted in the headrests of a vehicle parked on Salameh's street, and as Salameh passed by, the agents blew up the vehicle, killing him (Ben David, 2019).

Reactions: A Fatah spokesman claimed that Salameh was aware that Israel would kill him because it saw him as responsible for the murder of Israeli athletes in Munich. The targeted killing operations carried out in the wake of the terrorist attack in Munich, first and foremost that of Hassan Salameh, caused unrest among Palestinian terrorist leaders. Thenhead of the PLO, Yasser Arafat, with whom Salameh was close, went underground immediately after the killing, as did other senior members of terrorist organizations. There was a quick response to the operation, with Fatah firing Katyusha rockets at the city of Kiryat Shmona in northern Israel. One of the rockets even hit a school classroom only a few minutes after the children had left it. In response, the IDF shelled the organization's terrorist bases in southern Lebanon (Druckman, 2014).

REFERENCES

Ashkenazi, E. (2019, November 13). *From "Spring of Youth" to Yassin: A history of targeted killings*. Walla! News. https://news.walla.co.il/item/3323605

Barbing, A. (2019, November 18). *Larger than the sum of its parts: The complexity of targeted killings*. Israel Defense. https://www.israeldefense.co.il/node/40946

Ben David, A. (Director). (2019). Elimination list (Season 1 EPISODE 5). *Ali Hassan Salameh*. Reshet 13.

Ben-Israel, I. (2006). Dealing with suicide terrorism. In H. Golan & S. Shay (Eds.), *A ticking bomb* [*Petzatza metakteket*]. Tel Aviv: Maarachot. [Hebrew].

Benziman, U. (2011a, August 18). Pinui-Binui operation. *Ha'aretz*. https://www.haaretz.co.il/misc/1.832607

Benziman, U. (2011b, August 18). Sharon's road map. *Ha'aretz*. https://www.haaretz.co.il/misc/1.834786

Berger, G. (2004, April 19). *In his last days, Rantissi walked around disguised as an elderly man*. News1. https://www.news1.co.il/Archive/001-D-44320-00.html

Bohbot, A. (2013, June 25). *A rare glimpse: The ISA's secret methods of counterterrorism*. Walla! News. https://news.walla.co.il/item/2653566

Bohbot, A. (2014, August 20). *Allah saved me: All the assassination attempts of Muhammad Deif*. Walla! News. https://news.walla.co.il/item/2777325

Druckman, Y. (2014, January 18). *The Israeli revenge assassination that stunned Arafat*. Ynet. https://www.ynet.co.il/articles/0,7340,L-4478017,00.html

Frisch, F., & Waked, A. (2002, September 27.) *Shabak believes that Muhammad Deif was not killed*. Ynet. https://www.ynet.co.il/articles/0,7340,L-2139673,00.html

Ganor, B. (2015, December 9). Information theory: The role of the intelligence system in the international war on terror. *Ma'ariv*. https://www.maariv.co.il/journalists/Article-517126

Gross, M. L. (2003). Fighting by other means in the Mideast: A critical analysis of Israel's assassination policy. *Political Studies, 51*(2), 350.

Harel, A. (2011, August 22). Yassin lightly wounded in the bombing of a building where a meeting of senior Hamas figures was held. *Ha'aretz*. https://www.haaretz.co.il/misc/1.908721

Heller, O. (2014, August 20). A new leaf? *Globes*. https://www.globes.co.il/news/article.aspx?did=1000965263

Hemo, O., & Lachter, E. (2021, May 14). Muhammad Deif and six others: The next Hamas targets. *Mako.* https://www.mako.co.il/news-military/2021_q2/Article-5b74c6a4f0c6971027.htm

Israel Defense. (2012, June 12). *The terrorist attack that led to the establishment of "Kidon".* Israel Defense. "ודיכ" תמקהל האיבהש רורטה תפקת | Israel Defense.

Letz, Y. (2001, September 13). Agents were exposed in the al-Aqsa Intifada. *Globes.* https://www.globes.co.il/news/article.aspx?did=521979

Levy, S. (2012, November 15). Targeted killing: This is how you close a deadly circle. *Mako.* https://www.mako.co.il/pzm-magazine/Article-498a6e44a430b31006.htm

Levy, S. (2021, May 19). Wanted with nine lives: The reasons Israel wants to kill Muhammad Deif so badly. *Mako.* https://www.mako.co.il/pzm-magazine/Article-2f8833fb0158971027.htm

Levy, S. (2022, May 6). What is preventing Israel from eliminating the Hamas leadership? *Mako.* https://www.mako.co.il/pzm-magazine/Article-ed7fa8ec9ff5971027.htm

Ofek, Y., & Bachar, A., (2007). *Ali Hassan Salameh.* The Virtual Library of the Center for Educational Technology. https://lib.cet.ac.il/pages/item.asp?item=18366

Pinko, E. (2020, November 29). *The Assassination in Iran: Intimate intelligence gathering.* Israel Defense. https://www.israeldefense.co.il/node/46768

Reich, Y. (2004). The use of technology by terrorist organizations. In O. Kazimirsky, N. Grossman-Aloni, & S. Aludi (Eds.), *Aspects of terrorism and combatting terrorism* (pp. 1–183). Tel Aviv-Yafo: Ministry of Defense.

Reuters. (2001, August 07). *Annan's sharp condemnation of the assassinations' policy.* Ynet. https://www.ynet.co.il/articles/1,7340,L-992389,00.html

Rubina, P. (2014, August 10). Why didn't Israel eliminate Muhammad Deif? *Nrg.* https://www.makorrishon.co.il/nrg/online/1/ART2/605/206.html

Shaul, S., & Golan, H. (Eds.). (2004). *The limited conflict.* Ma'arachot.

Sofer, R. (2011, February 27). *Shehadeh's assassination report: "Intelligence failure, the lesson has been learned".* Ynet. https://www.ynet.co.il/articles/0,7340,L-4035142,00.html

Special Investigatory Commission on the targeted killing of Salah Shehadeh. (2011). https://www.gov.il/BlobFolder/news/spokeshchade270211/he/sitecollectiondocuments_pmo_32communication_spokemes_reportshchade.pdf

Stein, Y. (2003). By any name illegal and immoral. *Ethics and International Affairs, 17*(1), 127.

Waked, A., & Greenberg, H. (2006, July 12). *Muhammad Deif injured in Gaza airstrike.* Ynet. https://www.ynet.co.il/articles/0,7340,L-3274196,00.html

Zeitun, Y., & Levy, E. (2021, May 19). *Muhammad Deif survived assassination twice; Tonight: 122 bombs on Hamas's "metro"*. Ynet. https://www.ynet.co.il/news/article/rkgXprbzFd

Zeitun, Y., Levy, E., & Kais, R. (2014, August 21). *Minutes after the assassination: The house in Rafah that turned to ash*. Ynet. https://www.ynet.co.il/articles/0,7340,L-4561626,00.html

CHAPTER 4

The Legitimacy of Targeted Killings: A Death Penalty Under the Guise of Counter-Terrorism?

The terminology that Israel has chosen for the purpose of defining targeted killing operations is greatly significant, because it actually reflects Israel's position on this modus operandi, as well as the changing of the Israeli narrative over the years. In the 1970s, the targeted killings carried out around the world in the wake of the attack on Israeli athletes at the Munich Olympics were termed "*Hisul Ishim*"—"elimination of senior officials" by Israel (the label likely reflecting its desire to seek revenge on the perpetrators of this devastating attack). During the Second Intifada (the wave of terrorist attacks that took place in Israel between 2000 and 2005), Israeli officials began using the word "*sikul*" ("prevention" or "thwarting") instead of "elimination." "*Sikul*" is a "sterile" term with a positive connotation, designed to address the moral-legal controversy that may arise from such an operation in advance (Kremnitzer, 2006). The use of the term "*sikul memukad*" ("targeted prevention" or, as we use for the purpose of this book, "targeted killings") is intended to emphasize that this is a preventive action whose main purpose is to defend against future danger, and not an act of vengeful punishment (Yadlin & Kasher, 2003). The moral and legal validity of the action therefore derives from the State of Israel's right, and even moral obligation, to protect its citizens. The targeted killing is a preemptive military operation aimed at thwarting a particular attack, on the basis of intelligence information about terrorist organizations' intentions and plans to carry

© The Author(s), under exclusive license to Springer Nature Switzerland AG 2022
B. Ganor and L. Koblentz-Stenzler, *Israel's Targeted Killing Policy*,
https://doi.org/10.1007/978-3-031-13674-0_4

it out (Ganor, 2003). The targeted killing is not intended to take into account any past attack (Nevo & Shur, 2003) and therefore, according to the Israeli narrative, it should not be seen as an act of punishment or revenge.

Over time, reservations have also arisen regarding the use of the term "*sikul memukad*" to describe this course of action. Prof. Asa Kasher, an expert on military ethics, for example, argues that the term "*sikul memukad*" indicates a type of policy, a modus operandi that can be chosen or avoided, while in fact, it is an act of self-defense that is performed without choice.[1] ISA officials interviewed for this book also expressed some level of discomfort with the use of the term "*sikul memukad*," arguing that it does not necessarily reflect reality, and may even mislead the public to some extent. Indeed, over the last decade, the term used to describe this phenomenon has been "*pgiah monaat*" ("preventative strike"), which better illustrates the fact that the action is forward-looking, that its purpose is to prevent terrorist attacks, and that it is not an act of revenge.[2]

As stated, targeted killings are perceived in Israel as one of the most effective means of dealing with terrorism. Whether it was used to neutralize "ticking bombs," to deter terrorists and their leaders, or to disrupt the terrorist organizations' activities, the majority of the Israeli public and most decision-makers at both the political level and the operational, security and intelligence levels believe that this measure should be employed at the right time and place, while adhering to a regulated, consistent and critical decision-making process prior to the operation.

However, the use of targeted killings raises a number of fundamental moral-normative questions, such as: Does this measure not constitute an invalid method of punishment, a kind of death penalty without trial? Is it right to use this severe measure to punish and retaliate against particularly savage terrorists or their dispatchers? What influence do political considerations have? What about the influence of pressure from the public and/or the media on decision-making processes on this issue? And to what extent are targeted killings intended to satisfy the society affected by terrorism?

---

[1] Personal interview with Asa Kasher, February 23, 2022.

[2] Personal interviews with Arik "Harris" Barbing (February 21, 2022), Shalom Ben Hanan (February 21, 2022) and Oz Noy (February 16, 2022).

Or is this measure designed to strengthen national resilience and citizens' sense of personal security in the face of the terrorist threat?

The Normative Foundation—The Right to Life

Human rights were outlined for the first time in the 1948 United Nations General Assembly's Resolution on the Universal Declaration of Human Rights (Sabel, 2003). While this declaration does not constitute a binding legal norm, it has been adopted by many bodies around the world, including courts, as "reflecting fundamental norms of human rights." In order to give legal validity to the principles of the UDHR, several multilateral conventions have been adopted; one of these (relevant to the issue of targeted killing) is the 1966 International Covenant on Civil and Political Rights (CCPR). Israel is a signatory to this convention and reports on its implementation to the UN Human Rights Committee (Sabel, 2003). The CCPR allows for the infringement of certain rights in states of emergency or security instability, though it requires basic rights to be maintained even in these situations. According to the CCPR, "Every human being has the inherent right to life...No one shall be arbitrarily deprived of his life" (CCPR, Part 3, Article 6). This right is enshrined in the convention as a basic right that must be observed, as mentioned, even in emergency situations (ibid., Part 2, Article 4). The right to life has gained the status of a peremptory norm (*jus cogens*) in international law. That is, no state is allowed to deviate from this norm, even if it is not a signatory to the treaties that include it. Article 4 (1) of the CCPR (ratified by Israel in 1991) states that executions without trial are prohibited, even in cases of emergencies or armed conflict. Among the examples of arbitrary denial of the right to life that were cited in the Human Rights Committee's report on executions, the targeted killing of people not in government custody is mentioned (Kremnitzer, 2006). In October 2018, the UN Human Rights Committee adopted a "General Comment" on the right to life. This commentary includes 70 clauses. Among other things, paragraphs 22 and 63 state that the extraterritorial application of the right to life applies not only to territories controlled by the state, but also in cases where an act or oversight by the state occurs in areas located in the territory of another state, and impacts, in a direct and foreseeable manner, the ability of the people there to enjoy their right to life (Shany, 2019). The problem is that both those who oppose targeted killing and those who support it see the right to life as a supreme value. Thus, the challenge faced by the State of Israel, like other democracies that use the measure of targeted killing as part of their counter-terrorism policy, is to find the balance between the need to protect Israeli citizens and their right to life in the face of terrorist threats and the right to life of the terrorist operatives themselves.

The Right to a Fair Trial

The right to a fair trial is also enshrined in the Covenant on Civil and Political Rights. The convention states that: "All persons shall be equal before the courts and tribunals... Everyone charged with a criminal offence shall have the right to be presumed innocent until proved guilty according to law" (CCPR, Part 3, Article 14). However, unlike the right to life, according to the convention, the right to a fair trial does not have to be maintained in a general emergency. This is despite the fact that a fair trial has also been recognized as a fundamental right in all conventions dealing with human rights (HCJ 769/02). Article 14 of the CCPR lays down minimum standards of due process, including the presumption of innocence. That is, every person is presumed innocent until proven guilty in court. It is also the right of every defendant to know the nature of the charge against him and to defend himself. The article stipulates that "Everyone shall be entitled to a fair and public hearing by a competent, independent and impartial tribunal established by law."

The presumption of innocence derives from the right to human dignity and was therefore adopted by Israel as a constitutional right upon the adoption by the Knesset of the Basic Law: Human Dignity and Liberty.[3]

As noted above, both sides—the proponents and opponents of the targeted killing of terrorists—base their arguments on the inalienable right to human life. Detractors of this counter-terrorism measure claim that even if it is a state's right to protect its citizens from a future threat, one can still not accept the killing of people as a policy (HCJ 769/02). In any case, the question arises regarding whether is it permissible to kill a person without trial and without giving him the opportunity to defend himself (Kasher, 2006). According to critics of targeted killings, the fact that the investigation, judgment, and execution of the sentence are all carried out by the executive branch, the Israeli government, is contrary

---

[3] Background document on the right to a fair trial: Procedural limitations—general principles, submitted to the Knesset's Constitution, Law and Justice Committee, p. 45.

to the principle of separation of powers and the requirement by international law for an independent and impartial body to determine innocence or, alternatively, guilt and punishment (HCJ 769/02). Israel cannot rob terrorists of the right to life through a procedure carried out outside of the judicial system, in a way that violates the basic principle of humanitarian law, which provides for the protection of citizens (Kremnitzer, 2006). Opponents of the measure argue that moreover, how can a state that has removed the death penalty from its criminal code adopt a policy of targeted killing?[4]

There is no question that the terrorists who are targets of targeted killing operations do not enjoy the basic right to a fair trial—they are not brought before the court, no lawyer is appointed for them, and they cannot defend themselves against the indictments made against them (Ganor, 2003). In light of this, opponents of targeted killings state that the absence of a fair legal process and the denial of the right to be heard from a person whose life is at stake are inconsistent with the legal means and procedures required by a democratic regime (Kremnitzer, 2006). In their view, instead of killing the terrorist, he should be arrested and brought to justice. Doing so would preserve the human rights to life and a fair trial (Kremnitzer, 2006). This claim was also heard by, inter alia, MK Zehava Gal-On from the left-wing political party Meretz, following the killing of Raed Karmi, one of the leaders of the al-Aqsa Martyrs Brigades, in 2002. She called the murder of the two Israeli restaurateurs In Tulkarem in 2001, for which Karmi was responsible, horrific, but said that "it is not possible for the State of Israel to continue its policy of killings. The people responsible for the murder should have been arrested by the Palestinian Authority, but the State of Israel cannot carry out

---

[4] In the State of Israel, the death penalty was imposed until 1954, by virtue of the British Mandate Criminal Law Ordinance (Bendet, 2016). However, only one execution was carried out during this period. In 1948, with the establishment of the state, Meir Tobianski, an IDF officer accused of spying against Israel during the War of Independence, was executed. A year after the sentencing, it emerged that Tobianski had been falsely accused, and against this background, in 1954 the Knesset enacted a law abolishing the death penalty for a murder conviction. Since then, Israeli law has stipulated that a convicted serial killer—whether he is a Jewish or Arab Israeli—will be sentenced to a number of cumulative life sentences, but will not be executed (The only exception to this principle is the Nazis and Nazi Collaborators [Punishment] Law, enacted in 1950, on the basis of which the Nazi war criminal Adolf Eichmann was convicted and executed in Israel in 1962).

executions without trial, and any such assassination will lead to the next assassination against us" (Frisch & Waked, 2002).

On the other hand, supporters of targeted killings maintain that the crime of terrorism is a unique offense that does not fall under the regular criminal code. For example, the State Commission of Inquiry established by Israel to examine the ISA's interrogation methods with regard to terrorist activity states that: "... in all democracies there is a basic recognition that a terrorist is not a regular criminal. The ordinary criminal, no matter how horrible his crimes, does not threaten the very existence of society. The terrorist, on the other hand, openly declares his intention to destroy the foundation of the society, the foundation of the regime, and in the case of Israel, to eliminate the state itself, and to expel or kill its inhabitants" (Perry, 2002).

The main argument posed by Israeli supporters of targeted killings is that, as stated above, in carrying out this action no legal procedure is required at all, since it is a legitimate act of war, one of thwarting and prevention, and not a punitive action, or worse, a death sentence. Moreover, the demand to arrest the terrorist rather than eliminate him is not applicable in reality. According to supporters of the measure, in many cases, arrest is not possible at all because the terrorist is not in the territory of the state or in territory over which Israel has effective control (David, 2003). The Palestinian Authority's policy in the past of harboring terrorists wanted by Israel has also undermined Israel's ability to apply this alternative course of action. Elyakim Rubinstein, Israel's former attorney-general, argued in 2003 that the Palestinian Authority does not have a proper legal system, which was one of the main reasons that the State of Israel had to increase its self-defense activity and use targeted killings. He claims that not only can Palestinian law not impose its authority on the terrorists in the Palestinian Authority, but they are actually encouraged by the PA (Rubinstein, 2003). Indeed, during the Al-Aqsa Intifada (2000–2005), the Israeli public was exposed to many cases in which Israel transferred to the Palestinian Authority names of wanted terrorists in its territory, but the PA refrained from responding to Israel's request and these terrorists continued to attack Israel from its territory (Harel & Hass, 2001). Moreover, unlike terrorists operating from the West Bank, where Palestinian Authority security forces are active and, should the PA want to extradite them to Israel, it is able to, since June 2007, when Hamas took control of the Gaza Strip, Gaza has become an extraterritorial area for

Israel, with terrorists operating there under the auspices and protection of Hamas.

The dispute between supporters and detractors of targeted killings regarding the need to arrest terrorists and bring them to justice in Israel was in fact settled by the Israeli Supreme Court, which ruled that a civilian taking a direct part in terrorist activities should not be attacked if less harmful measures can be taken against him. Therefore, if he can be arrested and prosecuted, this should be preferred. However, arrests, investigations, and trials are not measures that can always be taken (HCJ 769/02). In other words, whenever possible, an arrest should be preferred over a targeted killing, but if an arrest is impossible or involves significant risk to the military forces, the targeted killing operation is legal and permissible.

In any case, the answer to the dilemmas created by the tension between these two basic rights—the right to life and the right to a fair trial—and the need to thwart terrorist attacks and protect the lives of the country's citizens naturally depends on the following fundamental question: Are targeted killings a counter-terrorism measure that constitutes the preventative act of thwarting terrorist attacks, or are they an act of punishment and revenge that do not allow for the due process of law?

DEATH PENALTY WITHOUT TRIAL?

One of the characteristics of the terrorist phenomenon is that it is a long-term threat, though not necessarily a continuous one. That is, the occurrence of a terrorist attack does not constitute the end of the threat; further attacks may take place after it (Shaul & Golan, 2004). In light of this, opponents of targeted killings claim that these operations are retaliatory actions, directed against terrorist operatives who were previously involved in carrying out attacks, whereas advocates of this method claim that even if there is no concrete intelligence that the target is initiating, planning or preparing terrorist attacks, because he has been involved in carrying out attacks in the past, he is likely to carry out further attacks in the future, and therefore the operation should be executed as an act of thwarting and preventing terrorism (Yadlin, 2004). Opponents of targeted killings also argue that the decision to carry out this action based on the terrorist's past involvement in terrorist attacks is an easy and convenient "way out" for decision-makers and security officials who have difficulty obtaining concrete intelligence about the terrorist's future plans

(Kremnitzer, 2005). According to them, it is in fact an extreme punishment under the guise of counter-terrorism; by eliminating the terrorist, the state is effectively imposing the death penalty on someone acting against it. The decision-makers and security officials who decide upon the targets for elimination and give the green light to the operation are simultaneously fulfilling the role of prosecutor, judge, and executor, according to this claim. In contrast to an ordinary judicial proceeding, in the case of the targeted killing of a terrorist, he is not aware that his fate is at stake and thus has no possibility of defending himself or appealing the decision, therefore his right to a fair trial has been violated.

In this context, former Justice Minister Dan Meridor presents a clear principled stance against the use of targeted killings (except in the case of ticking bombs). Meridor makes a distinction between a soldier carrying out a military operation designed to kill an enemy soldier and an operative sent on a mission to intentionally kill a specific terrorist. He argues that the classic dichotomous distinction between wartime and peace is the product of a declaration of war. This dichotomy also had a legal impact. The problem is that due to developments in technology and globalization, this dichotomy has blurred, and with it, the front line. Wars are no longer being waged at the front. Thus, in Meridor's view, the state should not enter into the gray area of targeted killing, "to a place in which we are not more powerful. To a place where the enemy can do the same thing. Apart from exceptional cases, in which the anticipated benefit is very great and there is no better alternative, the long-term risk to Israelis or Jews around the world as a result of such an act should be considered."[5] Meridor adds that "there is a strict prohibition on targeted killings (except for in cases of self-defense) in areas under Israel's control (such as the territory of the state and the territories under its military control), because in such a case conventional enforcement measures should be taken, and not targeted killings."[6]

Indeed, the moral basis of the laws of war (humanitarian law), perceives war as impersonal, as carried out by anonymous soldiers. Once a war or armed conflict has broken out, enemy soldiers can be killed, wounded, or captured, at any time and not only when they are in the course of military action, as an act of self-defense and regardless of the role in

[5] Personal interview with Dan Meridor, February 16, 2022.

[6] Ibid.

which they serve (Kremnitzer, 2006). The philosopher Michael Walzer says this regard: "It is not against the rules of war as we currently understand them to kill soldiers who look funny, who are taking a bath, holding up their pants, reveling in the sun, smoking a cigarette" (Walzer, 2006, 142). The soldiers on both sides are, therefore, perceived as representatives of their armies and countries. As part of a war machine, they kill and are killed solely due to this (Kremnitzer, 2006). Jean-Jacques Rousseau himself pointed this out, saying that, "War is not a relationship between man and man, but between state and state, in which individuals become enemies only by accident, not as men... not even as a members of their own nation, but as its defenders" (Rousseau & Betts, 1999). Hence, as long as the soldiers are not committing crimes, they have no legal responsibility for their actions.

Against this backdrop, those who disagree with the use of targeted killings say that marking a terrorist as worthy of death because he is a soldier in the enemy army is immoral, as it disregards any respect for his individual humanity. Thus, this action changes the conceptual and moral infrastructure of the laws of war (Kremnitzer, 2006). In response to this argument, proponents of targeted killings say that if one compares the act of killing, aimed at a specific person, to the killing of an anonymous soldier during a war, the targeted killing is more moral and right, as it allows for the selective killing of a person who has taken and is still taking an active part in terrorist acts. This is different from killing anonymous people simply because they are the "enemy" (Meisels & Waldron, 2020; Kremnitzer, 2006).

Military ethics expert Prof. Asa Kasher dismisses the legal dilemma on the issue of targeted killing, saying, "I think this whole legal concept is nonsense. Targeted killing is an act of self-defense. In war, a military force, for example, one armored brigade attacks another, so you're going to take them to court? It's nonsense. It's a war. I defend myself against those who attack me... trying to make a targeted killing look like punishment or revenge? It's not true. It's self-defense."[7] Indeed, the main response to the moral and ethical arguments raised by critics of targeted killings is derived from the following questions: Are targeted killings a punitive measure or a military action? What are the considerations underlying the decision to carry out a targeted killing? What is the goal that the

---

[7] Personal interview with Asa Kasher, February 23, 2022.

targeted killing is intended to achieve? and more. As mentioned, the issue was brought before the Israeli Supreme Court; the court resolved the dilemma by ruling that targeted killings must be carried out only for the purpose of preventing an attack and not as a punishment since it is not a sanction for acts committed in the past, but a measure designed to prevent a future attack (Rosenzweig, 2014). However, though the legal issue has been resolved, the ethical debate remains—can (even if only theoretically) a targeted killing also be justified as a means of punishment? This question was posed to various Israeli decision-makers at both the political and the military-security echelons.

Former Prime Minister Ehud Olmert says in this context:

> "We say that targeted killing is when we know in advance who will bear this consequence, who will be eliminated. Then you ask yourself, is this permissible? Is it prohibited? Is it moral? Is it immoral? The death penalty? Not the death penalty?... When it comes to targeted killings, the moral question arises, more so than in a routine operation in which it is not debated." Olmert answers these questions by saying, "Let's put things into context. War is not a nice thing, it's something in which people are killed, and there is no escaping that. Now, what distinguishes a targeted killing from an ordinary operation is the fact that here, you know in advance that you're going to target someone in particular. You're not embarking on a wide-ranging operation, you're going to eliminate someone whose identity and everything about him you know, for specific reasons...He's a ticking bomb, he's a murderer who may continue to order murderous activities, he has done things in the past for which he should be punished. Admittedly, without trial and without defensive lawyers, etc. Which of these considerations are legitimate? Which are not?"[8]

Olmert relays that he discussed these questions with US President George W. Bush: "It was very interesting to hear what the American approach was on this matter. Bush told me he would bring in NSA or CIA officials or the Special Operations Commander. He would ask them a question – if the specific man you're talking about continues to live, is there a danger that innocent people will die? 'If there is a high degree of certainty that innocent people will die,' he said, 'then I can justify the action. If not, then there's a problem ...'"[9] In this example, Olmert

---

[8] Personal interview with Ehud Olmert, March 3, 2022.

[9] Ibid.

answers the ethical questions raised and in fact determines that the moral issue relates to the future. Whether or not there is a reason to punish the target, the question is whether that terrorist is considered to pose a future risk to innocent lives.

Former Defense Minister and IDF Chief of Staff Moshe (Bogie) Ya'alon believes that it is legitimate to carry out targeted killings for the punitive purposes:

> I think it is right to use targeted killings for punishment as well. It is true that in recent years we have limited ourselves to cases of ticking bombs in the vast majority of cases. But I can mention, for example, the 'Committee X-period', the settling of accounts with the Munich murderers. It makes sense that someone who carries out an attack of a certain kind knows that he might not die a natural death. And it's a deterrent. Therefore, the pursuit of the Munich murderers, who no one checked whether they were active or inactive, but where it was simply decided to settle accounts with them, I see this as an important tool for deterrence.[10]

It is interesting to note that Ya'alon justifies his view that the use of targeted killings should be allowed for punitive purposes in terms of deterrence as well. That is, here again, the arguments are future-oriented—deterring others from committing similar terrorist acts.

The question can therefore be honed, and rather than using the term punishment, one can address the question of targeted killing as an act of revenge. In this context, it is interesting to note that in a national opinion poll conducted in Israel by the International Institute for Counter-Terrorism (ICT) at Reichman University in early 2022, in order to evaluate the Israeli public's views on targeted killings, 51% of respondents said that in their opinion, a targeted killing should be carried out even when it is an act of revenge, following the occurrence of a mass casualty terrorist attack. 10% of respondents completely objected to such an action, and 29% responded that it was conditional on the specific circumstances of the case.[11] In this regard, former Prime Minister Olmert says:

---

[10] Personal interview with Moshe (Bogie) Ya'alon, February 17, 2022.

[11] National Public Opinion Poll on Targeted Killings, conducted for the International Institute for Counter-Terrorism (ICT) by *Ma'agar Mochot*, February 21, 2022.

Revenge is certainly a legitimate consideration in the fight against such bodies [terrorist organizations]. It should be understood that a commander in a terrorist organization, the head of a terrorist organization, is from the outset the leader of a system that has decided in its very establishment to violate all the rules and not recognize any law, any of the fundamental norms that we live by, including during conflicts between armies... A terrorist organization excludes itself in advance from these rules by its behavior. It also excludes itself from the possible protections it might enjoy. There can't be a situation in which a terrorist organization says, 'I am not limited by anything, but you are limited by all the conventions you have signed'.[12]

Asa Kasher, on the other hand, states that "this is out of the question. Revenge is a primitive interaction that all of civilization wants to uproot. When someone does something bad to me, I can defend myself, and after the fact, bring him to justice. On the civilian level. We do not avenge; someone who avenges is a criminal. I can defend myself and then afterwards bring him to trial... If the principal, or only, motivation is revenge, it's wrong ... Deterrence is a by-product. I carry out a targeted killing to defend myself, and then it can also be a deterrent." Despite this decisive and clear position, in reference to the concrete example of the targeted killings carried out by Israel in the wake of the Munich Olympics attack, Kasher says, "Munich was an elimination and deterrence operation. They [the terrorists] carried out the attack in Munich. They are dangerous people and they could do it again."[13]

Discussing the Mossad's actions after the Munich attack, former Mossad Chief Shabtai Shavit says:

If you take the Munich case, then I cannot rule out the claim that the targeted killing operations the Mossad carried out after Munich had an element of revenge. But I can say that the element of deterrence was combined with revenge. I can empirically prove that targeted killing operations caused the other side to spend at least part of their time defending themselves. Many terrorists, especially at the command level, key people in the organizations, saw themselves as potential targets, so mentally and practically much of their time was devoted to surviving and defending themselves. They imposed on themselves rules of conduct that made it

---

[12] Personal interview with Ehud Olmert, March 3, 2022.
[13] Personal interview with Asa Kasher, February 23, 2022.

difficult for them to do what they wanted to do under conditions of complete freedom.[14]

An example of Shavit's claim arises from the words of another former Mossad official, Amnon Sofrin, who cites the case of the elimination of Fathi Shaqaqi in Malta, decided upon by then-Prime Minister and Defense Minister Yitzhak Rabin immediately after the double suicide bombing at Beit Lid junction by members of Shaqaqi's organization, the PIJ.[15] Former Head of the Mossad Yossi Cohen rules out the possibility of carrying out a targeted killing as an act of revenge, saying "I learned from Meir Dagan [former Mossad chief] that we do not avenge, we thwart, to prevent future terrorism."[16] Former Director of the Counter-Terrorism Bureau at the Prime Minister's office Nitzan Nuriel says categorically, "To the best of my knowledge and throughout my involvement in these processes as director of the Counter-Terrorism Bureau, I don't remember the justification of revenge even being alluded to."[17]

Former senior ISA official Oz Noy proposes a distinction between targeted killings that are carried out for the tactical purpose of thwarting concrete attacks and targeted killings that are carried out for strategic purposes: "During the Second intifada, there were operations whose goal was very focused, to thwart a developing attack. In previous years, there were operations whose goals were different, more strategic, with very long-term consequences. For example, the attacks on Black September after the Munich attack."[18] Referring to the issue of revenge, Noy states that if the action is performed only out of revenge, "I think it should be a very, very rare event...and it must also achieve far-reaching perceptual effects that create something more."[19]

The quasi-judicial procedure employed during Operation Wrath of God by "Committee X" in the 1970s following the massacre at the Munich Olympics, which was ostensibly intended to prevent arbitrary

---

[14] Personal interview with Shabtai Shavit, February 17, 2022.

[15] Personal interview with Amnon Sofrin, February 22, 2022.

[16] Personal interview with Yossi Cohen, May 1, 2022.

[17] Personal interview with Nitzan Nuriel, February 14, 2022.

[18] Personal interview with Oz Noy, February 16, 2022.

[19] Ibid.

targeted killings stemming from a desire for revenge alone, did not satisfy opponents of targeted killings; they claimed that such a policy, carried out through a "court" composed of politicians and military officials playing the roles of prosecutor, judge, and jury, was not an acceptable solution to the moral dilemma the use of this measure presents, because this group of these people was deciding on the death penalty, with the defendant having no right to appeal (Dershowitz, 2003; Zonder, 2001).

It was also problematic in their view due to the fact that it is highly doubtful whether this legal arrangement met the standards of the due process of law, since the defendant was unaware of the fact that he was being prosecuted and did not get the opportunity to defend himself, with only a particular minister to reluctantly defend him. (It is reasonable to assume that a terrorist operative would not want an Israeli minister defending him) (Ganor, 2003; Zonder, 2001).

The opponents of targeted killings maintain that the court alone is the body that should be responsible for conducting an orderly legal process, subject to judicial review, in order to ensure that the decision-making process is as moral and ethical as possible; in this way, there is more accountability and transparency of the process vis-à-vis the public. (Meisels, 2004).

In any case, many years later, in 2006, the question of whether targeted killing as a punitive measure necessitated a judicial or quasi-judicial process was decided in a Supreme Court ruling on a petition on targeted killings, which determined that there is an armed conflict between Israel and terrorist organizations in Judea and Samaria and the Gaza Strip. Hence, targeted killings are combat operations carried out under international humanitarian law and not an act of law enforcement or self-defense by the state (Rosenzweig, 2014).

Even in later targeted killings carried out in the 1970s, it could be seen that revenge was at the forefront of decision-makers' minds. For example, Operation Spring of Youth, which took place in Lebanon in 1973, was carried out following terrorist attacks on Israeli targets in Cyprus by Palestinian terrorists (Israeli Air Force, Operation Spring of Youth). As part of this operation, three senior PLO members were killed in their homes by Israeli special operations units that arrived in Beirut by sea. More than 20 other PLO activists were also killed in this operation. One of the participants in the operation claimed that the initial instruction was to abduct the PLO leaders and not to shoot them; however, in a briefing given by then-IDF Chief of Staff David Elazar before the operation, they were apparently told: "Kill the bastards" (Zonder, 2001). This statement reveals the real intention of the operation—to kill the terrorists—and the centrality of the element of revenge.

This systematic campaign came to an end in July 1973, when a decision was taken to slow it down in the wake of the operational failure in which Mossad agents misidentified Hassan Salameh and inadvertently shot an innocent Moroccan waiter. It was against this background that Israel's policy of targeted killings was changed, and it was determined that such an act could indeed be an option in certain circumstances, but its use must be careful, intelligent, and rare. It was advised to eliminate only senior leaders of terrorist organizations who were considered operatives, and whose elimination would severely impair the organization's operational capacity (Melman, 2004). This policy was changed again years later, and since the 1990s Israel has established that it carries out targeted killings only for the purpose of self-defense, in order to prevent a future terrorist attack that could harm its citizens (Ganor, 2003).

The motivation of revenge in targeted killings is, on the face of it, natural and understandable in light of the atrocity of a particularly severe terrorist attack or a wave of attacks that has traumatized the country and caused many casualties. However, it is obvious to most that it is impossible to morally or legally justify a targeted killing when revenge is the only, or even the central, motive. The desire for revenge may accompany other motives, principally the desire to thwart and prevent terrorism. Indeed, Israeli advocates of targeted killings, decision-makers, security officials, jurists, and academics emphasize that targeted killings are an act of prevention and not one of revenge. Their main argument is that it is the State of Israel's duty, as a democratic state, to protect its citizens and that the fundamental and supreme right of every person is the right to life. It is the duty of the state to ensure its security to the best of its ability, and to protect the lives of its citizens and their fundamental rights (Kasher, 1996). Asa Kasher argues that not only does the state have a duty to protect its citizens, but that this is a moral duty, (ibid.) because sitting passively, waiting for a deadly attack on the citizens of the state, is no more moral than taking preventive action for the purpose of self-defense (Zamir, 2007). This duty is reflected in the words of Former Air Force Commander and IDF Chief of Staff, Maj. Gen. Dan Halutz, who says, "Every time we set out to carry out a targeted killing, we also think of the 29 people killed at the Park Hotel [an attack carried out on the night of the Passover Seder in 2002] and the 22 people killed at the Dolphinarium [an attack that took place in 2001, and in which all of the victims were teenagers] and the bus that exploded in Jerusalem [an attack that took place in 2003 and killed many children]. This, too, is being taken into account" (ibid., pp. 110–111).

The prevailing view in Israel, therefore, is that the killing of a terrorist who threatens the right to life of Israeli citizens is a justified, moral, and essential act to save their lives. In the name of the sanctity of life, every effort should be made to prevent terrorists from taking the lives of civilians (Ganor, 2003). According to the proponents of targeted killings, such actions may indeed be carried out after the terrorist attack has already taken place, but even then, it is not an act of revenge, but an act of prevention. Israeli legal scholar Emanuel Gross maintains that targeted killing operations are intended to prevent further attacks, which are sometimes not known to the public, given that has not yet been carried out. In such cases, therefore, the targeted killing may appear to the outside observer, who is unfamiliar with security and intelligence matters, as an act of revenge or punishment, even though it is not (Gross, 2004).

Brig. Gen. (Res.) Gal Hirsch also rejects the definition of targeted killing as an act of revenge, but he suggests treating this element as one of many factors (and perhaps even a marginal one) involved in carrying out a targeted killing. Hirsch emphasizes the importance of delivering the messages of Israel's "long memory" and "closing of accounts" for the purpose of future deterrence. In his words, "the first message is prevention. The second message is deterrence, and the third message is know that we will not forgive and we will not forget...Central Command's modus operandi was to prevent the next attack and create deterrence. Of course, we also have to underscore and preserve the narrative that whoever messes with us will not come out unscathed. But first and foremost it's about prevention and long-term deterrence."[20] This approach is also consistent with the words of Daniel Reisner, who refers to the motive of revenge as an illegal one: "We have determined that the target must represent a tangible and real danger. It cannot be a punishment for the past." The tangibility and imminence of the danger sometimes make it difficult to substantiate the deterrence element in carrying out targeted killing operations. When asked about deterrence, Reisner replies

---

[20] Personal interview with Gal Hirsh, February 20, 2022.

that while it may be a side effect, "it cannot be the main reason" for such an action.[21]

The solution to the revenge dilemma, as mentioned, is the fact that punishment or revenge cannot serve as a motive or justification for a targeted killing operation. However, because the targets are often savage terrorists who were involved in carrying out mass casualty terrorist attacks, the elements of punishment and even revenge may accompany the core purpose of the strike, and reflect the feelings of operational, intelligence, and security officials, the decision-makers at the political level, and indeed the entire Israeli public, once they are informed of the death of an arch-terrorist.

Although targeted killing operations are primarily intended to prevent future terrorist acts, they still must be carried out with the necessary caution and only as a last resort. Kasher claims that the phrase "If someone comes to kill you, rise up and kill him first" is morally wrong because it expresses an incorrect directive: "Once you are in danger of being killed, the first action to be taken is to kill the source of the danger." According to Kasher, the correct expression to use in these cases is: "If someone comes to kill you, do whatever it takes to thwart his desire to kill you. If there is no choice but to kill him, rise up and kill him first; if there is an alternative to killing him, kill his desire without rising up to kill him first" (Kasher, 1996). That is, Israel must act according to the "light to heavy" principle: Israeli decision-makers must ask themselves, "Is it possible to arrest the person and imprison him until the violence ends?" If so, this is what should be done. If it is not possible to arrest the person, but only to strike him from a distance, then there is no choice and there is a very strong justification to target him (Zonder, 2001).

TARGETED KILLING AS A MEANS OF SATISFYING PUBLIC OPINION

In a democracy where the government is attentive to the feelings of the public, and the very continuation of the regime of one leadership or another is dependent on the will of the electorate and public opinion, decision-makers find themselves compelled to carry out resolute offensive action to combat terrorism; targeted killings may serve as a convenient

---

[21] Personal interview with Daniel Reisner, April 8, 2002.

way to respond to the will and demands of the people and thereby serve the political needs of the government. Naturally, the public's demand for more resolve in the country's counter-terrorism activity is more pronounced when waves of terrorism or particularly severe terrorist attacks occur. These calls are sometimes accompanied by a demand for revenge against anyone who had a hand in carrying out the attack. In light of this, detractors of targeted killings argue that this course of action is liable to be carried out as a result of the will or need of political decision makers to please the public and satisfy its desire for revenge (Ganor, 2003).

Moreover, the influence of public opinion on the political leadership's decision to employ the use of targeted killings may stem not necessarily from political considerations, electoral interests, or foreign policy considerations, but rather from an understanding of the psychological aspects of terrorism and the terrorists' aspiration to erode national security and the citizens' sense of personal security. In this context, decision-makers may take offensive counter-terrorism measures in order to show the public that the country's security agencies and leadership are working to maintain public safety and combat terrorism, and that they will not shy away from using even severe measures such as targeted killings to achieve this goal. Targeted killing operations may therefore be an outgrowth of the desire to strengthen the public in times of distress due to the proliferation of terrorist attacks, and to bolster national resilience and personal security.

The degree of the impact of public opinion on the decision-making process in targeted killings can be understood from interviews with political decision-makers and heads of the defense establishment in Israel.

Former Prime Minister Yitzhak Shamir said in this regard that the stances of the public influence decision-makers "on everything." In his words, "Some popular article in a newspaper will affect the decision maker. On the political echelon. It may have a positive or negative effect. Public opinion polls less so. But they also have an effect." Shamir said that he himself faced pressure from the public on an issue about which he had to make a decision (he was most likely referring to his decision to acquiesce to the US administration's request to refrain from responding to the Iraqi missiles fired on Israel during the Gulf War). "Every day I had to read newspaper articles that attacked [this decision] using all possible arguments, and I had to deal with this doubly. First, I would tell myself personally that [the author] is not right and why he is not right. And secondly, I would have to explain it [my decision] to the public... It's a war of opinions."[22]

Another prime minister, Benjamin Netanyahu, said that the impact of public pressure on his decision-making processes on counter-terrorism in general and targeted killings, in particular, was minimal.[23] On the other hand, Meir Dagan, who served as the prime minister's adviser on counter-terrorism during Netanyahu's first term and later served under Netanyahu as head of the Mossad, said in this context that "If there were no terrorist acts, the issue of terrorism would never be discussed by the prime minister. The only thing that places this issue on the prime minister's desk is the public reaction and the effectiveness of the public response to these events. This forces the decision makers to deal with it" (Ganor, 2003).

Rafi Eitan, who served as a counter-terrorism adviser to other prime ministers, determined that public opinion does have an impact on the decision-making process regarding the war on terror. "Absolutely yes," he said. "I think that many times when I sat with Begin and also with Shamir or with Yitzhak Rabin when he was defense minister, the question of what it would look like in the eyes of the public was on the agenda."[24] Amnon Lipkin-Shahak, who served as IDF chief of staff and as a minister in the Ehud Barak government, also addressed this question, saying, "Very much. The public has a huge influence. Public opinion has an effect. It's the public, the media...[to what extent] cannot be measured, certainly not accurately, but there is no doubt that the public and the media have an influence on decision makers...This impact is usually in the direction of action, not in the direction of restraint."[25]

Former ISA Chief Carmi Gillon explains the reasons and motives behind the public's influence on these issues. "If you ask me when the chances of approval [of counter-terrorism operations] are higher, it's certainly when it's the public atmosphere invites such things. Because a prime minister... is at the end of the day also a political creature. The public is important to him... Yitzhak Shamir was a political man, even

---

[22] Personal interview with Yitzhak Shamir, November 18, 1996.

[23] Personal interview with Benjamin Netanyahu, December 20, 1999.

[24] Personal interview with Rafi Eitan, October 30, 1999.

[25] Personal interview with Amnon Lipkin-Shahak, December 23, 1999.

though he managed the system beneath him in a very rigid and institutionalized manner, Begin definitely, and Rabin as well. Ultimately [there is] the ballot box. There is a lot of populism regarding this matter...".[26]

Former IDF Chief of Staff and Foreign Minister Gabi Ashkenazi believes that the public's influence on the decision-making processes in counter-terrorism stems from the fact that the public is required to pay a price as a result of these decisions. "The problem is that today, the public is part of the combat arena. When terrorists explode here, the public demands that it stop, and this affects the decision maker... I think it cannot be said that public opinion doesn't have an impact, but I would say that it is in very special cases. They're not exactly looking at public opinion when planning a significant targeted killing. But they do embark on an operation in Gaza depending on what happens in Sderot (a small city bordering the Gaza Strip)."[27] Ashkenazi therefore distinguishes between specific and surgical counter-terrorism operations such as targeted killings, with regard to which he claims the influence of the public is smaller, and the strategic decision of embarking on a broad military operation when the scale of terrorism is severely harming the fabric of life in the country, which creates significant public pressure on decision-makers. Referring to the difference in the public's impact on decision-making processes at the military level versus the political level, Ashkenazi says, "The army cannot ignore what society thinks...The military, of course, takes it into consideration. But you don't take action because of this pressure. I think the military stays in the realm of professional considerations. The military looks at strategic conditions, not just public opinion. The army does not justify its actions because of public opinion.... The Israeli public is the customer of the activity, you serve the public... you give it a result [because] it paid a price."[28]

Another former IDF chief of staff and former commander of the Air Force, Dan Halutz, warns against giving too much consideration to public opinion in the field of counter-terrorism and targeted killings: "Public opinion must not be ignored, but I think the Israeli leadership would be making a mistake if it included it as a key element in the decision-making

---

[26] Personal interview with Carmi Gillon, November 24, 1999.

[27] Personal interview with Gabi Ashkenazi, March 2, 2022.

[28] Ibid.

process."[29] Halutz explains that in some cases the Israeli public does not see the whole picture: "There may be a situation in which the State of Israel has tremendous security challenges that are hidden from the public eye. For example, the whole campaign that is taking place against the Iranian nuclear program is hidden from the eyes of the Israeli public…In these cases, bowing to public pressure will naturally be a mistake." Halutz believes that the stances of the public should be only one component (and not necessarily the main one) in decision-makers' deliberations, one that should be assessed along with many other important elements, and regrets that in practice this has not always been the case.[30]

In conclusion, based on an analysis of the statements of political and military decision-makers, it seems that public opinion does have an important place in decision-making processes in the field of counter-terrorism, including with regard to targeted killings, but the extent of this influence varies depending on the views and characteristics of the prime minister and his or her staff, changes in circumstances, and, especially, the scope and nature of terrorism during the period in question. But can the influence of the public extend to the point of a decision being made to carry out a targeted killing only for the purpose of boosting morale? Or only for the purpose of strengthening national resilience and the citizens' sense of personal security? To these questions, former Prime Minister Ariel Sharon replied, "If you are asking me whether targeted killing operations should be carried out in order to boost morale among the citizens, then, in my opinion, the answer is no."[31]

Lior Lotan, former Special Negotiator on Hostages and Missing Persons for Prime Minister Netanyahu, reinforces this position, stating, "No, no and no. It doesn't factor into the equation at all. National resilience is important because it ultimately produces the state's capabilities. But national resilience is not something that is achieved by attacking the other side…I don't believe in building morale by way of striking the enemy."[32]

Meir Dagan, however, thought otherwise, and supported the carrying out of counter-terrorism activities in order to strengthen public morale.

---

[29] Personal interview with Dan Halutz, March 3, 2022.

[30] Ibid.

[31] Personal interview with Ariel Sharon September 13, 2000.

[32] Personal interview with Lior Lotan, April 17, 2022.

"Unequivocally, yes. Even when you know that this [action] does not solve the problem, the effect you achieve in the public consciousness is important... Because terrorism is about the war over public consciousness, I have no doubt that these reactions after a terrorist attack are important."[33]

Lipkin-Shahak clarified that "If that is the only goal, you need a very good reason to carry out such an operation. Morale would have to be very significantly low, and there would have to be a very dire need to take action to respond to this. Otherwise, one should refrain, because I believe that ultimately the public is extremely resilient, even in difficult times of terror."[34] Former Prime Minister Yitzhak Shamir also did not rule out the possibility of carrying out counter-terrorism activities on the basis of considerations of morale. "It depends on the price of the action. What is its impact on the enemy? There are no rules here. It depends on each individual case. I would not preclude it and I would not say we should do it in every case. It's always better for the action to also have a practical effect."[35] Unlike Shamir, who referred to the "practical effect" as a by-product, former Defense Minister and IDF Chief of Staff Moshe (Bogie) Ya'alon says the reverse: "There is no doubt that one of the by-products of targeted killings is to raise morale, improve morale. But you don't do it because of that. There's no doubt that it's an important by-product."[36]

It arises, then, from these statements, that boosting morale is likely to be one goal of counter-terrorism activity in general and targeted killing in particular, but it is one of several goals, and in any case, it is an important outcome of counter-terrorism; however, this goal is not a key component of the decision-making process. Moreover, as much as the element of morale may be relevant to the decision-making processes at the political level, it is not a legitimate consideration and therefore does not exist at the military-operational level. In the words of former ISA official Oz Noy, "What? No way. There can be no such thing. No way. It's possible that the politicians above will make these calculations, but the operational ranks? No way."[37]

---

[33] Personal interview with Meir Dagan, December 2, 1999.

[34] Personal interview with Amnon Lipkin-Shahak, December 23, 1999.

[35] Personal interview with Yitzhak Shamir, November 18, 1996.

[36] Personal interview with Moshe (Bogie) Ya'alon, February 17, 2022.

[37] Personal interview with Oz Noy, February 16, 2022.

And what about the role of the media in reflecting public opinion and applying pressure on decision-makers with regard to counter-terrorism in general and targeted killings in particular? Rehavam Ze'evi ("Gandhi"), who served as the prime minister's adviser on counter-terrorism and as a minister in the Israeli government, said in this context, "Our public has become a factor. The Israeli domestic factor is gaining more and more influence because of the intensification of the media. Our transparency vis-à-vis the media. And because of a process called democratization."[38] The decision-makers interviewed on the subject emphasize the impact of the media in creating pressure on decision-makers to respond to terrorism, mainly following the occurrence of terrorist attacks, or as a result of political and other processes. These decisions are made under time pressure and therefore may be hasty.[39] Meir Dagan explains, "The role of the press is a positive one because it forces decision makers to engage in the matter. However, it forces them to engage in actions whose purpose is to please the public and not to fight terrorism. In fact, a real war on terror can take place in times when there are no terrorist attacks. In relative quiet...".[40]

In summary, the Israeli public, as well as decision-makers and defense chiefs, not only believe that targeted killings are an important and effective tool in Israel's toolbox as it faces a serious terrorist threat, but that it is also a legitimate and moral one. The motives of punishment and revenge may accompany the decision to carry out a targeted killing, but they do not constitute a justification for such an action or even a key element in the decision-making process. The standpoints of the public and the Israeli media on the subject may influence the considerations of political decision-makers by virtue of Israel being a democratic state, and their desire to prove that they are doing everything in their power to restore personal security to the citizens in the face of terrorist attacks. However, they do not affect the deliberations of the security establishment, which operates according to the criterion of the degree of danger the target represents in the future.

[38] Personal interview with Rehavam Ze'evi ("Gandhi"), November 29, 1999.

[39] Personal interview with Yaakov Perry, December 4, 1998.

[40] Personal interview with Meir Dagan, December 2, 1999.

Case Study—Ghassan Kanafani

Background: Kanafani had served as the spokesman for the Popular Front for the Liberation of Palestine, led by George Habash, since the late 1960s. As well as being the organization's spokesman, Kanafani was one of the most respected Palestinian writers in the Arab world (Yudilevitch, 2008). In 1972, the PFLP carried out a terrorist attack on Israel's International Airport in Lod, which killed 24 people and injured 71.

The operation: On July 8, 1972, the targeted killing operation was carried out, ostensibly by the Israeli Mossad, by placing an explosive device in his car in Beirut, Lebanon. Killed along with him was his brother's daughter, who was with him in the car (Darraj, 1999).

Background of the operation: After the airport massacre, Kanafani was sentenced to death by Golda Meir's "court" (Committee X) as part of the elimination campaign following the murder of the Israeli athletes in Munich (Yudilevitch, 2008). In a photo taken in Lebanon in the weeks before the attack, Kanafani was seen with one of the Japanese terrorists trained by the PFLP in preparation for the attack at the airport, which is likely what revealed his involvement in the operational aspects of the planning of the attack (Amior, 2015). According to another version of events, Kanafani was mistakenly added to the elimination list after the Munich Olympics. In a 2005 interview with Israeli daily *Yedioth Ahronoth*'s military analyst, Eitan Haber claimed that "Today, the Mossad also half-heartedly admits that there were those who fell victim to injustice following the decision to create an atmosphere of deterrence and fear among Palestinian communities in Europe... the most senior and prominent among those sentenced to death by Golda's 'court,' even though they had no direct connection to terrorism in general and to Munich in particular, was Kanafani." According to Haber, Kanafani was considered an easy target since he was a spokesman for the PFLP (Yudilevitch, 2008).

Consequences of the action: After the operation, newspapers in Beirut wrote that it constituted an Israeli response to the act of terrorism at the Israeli airport (*The death of Kanafani*, 1972). The fact that Kanafani's niece was also killed with him muddied the action, which was already considered by many to be reckless (Yudilevitch, 2008).

The 1972 targeted killing of Kanafani that was most likely carried out by Israel illustrates the central dilemma presented in this chapter—the use of this counter-terrorism measure to thwart and prevent terrorism,

4 THE LEGITIMACY OF TARGETED KILLINGS: A DEATH PENALTY ... 109

versus its use to exact revenge and punishment. Assuming that this operation was indeed accompanied by a quasi-judicial proceeding involving Committee X, a retrospective examination establishes that this procedure did not prevent a targeted killing operation whose benefit was questionable and which certainly did not give Kanafani any opportunity to claim his innocence. Supporters of this operation may argue that even if the PFLP spokesman was not a link in the chain of the decision-making and execution of the attack on the Israeli airport, his killing deterred other PFLP members from continuing to carry out major attacks in Israel in the years that followed.

REFERENCES

Amior, H. (2015, January 15). *According to Dror Etkes of Ha'aretz, Israel also kills journalists. Really?* Presspectiva. https://presspectiva.org.il/%D7%A2% D7%95%D7%93-%D7%94%D7%A9%D7%95%D7%95%D7%90%D7%95%D7% AA-%D7%91%D7%99%D7%9F-%D7%99%D7%A9%D7%A8%D7%90%D7% 9C-%D7%9C%D7%91%D7%99%D7%9F-%D7%94%D7%9E%D7%97%D7%91% D7%9C%D7%99%D7%9D-%D7%9E%D7%94%D7%A4/

Bendet, S. (2016, May 21). Two executions and countless disputes: The punishment that no one in Israel is happy to carry out. *Walla! News.* https://news. walla.co.il/item/2963189

Darraj, F. (1999). Ghassan Kanfani. In A. Ophir (Ed.), *Fifty to forty-eight: Critical moments in the history of the state of Israel.* Van Leer Institute Press and Hakibbutz Hameuchad.

David, S. (2003). Israel's policy of targeted killing. *Ethics & International Affairs, 17*(1), 122.

Dershowitz, A. (2003). *Why terrorism works: Understanding the threat, responding to the challenge.* Yale University Press.

Frisch, F., & Waked, A. (2002, January 14). *The Palestinians: IDF assassinates senior Tanzim leader Raed al-Karmi.* Ynet. https://www.ynet.co.il/articles/ 0,7340,L-1539788,00.html

Ganor, B. (2003). *The counter-terrorism puzzle—A guide for decision makers.* Mifalot.

Gross, E. (2004). *Democracy's struggle against terrorism—Legal and moral aspects.* Nevo.

Harel, A. & Hass, A. (2001, August 6). The IDF publishes a list of seven "candidates for assassination." *Ha'aretz.*

HCJ 769/02. (2006). *The Public Committee against torture in Israel v. The Government of Israel, 62*(1), 507.

Israeli Air Force. *Operation "spring of youth."* http://www.iaf.co.il/Templa tes/FlightLog/FlightLog.aspx?lang=HE&lobbyID=40&folderID=48&subfol derID=322&docfolderID=842&docID=7220&docType=EVENT

Kasher, A. (1996). *Military ethics.* Ministry of Defense.

Kasher, A. (2006). Principles of military counter-terrorism. In D. Meridor & H. Fass (Eds.), *The battle of the 21st century: Democracies fighting terrorism* (pp. 276–277). Israel Institute of Democracy.

Kremnitzer, M. (2006). *Is everything kosher when dealing with terrorism?* The Israel Democracy Institute.

Meisels, T. (2004). Targeting terror. *Social Theory and Practice, 30*(3), 297–326.

Meisels, T., & Waldron, J. (2020). *Debating targeted killing: Counter-terrorism or extrajudicial execution?* Oxford University Press.

Melman,Y. (2004, March 23). Assassinations were once a last resort today, today they are carried out wholesale. *Ha'aretz.*

Nevo, B., & Shur, Y. (2003). *Morality, ethics and law in wartime.* The Israel Democracy Institute.

Perry, Y. (2002). Counter-terrorism and human rights. In *The fight against terrorism and the rights of the individual: A dialogue in memory of Col. Uzi Yairi,* 12. The Interdisciplinary Center Herzliya.

Rousseau, J., & Betts, C. (Ed.). (1999). *Discourse on political economy and the social contract.* Oxford University Press.

Rosenzweig, I. (2014). Targeted killings during high and low intensity warfare. In P. Sharvit & A. Kurz (Eds.), *Law and national security: Selected issues* (pp. 41–52). INSS.

Rubinstein, E. (2003). On security and human rights in the era of the war on terror. *Law and the Military, 16*(4), 764–778.

Sabel, R. (2003). *International law.* The Hebrew University.

Shany, Y. (2019). *The UN Committee on Human Rights and the right to life.* ICON-S-IL Blog. https://israeliconstitutionalism.wordpress.com/2019/03/ 05/%D7%94%D7%95%D7%95%D7%A2%D7%93%D7%94-%D7%9C%D7%96% D7%9B%D7%95%D7%99%D7%95%D7%AA-%D7%94%D7%90%D7%93%D7% 9D-%D7%A9%D7%9C-%D7%94%D7%90%D7%95%D7%9D-%D7%95%D7% 94%D7%96%D7%9B%D7%95%D7%AA-%D7%9C%D7%97%D7%99/

Shaul, S., & Golan, H. (Eds.). (2004). *The limited conflict.* Ma'arachot.

The death of Kanafani. (1972, July 10). Al Hamishmar. https://www.nli.org. il/he/newspapers/?a=is&oid=ahr19720710-01&type=staticpdf&submitted= 1&e=-------he-20--1--img-txIN%7CtxTI-------------1&g-recaptcha-response= 03AGdBq26Z_xZzka4-6jz90N4HkgeaKbP4qg2A49-u1i64OiCkZInf20De3 U09imGz3Hcua4DtAWu5FHuNOEmCg

United Nations (General Assembly). (1966). International covenant on economic, social, and cultural rights. *Treaty Series 999* (December), 171.

Walzer, M. (2006). *Just and unjust wars: A moral argument with historical illustrations.* Basic Books.

Yadlin A. (2004) Professional and ethical dilemmas in the use of force in fighting terrorism. In S. Shaul & H. Golan (Eds.), *The limited conflict* (p. 13). Ma'arachot.

Yadlin, A., & Kasher, A. (2003). Ethics in fighting terrorism. *National Security* (2–3).

Yudilevitch, M. (2008, April 7). *Faithful to the original.* Ynet. https://www.ynet.co.il/articles/0,7340,L-3528768,00.html

Zamir, E. (2007). The moral fight against terrorism. *Ma'arachot* (414), 36. Ministry of Defense.

Zonder, M. (2001, July 27). *Shooting and not crying.* NRG. http://www.nrg.co.il/online/archive/ART/169/638.html.

CHAPTER 5

The Principle of Distinction in Targeted Killing—Who Do You Target?

The determination of who can be targeted in a targeted killing operation is a major issue underlying any assessment of the legitimacy of this action. Because Israel regards targeted killings as a legitimate military action in the framework of the war on terror, and not as a punitive action in the fight against crime, it is the principles of international law that must be applied to such operations, and in particular the principle of distinction. The fundamental norm of humanitarian law is that causing intentional harm to civilians is prohibited; hence, the questions and dilemmas surrounding the deliberate harming of terrorists who, on the one hand, are not necessarily soldiers—they do not always wear uniforms and do not necessarily carry their weapons openly or belong to a chain of command with a clear hierarchy—and on the other hand, they are not uninvolved civilians, since they engage in combat and carry out attacks to harm those whom they define as their enemies. The issue of the definition of terrorists as a legitimate target has been discussed by Israeli decision-makers and legal entities, who see them as unlawful combatants, whereas the Supreme Court has chosen to define them as civilians directly involved in hostilities, and therefore legitimate targets (HCJ 769/02, 2006). However, even if we accept the claim that terrorists are legitimate targets for targeted killings, we still must address a number of questions derived from this conviction, including: Should we distinguish between the military and the political echelons with regard to targeted killing

© The Author(s), under exclusive license to Springer Nature Switzerland AG 2022
B. Ganor and L. Koblentz-Stenzler, *Israel's Targeted Killing Policy*, https://doi.org/10.1007/978-3-031-13674-0_5

113

operations? Is intentional harm at the political level permissible and legitimate? What are the criteria that determine the degree of legitimacy of the elimination of one terrorist or another? Is the target's seniority a relevant factor? Or is his operational role, the degree of his personal involvement in the execution of terrorist attacks, and the immediate or future danger he poses? This chapter will delve into these questions.

First, we will examine the question of the **distinction between the military and the political echelons**. The philosopher Michael Walzer argues that there is a moral distinction, backed by international law, between people whom it is permissible to kill and those whom it is forbidden to kill once a war has broken out. Among those who cannot be killed are people who are not carrying weapons and those who do not pose an immediate threat (such as political figures and leaders). These are naturally not military personnel, and therefore cannot be considered legitimate targets for attack. According to Walzer, "If their support for the government or the war were allowable as a reason for killing them, the line that marks off immune from vulnerable persons would quickly disappear" (Walzer, 2006, p. 202). Walzer explains that one of the reasons behind the separation between people whose killing is permissible and legitimate in a state of war (i.e., soldiers), and people whose killing is illegitimate (i.e., political figures), is the fact that the soldier's activity threatens a given country, while the unjust or oppressive nature of the conduct of a political activist is a matter for political judgment (Walzer, 2006, pp. 237–238). Kremnitzer, on the other hand, states that, "Targeted killings are used to eliminate a particular person: a political or military leader, a commander or an operative in a terrorist organization, or a person responsible (according to intelligence information) for terrorist acts" (Kremnitzer, 2006, p. 5). For him, the range of legitimate targets is broader and includes political leaders and heads of terrorist organizations.

In contrast, Yael Stein, an Israeli human rights activist, claims that the problem with Israel's targeted killing policy is that there are no guidelines that create a distinction between those terrorist operatives who are a legitimate target for elimination and those who are not. In her view, the evidence for this is that Israeli officials speaking about the policy at the outbreak of the Second Intifada in the early 2000s deliberately refrained from declaring who they see as a legitimate target. As an example, she cites the words of then-Prime Minister of Israel Ehud Barak: "We will strike against anyone who hurts us. We have the ability to do so" (Stein, 2003, p. 135).

In this context, it is worth remembering that it is often difficult to distinguish between the political and military-operational echelons in the terrorist organizations; the heads of the organizations and their senior officials, despite being identified as the political representatives of the organization, are also sometimes those who dictate its terrorism policy. Indeed, many decision-makers in Israel believe that the terrorist organization should be treated as a whole, that is, a semi-military body that carries out terrorist attacks as part of the joint efforts of various officials. In other words, there should be no distinction between the administrative, political and semi-military elements, because all of the organizations' members together build up its capability to carry out terrorist attacks against Israeli citizens. It is possible then, for example, for the person in charge of the political wing of a particular terrorist organization to also be a member of the organization's leadership, and therefore also be responsible for shaping its terrorist policy (Ganor, 2003). **Asa Kasher** asserts that when it comes to terrorist organizations, there is no difference between a political and a military leader. "It's problematic," he says. "On the one hand, it makes sense to maintain distinctions between soldiers and civilians, but sometimes it's a pretense. What, was Arafat not involved in the terrorist organizations' every move? What is a political leader? If I can prove that Hamas helps the poor, does that make it the political echelon?" Kasher states that "The head of Hamas is the effective ruler of Gaza, and I can't give him immunity as a political leader. As long as he is not responsible for cultivating threats, he is immune… he is not a political leader dealing with diplomacy, but a terrorist who sent missiles to Jerusalem. So he is a terrorist."[1]

In 1998, **Lt. Gen. Moshe (Bogie) Ya'alon**, who was serving as head of Military Intelligence at the time, referred to the manner in which Hamas had been carrying out attacks since the mid-1990s:"When Hamas sets out on a suicide attack, the operation is the result of a decision by the system, by the leadership that sits mainly abroad, in Jordan and Damascus and other countries in the world. These people formulate a strategy of terrorist attacks that is then passed down to people on the ground. On the ground, the potential always exists, but it is not put into action without instructions from above" (Figel, 1996). However, Amin al-Hindi, the former commander of the Palestinian General Intelligence Service in

---

[1] Personal interview with Asa Kasher, February 23, 2022.

Gaza, claimed in 2001, following the wave of targeted killings carried out by Israel, that Israel did seek to assassinate Palestinian activists regardless of whether the target was a political or military figure, or even a journalist ("Annan's strong condemnation of assassination policy," 2001).

A case study that exemplifies the blurring of the distinction between a political and a military leader is the case of Thabet Thabet. In December 2000, following the wave of terrorism that befell the State of Israel, the secretary general of the Fatah movement in Tulkarem, Dr. Thabet Thabet, was killed when snipers fired at his vehicle. Thabet was considered the "number three" in the organization, after the senior political echelon which included Yasser Arafat, the head of the Palestinian Authority, and Marwan Barghouti, Fatah's secretary general in the West Bank. Israel's claim was that under Thabet's command, a terrorist cell repeatedly shot at Israeli settlements and IDF soldiers, seriously injuring three soldiers. This cell received weapons and ammunition from Thabet (HCJ 474/02, 2011; Waked, 2001). Thabet's killing provoked allegations by the Palestinian Authority that it constituted an escalation of Israel's targeted killings because he was a political figure who had nothing to do with Fatah's military activities (Waked, 2001). Israel justified the decision to kill him, saying that Thabet was responsible for a series of shootings by Fatah's Tanzim faction at Israeli targets in Tulkarem (HCJ 474/02, 2011). Thus, Israel tried to show that this was one unified terrorist organization, meaning that despite Thabet being a political figure, he was personally responsible for those shootings.

Here, the question arises regarding the strength of the connection between the target and the occurrence of a future terrorist attack. To what extent is the connection certain, and what is the degree of the imminence of the danger the terrorist poses? Is the danger immediate and tangible, or distant? **Asa Kasher** believes that the legitimacy of carrying out targeted killings is derived from the degree of danger posed by the target in terms of terrorist attacks that must be thwarted and the absence of other alternatives. For him, it would not be legitimate to target a driver driving a terrorist, "because there is no problem in bringing someone else to be a driver. But if he is currently taking part in an immediate threat, he can be targeted because it is a 'developing event.' The question is – is he now a partner in creating the threat? Is he now part of the plan? There is a difference between 'he is planning to drive,' in which case he is replaceable, and 'he is now driving,' in which case he can be targeted."[2]

Shalom Ben Hanan assesses this issue according to what he calls "the test of near certainty." In his words:

> A target for killing must meet the criteria of a 'clear and present danger.' How great is the danger and how imminent is it? The intelligence and/or evidential material must be solid and real in order for targeted killing to be approved. This is sometimes referred to in legal parlance as a test of 'near certainty.' A decision on a targeted killing will only be made if it can be proved with near or absolute certainty that this measure is the only tool that will prevent future risk to the lives of civilians or soldiers. This is the principal test, and it is not related to the rank of the target, who may be a senior terrorist or a simple operative.[3]

Former Prime Minister **Ehud Olmert**, on the other hand, believes that there is no need to take into account the degree of the target's current and immediate involvement when gauging the legitimacy of a targeted killing operation. To justify his argument, Olmert refers to the killing of Imad Mughniyeh—a senior Hezbollah official and the head of the organization's military wing, who was responsible for many terrorist attacks against Israel, the United States, France, and many other countries—and asks a rhetorical question: Is it illegitimate to target Mughniyeh even if there is no up-to-date information on plans for a concrete terrorist attack that he is involved in?[4]

Former Justice Minister **Dan Meridor**, who takes a critical principled stance on the use of targeted killing and prefers to limit it mainly to cases of ticking bombs, nonetheless maintains that the definition of a ticking bomb must not be limited to the time at which the terrorist is already on his way to his destination. "It does not have to be immediate in the sense of the time that the attack is going to take place. It's the time frame in which I can stop the attack."[5] **Ben Hanan** explains that although it is possible to point to a hierarchy of ticking bombs at various levels in the

---

[2] Personal interview with Asa Kasher, February 23, 2022.

[3] Personal interview with Shalom Ben Hanan, February 21, 2022.

[4] Personal interview with Ehud Olmert, March 3, 2022.

[5] Personal interview with Dan Meridor, February 16, 2022.

terrorist organizations against whom it would be legitimate to carry out a targeted killing, the common denominator for all of them is the near certainty that the particular target will "kill the next citizen. Sometimes it will take him weeks, sometimes it's a matter of days, sometimes the intelligence is such that you have only a few hours [before the attack], and sometimes you target the wanted person when he is literally on his way to carry out the attack."[6] In contrast to this test of near certainty, former IDF Chief of Staff **Moshe Ya'alon** says that in his opinion, the targeted killing of a terrorist who has "retired" is also legitimate, as it has a deterrent effect on the next in line, bestowing upon them the knowledge that "we are settling the account."[7]

As mentioned, in its ruling on the petition against targeted killings, the Israeli Supreme Court discussed the classification of the status of terrorist operatives. The discussion on this issue opened with the question of whether the terrorists are combatants, civilians, or unlawful combatants. It is from this designation that the terrorists' rights and obligations as combatants or civilians are derived, as is the degree of legitimacy of the deliberate harm inflicted on them (Intelligence & Terrorism Information Center, 2006). The petitioners' claim was that according to the laws of war, there are only two statuses—combatants and civilians. Combatants are legitimate targets for attack, on the one hand, but they enjoy rights granted to them by international law, such as immunity from prosecution and the right to the status of prisoner of war. Civilians enjoy the protections and rights conferred on them by international law in times of war—for example, they cannot be the targets of an attack (HCJ 769/02, 2006).

The position of the respondents to the petition, representing the state, was that the terrorists, in fact, constitute a third category, that of "unlawful combatants," as they participate in the hostilities, but not in a lawful manner, and they therefore cannot enjoy the rights given to combatants. The Supreme Court did not accept the respondents' position and ruled that although the terrorists are not considered combatants, they are also not citizens with immunity (according to Article 51(3)

---

[6] Personal interview with Shalom Ben Hanan, February 21, 2022.

[7] Personal interview with Moshe ("Bogie") Ya'alon, February 17, 2022.

of the First Additional Protocol to the Geneva Conventions[8]), but are considered civilians who are "directly participating in the hostilities" and therefore lose the protection to which uninvolved civilians, who are not involved in terrorist acts, are entitled (Intelligence & Terrorism Information Center, 2006). At the same time, the terrorist does not enjoy the privileges granted to a lawful combatant, such as recognition of POW status, as he is a civilian playing the role of a combatant.

The ruling was based on the premise that there is an armed conflict between Israel and the terrorist organizations in Judea, Samaria, and the Gaza Strip, so the act in question is a combat operation carried out in the framework of international humanitarian law, and not an act of law enforcement or self-defense (Rosenzweig, 2014).

Sharon Afek, who previously served as the IDF's chief military advocate general, explains that the Military Advocate General's Corps regards the war on terror as fitting the definition of an "armed conflict," and therefore the relevant laws for inspecting the issue are the laws of armed conflict (that is, the laws of war), and not policing laws. The reason for this is, first and foremost, is the factual situation—within the Palestinian terrorist organizations there are very many terrorist operatives, equipped with significant arms, on the scale of an army, and they cause damage and casualties on the same scale as an armed conflict. This decision had many implications, including with regard to the weapons used against the terrorist operatives, the regulations on opening fire, and the issue of tort claims. The legal thesis developed by the Military Advocate General (the Department of International Law) was revolutionary at an international level, stating simply that just as in a theoretical war with Syria it is permissible to deliberately harm a Syrian general, it is also permissible to do the same in Gaza (a place over which Israel does not have control) to a leader of a terrorist organization who is leading the fight against Israel. Even if the head of the terrorist organization, is, for example, a university professor by day, and at night, sends suicide bombers into Israel, he is a legitimate target for attack. According to Afek, "Not only does he not have more privileges than the Syrian general, he actually has much fewer, and is a legitimate military target."[9]

---

[8] The article states that "civilians shall enjoy the protection afforded by this Section, unless and for such time as they take a direct part in hostilities.".

[9] Personal interview with Sharon Afek, March 13, 2022.

In this situation of armed conflict, it is forbidden to attack civilians, but a combatant belonging to the enemy forces, or a civilian taking an active part in the hostilities, may be attacked, provided the attack is not likely to cause collateral damage that is disproportionate to the military benefit anticipated from this operation (Rosenzweig, 2014); however, targeted killings are only permissible against terrorist operatives who are taking a direct part in the hostilities.

Daniel Reisner, who represented the position of the state in this petition, clarifies that:

> If we are in a state of armed conflict, then in armed conflicts there are basically two types of people, combatants and civilians. Now, you are allowed to kill combatants, but they are allowed to fight. You are not allowed to kill civilians, and they are not allowed to fight. The question is, what is the law for people who are not combatants, but who fight you? And we argued that international law recognizes this group [unlawful combatants] and that it is permissible to kill them, and that they are not prisoners of war. That is, there is such an 'in-between' group. The Supreme Court said, 'You have not convinced us that this group is considered combatants.' The court didn't claim that they do not exist in reality, but was not sure that there is such a legal category. Therefore, it said, 'I want to say that they are terrorists. That is, civilians who are terrorists ...when they take part in the fighting, you can kill them.'[10]

The Supreme Court did not content itself with this declaration, but went on to define the actions that should be considered direct involvement in hostilities beyond the execution of the terrorist attack itself: dispatching terrorists to carry out the attack; deciding on the execution of the attack; gathering information about the army; operating weapons used by terrorists, supervising their operation, or providing services for them, and any other action that constitutes a function played by combatants (Intelligence & Terrorism Information Center, 2006). In this context, the Supreme Court also ruled that the hostile act does not only include the use of weapons and that the hostile acts themselves can be directed at both military targets and at the civilian population. Unlike those who take a direct part in hostilities, the court emphasized that those taking an indirect part in terrorist acts cannot be harmed; these may include those

---

[10] Personal interview with Daniel Reisner, April 8, 2022.

who sell food or drugs to terrorist operatives, those who provide logistical support, such as propaganda and financial aid, or those who conduct general strategic analyses (Ibid). These distinctions raised the matter of the length of time a terrorist operative takes part in hostilities. The answer given in the ruling is that because there is no consensus in the legal literature on the length of the period in which a terrorist operative loses the protection afforded to him as a civilian, each case must be examined on its own merits (Intelligence & Terrorism Information Center, 2006). **Reisner** clarifies, "The problem is that international law says you are only allowed to kill them while they are taking part in the hostile act. So we asked, and what if he throws away the weapon? Aharon Barak [former president of the Supreme Court] solved this problem by saying …'if he has not given up his intention to fight, he becomes a legitimate target.' Barak therefore solved the problem by defining the phrase 'for such time as they take a direct part in hostilities' as something large and broad."[11] **Reisner** illustrates the implications of this decision by saying, "If there is information that the terrorist is planning further attacks, then the answer will be that they will approve [the targeted killing]. But if he's announced to all his friends, 'That's it, I'm retiring from the war, I've done my part for the homeland, etc.', then the answer will be no. As long as he has not publicly announced his retirement and has already carried out one or two attacks, then it can be assumed that he is a legitimate target. That is what came out of the Supreme Court ruling."[12]

Avi Eliyahu believes that the legal considerations, including the principle of distinction that classifies the degree of legitimacy of targeted killings of various types of operatives in terrorist organizations, are overly dominant, and have in fact taken over the operational decision-making processes, thereby undermining the effectiveness of this measure. He says that there has been a "process of the over-involvement of jurists, of legal issues, in military combat." Eliyahu refers to this process as the "Goldstone Effect" (named for Richard Goldstone, who was appointed in April 2009 to head the United Nations Human Rights Council's fact-finding mission to investigate the actions of the IDF and Hamas during Operation Cast Lead). Eliyahu says, "I think there is an unhealthy process here, and it stems from serious mistakes. But as someone who has been

---

[11] Ibid.
[12] Ibid.

there at these junctions and seen the legal world's takeover of the military's assessments through the act of targeted killing, then I think there is over-involvement here. And it troubles me."[13]

In any case, former Mossad Chief **Yossi Cohen** believes that the principle of targeted killing as a legitimate act of war applies not only to ISA and IDF operations in Gaza or the West Bank, but to Mossad operations as well. "The executive branch has the authority to decide to go to war, and in war there are laws. Targeted killings are a kind of small war, and are part of a larger and covert campaign. They are a military, wartime action, and the laws that apply to them are like those that apply to any other army going to war."[14]

THE TARGET PROFILE AXIS

As discussed, the question of the targeted killing of a terrorist leader or senior member of an organization is one of many that examines the legitimacy of this measure with regard to the profile of the target. The following model presents an axis that assesses the profile of the person being targeted. This axis addresses the target's status and role in the terrorist organization and the extent to which he is involved in terrorist activities. The left side of the axis reflects an absence of direct operational involvement in terrorist activity, or low and indirect involvement, while the right side of the axis reflects a high and concrete involvement in the carrying out of attacks. The different types of profiles of terrorist operatives and the degree of their involvement in terrorist attacks are therefore arranged from right to left, representing a decreasing level of involvement and a diminishing of the degree of imminent danger they pose.

Detailed below are the various levels of involvement (Fig. 5.1):

The first three profiles (from the right) in the Target Profile Axis are operatives involved in the execution of concrete or ongoing terrorist attack:

> **1. Ticking bomb**—Inherently, the highest level of involvement in carrying out attacks is that of the "ticking bomb." This operative is involved in carrying out a concrete terrorist attack, whether as the

---

[13] Personal interview with Avi Eliyahu, April 6, 2022.

[14] Personal interview with Yossi Cohen, May 1, 2022.

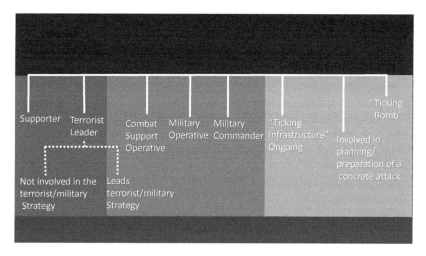

Fig. 5.1 The target profile axis

perpetrator himself, his dispatcher or his commander, or as someone providing immediate operational assistance to the perpetrator. With this type of terrorist operative, there is near certainty that he is about to carry out an attack, having completed all the planning and preparations.

Example: In November 2019, Israel killed Abu al-Ata, commander of the northern brigade of Islamic Jihad in the Gaza Strip. The IDF spokesperson issued a statement after the attack, saying that "Abu al-Ata was responsible for most of the Palestinian Islamic Jihad's activity in the Gaza Strip and was a ticking bomb. He directly orchestrated terrorist attacks and attempts to harm Israeli citizens and IDF soldiers in various ways, including rocket fire, sniper fire, launching drones, and more" (Frisch & Bar Gefen, 2001; Landau, 2019; Levy, 2019).

Former Defense Minister **Shaul Mofaz** believes that targeted killings are, first and foremost, a means of thwarting ticking bombs. Mofaz defines such a target as "someone who has set out to carry out a terrorist attack in Israel or an attack on the security forces." He maintains that the legitimacy of the targeted killing stems from the fact that the operation is a "Preventive and not a punitive step. We do not punish someone with a targeted killing after he has carried out the attack, even if there is intelligence on him – it's irrelevant. It is only relevant when it's in order to prevent a serious attack. There should be at least two indications in identifying him."[15]

The vast majority of the Israeli public believes that targeted killings should be carried out against someone who is defined as a ticking bomb—a person who is about to carry out an attack in the near or immediate future. A national public opinion poll conducted by the International Institute for Counter-Terrorism (ICT) at Reichman University in early 2022 shows that 83 percent of Israelis believe it is important to carry out targeted killings against ticking bombs. 70 percent defined this act as "extremely important," and 13% as "important."[16]

Former Justice Minister **Dan Meridor**, who has expressed reservations in principle about the use of this measure in the state's counter-terrorism arsenal, does support its use against a ticking bomb. In his words:

> There are cases of prevention in real time. Just as criminal law provides you with the right to self-defense when there is a serious and immediate threat, when there is no other way. Someone is going to kill me, or my son, or someone I am responsible for, and there is no other way, so I shoot him. It's the classic 'rise up and kill'... I say that when there is an immediate threat of very severe harm or death, then, according to the rules of personal self-defense, I would allow or even demand from the army to strike and kill.[17]

Former Deputy Head of the Mossad **Naftali Granot** considers the issue of targeted killings with regard to ticking bombs to be relatively simple and understandable in all aspects, both legally and vis-à-vis its moral justification as an operational practice designed to thwart concrete terrorist attacks. Granot points out that targeted killings of this category of operative take place mainly during periods of escalation and waves of terrorism, such as the rise in suicide bombings during the Second Intifada. In his view, the targeted killing of a suicide bomber making his way to Israel can be likened to the neutralization of a terrorist infiltrating

---

[15] Personal interview with Shaul Mofaz, February 23, 2022.

[16] National Public Opinion Poll on Targeted Killings, conducted for the International Institute for Counter-Terrorism (ICT) by *Ma'agar Mochot*, February 21, 2022.

[17] Personal interview with Dan Meridor, February 16, 2022.

the country's borders with the intention of carrying out attacks in its territory.[18]

As stated, a ticking bomb refers to the stage at which the preparations for the attack have been completed and the terrorist has departed to carry it out. However, **Asa Kasher** believes that as long as the legitimacy to target a terrorist operative is there, it can be done not only at the stage at which he is departing on his mission, but also at earlier stages. If necessary, he says, he can also be "surprised" in his sleep. "It's unpleasant, inhumane, but I'm allowed to. He went to sleep. Tomorrow he will wake up to kill me."[19] Kasher adds that before carrying out a targeted killing, the question must be asked regarding whether "I can stop him otherwise. Can I catch him?... If I can catch him, I will learn who is behind him, I can interrogate him. If I can't, then I will kill him."[20]

2. An operative involved in the preparation or planning of a (concrete) attack

The second level of involvement in the execution of attacks is that at which an operative is involved in the preparations of a concrete attack and whose targeting is very likely to lead to its thwarting or disruption. This operative may be, for example, an "engineer" who possesses professional skills in preparing explosive devices, an intelligence gatherer who brings essential operational information to the planning of the attack, a driver who is supposed to drive the perpetrator to the destination of the attack, etc. This level of involvement also includes a terrorist operative who is involved in the planning of the attack or in the early stages of its preparation (such as recruiting the terrorists and training them for their mission), and whose elimination may prevent a concrete attack.

Example: In December 2011, Israel eliminated Issam Batash, a senior member of the Al-Aqsa Martyrs Brigades. Batash had been planning an attack in the Israeli city of Eilat, and was responsible for dispatching the perpetrator to his destination. He was killed in his car before the attack took place. In the past, Batash had been involved in attacks in which

---

[18] Personal interview with Naftali Granot, February 17, 2022.

[19] Personal interview with Asa Kasher, February 23, 2022.

[20] Ibid.

terrorist operatives from the Gaza Strip came to Eilat. In one of the attacks, three Israeli civilians were killed (Levy, 2011).

According to ICT's public opinion poll, the majority of the Israeli public believes that targeted killings should be carried out against "terrorist operatives involved in the planning or preparation of concrete terrorist attacks" (the poll did not highlight the urgency and imminency of the action). 78% stated that it was important to carry out targeted killings in such a case, with 53% describing it as being "extremely important," and 25% as "important."[21]

3. An operative involved in producing capabilities for a (general) attack—"ticking infrastructure"

This type of operative is a key link in the chain of the initiating, planning, preparing, and executing of terrorist attacks, and has been involved in their execution in the past. Although there may not necessarily be solid information about his current involvement in the preparations for a concrete terrorist attack, it is believed that he is indeed continuing his operational activities, and that his elimination will disrupt terrorist attacks and is very likely to prevent future attacks.

Example: In January 1996, Yahya Ayyash, dubbed "The Engineer" by Israel, was eliminated. Ayyash was the person who "imported" the modus operandi of suicide bombings from Hezbollah to the Palestinian arena; he developed special capabilities for the preparation and assembly of explosive devices that were used to carry out many suicide bombings against Israeli citizens in the mid-1990s. Ayyash was also involved in recruiting and training suicide bombers. His assassination was carried out using a booby-trapped phone that was passed on to him through a collaborator. Ayyash was replaced by Muhi a-Din Sharif, nicknamed "The Engineer 2," who was later also eliminated (Levy, 2011). Asa Kasher says in this context, "There is the engineer, who creates the means of terrorism. He never explodes. He never approaches the place, but he contributes directly to the threat. Without him, there would be no terrorist attacks. So if I can catch him, great, I will interrogate him. If I kill him, there will be a

---

[21] National Public Opinion Poll on Targeted Killings, conducted for the International Institute for Counter-Terrorism (ICT) by *Ma'agar Mochot*, February 21, 2022.

lull until there's a new engineer. I will try to catch him first, and if I can't, then there is no choice—I will kill him."[22]

Another terrorist who fits the profile of this level of involvement is Adnan al-Ghoul, who was targeted by Israel in October 2004. During the al-Aqsa Intifada in 2000, al-Ghoul became an expert in explosive devices and anti-tank weapons. He was considered by Israel to be the "father of Palestinian military industry." As such, he also oversaw the production and use of Qassam rockets and helped increase their firing range. Al-Ghoul also recruited the experts who assembled the rockets to be fired at Israel. He was involved in the execution of many concrete attacks, for example in preparing the explosive devices for the terrorist attacks that were carried out at Tapuah Junction and at the Dizengoff Center in 1996, during the holiday of Purim. In October 2004, after several unsuccessful attempts, al-Ghoul was killed by helicopter missiles fired at his vehicle, although it is unclear if he was involved in preparing a concrete terrorist attack at the time (Hess, 2019; Levy, 2011).

In contrast to ticking bombs, whose very definition connotes a concrete terrorist attack, those belonging to this category of operatives can be labeled "ticking infrastructure." These are terrorist operatives who are highly likely to be involved in future attacks, but who cannot currently be linked to the execution of a concrete attack. Former Prime Minister **Ehud Olmert** addressed the legitimacy of targeted killings against terrorist operatives belonging to this group: "He may not be in command of the operation, but he prepares the forces, he prepares the weapons for them, he teaches them how it [the attack] can be done, he is the dispatcher, he sits at headquarters but leads others to do it, and if he stays alive then they will kill people. I think in such cases, there is definitely justification for carrying out targeted killings."[23] **Oz Noy** believes that there is no justification for carrying out a targeted killing against someone who constitutes "ticking infrastructure" in the West Bank. He says the ISA knew of thousands of people in Judea and Samaria involved in preparations for attacks, and they were not targeted. In Noy's opinion, targeted killings in this territory should be limited to ticking bombs since Israel has effective control there and could arrest the perpetrators.[24] With

---

[22] Personal interview with Asa Kasher, February 23, 2022.

[23] Personal interview with Ehud Olmert, March 3, 2022.

[24] Personal interview with Oz Noy, February 16, 2022.

regard to the Gaza Strip, however, Noy maintains that the criteria are different because a targeted killing in Gaza is, in fact, an act of war that allows for the intentional harming of operatives and military commanders. "We are in a battle with the Gaza Strip," he says. "At any given moment, the fact that there are no casualties does not mean that there is no battle. It's an act of combat. It's something else. These are operatives in the Hamas military hierarchy who we are targeting. It's like in a war, when you target the command rooms, headquarters, supply bases and supply routes."[25]

Former IDF Chief of Staff **Gadi Eisenkot** says on this matter, "With regards to the target who is a direct and immediate threat [a ticking bomb], there is no dilemma, and the right thing to do is to take him down. When it comes to dispatchers, ideologues, commanders and leaders, I would make a matter-of-fact judgment."[26] Former ISA Chief **Avi Dichter** asserts, "First of all, the perpetrators of terrorism are undoubtedly very significant figures. There are figures who have certain knowledge, and they know they have no substitute. You really want to target someone like that, because even if there is someone to replace him, it will take time for them to really fill his shoes."[27]

4. Military commander in a terrorist organization

The military commander in a terrorist organization is responsible for the military and operational activities of the organization (depending on his level of seniority). This responsibility may be comprehensive (at the most senior levels of command) or regional (at lower levels of command). The elimination of the military commander (be he senior or regional) is likely to lead to a change in the organization's terrorism policy or disrupt its military-operational efforts.

Example: In July 2002, Salah Shehadeh, commander of the Izz ad-Din al-Qassam Brigades, Hamas's military wing, was killed at his home. Among other things, Shehadeh was involved in the abduction and murder of two IDF soldiers and in sending various terrorists into Israel. His

---

[25] Ibid.

[26] Personal interview with Gadi Eisenkot, March 2, 2022.

[27] Personal interview with Avi Dichter, March 11, 2022.

assassination, which caused extensive collateral damage, led to the establishment of a commission of inquiry and an in-depth examination of the principle of proportionality before carrying out a targeted killing (Levy, 2011).[28]

Former Prime Minister **Ehud Olmert** believes that targeted killings should be carried out against senior military operatives even when there is no concrete information about his intentions of executing an attack:

> You know he's the chief of staff of Hezbollah. You have no information about anything set to take place in the future. You have knowledge of what he's done. So you say, it makes sense that whoever has done what he has and is still in that role, and is actually the man who commands the army of Hezbollah... [You remember] his fighting spirit, dedication, and so on. And when he wants to carry out an operation, he will do it ... there is a high probability of this. Is this a sufficient justification? In my opinion, yes.[29]

Moreover, Olmert maintains that a military commander (for example Mughniyeh, the head of Hezbollah's military wing) should be targeted, even in the absence of an assessment that he is likely to be personally involved in initiating, planning, or carrying out attacks against Israel. Olmert says that Hezbollah is:

> a terrorist organization that poses a very significant threat in the immediate- or very short-term. Is it legitimate to carry out a targeted killing if the elimination of this person causes damage to the organization? Not necessarily because he is currently active, but because you would be harming the fighting spirit of the organization. You are also undermining the myth surrounding his character when you catch him in such a way that presents him as a failure – how could he not have avoided it? How was he followed? How was he exposed? How did they know where he was going? When he was going to be meeting people? Which route he would take? And all these things ... the answer is definitely yes. I certainly [would target him], even if I didn't know anything about his future plans.[30]

---

[28] For more details about the case study of Salah Shehadeh, see Chapter Two.

[29] Personal interview with Ehud Olmert, March 3, 2022.

[30] Ibid.

The public opinion poll conducted by the International Institute for Counter-Terrorism at Reichman University also posed this question, and found that 77% of respondents believe that targeting a "military commander of a terrorist organization" (without any reference to his degree of involvement in the preparation or execution of terrorist attacks) is legitimate.[31] Thus, in assessing the importance of the use of targeted killings as a counter-terrorism measure, the Israeli public does not attach much significance to the direct involvement of this or that terrorist operative in the execution of concrete terrorist attacks, nor to the degree of urgency in thwarting these attacks. The vast majority of the Israeli public believes that as long as the target is an operative belonging to the military forces of the terrorist organization, then targeted killings are an "important" or "very important" measure in Israel's counter-terrorism toolbox.

5. Military operative
The terrorist organizations' military operatives are less active than the military commanders and they serve as the fighting force of the organization. Some of them help the terrorist organization recruit the operatives who will carry out future attacks, and some perform routine and special military missions. As such, military operatives constitute a legitimate target for counter-offensive action, including, if necessary, targeted killings.

Indeed, former Chief Military Advocate General **Sharon Afek** draws attention to the fact that over the years, the laws of war have developed to address the issue of targeted killings, among others, and in particular, the matters of civilians taking part in hostilities and organized armed groups. This development is related to the fact that some of the terrorist organizations have transformed into terrorist armies (especially hybrid terrorist organizations that control territory and populations, such as Hezbollah and Hamas). Afek points out that, to his understanding, this Israeli legal concept is also the approach taken by the US military.[32]

---

[31] National Public Opinion Poll on Targeted Killings, conducted for the International Institute for Counter-Terrorism (ICT) by *Ma'agar Mochot*, February 21, 2022.

[32] Personal interview with Sharon Afek, March 13, 2022.

6. A terrorist operative involved in administrative terrorist activity **(combat support)**

This type of terrorist operative is involved in the administrative-operational activities of a terrorist organization, and in this framework, he assists in its day-to-day functioning. The "infrastructural" terrorist operative may engage in, inter alia, the organization's computer department, the procurement of weapons, fundraising, and more. His activities help facilitate the terrorist attacks carried out by the organization. His elimination, therefore, is likely to disrupt such actions.

In this regard, **Lior Lotan**, former Special Negotiator on Hostages and Missing Persons for Prime Minister Netanyahu, believes that targeted killings should be aimed at those holding an effective role in the terrorist organization, that is, an operative who contributes to the organization's ability to harm Israel (which is not necessarily directly related to the organization's hierarchical structure.[33]

Example: In May 2019, Hamad Hadri was killed by a missile fired at his vehicle. Hadri had been responsible for large-scale cash transfers from Iran to terrorist organizations in the Gaza Strip, through an exchange company he ran (Hess, 2019).

Asa Kasher, as mentioned, believes that targeted killings should be determined by the degree of danger posed by the specific target. For example, he does not think that they should be carried out against cash couriers, because they do not contribute directly to the threat. On the other hand, he says, operatives involved in the production of the weapons required for the attack (the engineer), the planner, the driver, or even the imam who incites the perpetrators, should be targeted (in the absence of any other alternative).[34] Regarding the question of the legitimacy of targeting infrastructural operatives, **Daniel Reisner** emphasizes that the first circle of targets in targeted killings includes the perpetrators, their dispatchers, and their commanders, and does not include combat support operatives. "At first, we did not let it [happen]", he says. "In the early years, we targeted only actual commanders, and over the years it was expanded, for example, to those who prepare all the explosive belts

---

[33] Personal interview with Lior Lotan, April 17, 2022.

[34] Personal interview with Asa Kasher, February 23, 2022.

in the territories. [We're talking about] major players, not a logistical assistant."[35]

Former Director of the Counter-Terrorism Bureau at the Prime Minister's office **Nitzan Nuriel** cites the example of the Hamas technological system, which he says special efforts were made to damage during Operation Guardian of the Walls in Gaza in May 2021. He says that the premise for this was that when technology experts are eliminated, it takes a long time to train the next generation. Thus, the targeting of technology professionals who, for example, are preparing sophisticated bombs, impairs the organization's capabilities for a significant period of time, even if it is difficult to prove how many attacks were avoided by doing so.[36]

7. Political/ideological leader

The political leader of a terrorist organization, or its ideologue—the organization's spiritual leader—may carry indirect responsibility for its terrorist attacks whether by way of incitement, calling for terrorist attacks, or explicitly permitting them on the basis of an ideological or religious interpretation. Opponents of targeted killings, however, argue that the political leader is not necessarily involved in initiating, directing, or preparing operationally for terrorist attacks.

On this subject, former Prime Minister **Ehud Olmert** says, "The head of a terrorist organization? Certainly. If I could have targeted Nasrallah during the Second Lebanon War, I would have. The truth? We tried, but we didn't have good intelligence, so we didn't do it... we had an idea where he was at a specific point, and we fired there and it was a direct hit, but it turned out he wasn't there—he'd run away."[37]

Former Mossad Chief **Shabtai Shavit** explains why he believes the head of a terrorist organization to be a legitimate target:

> The spiritual leader of the organization is the one who makes the decisions, and he then becomes a partner in knowing and deciding on terrorist

---

[35] Personal interview with Daniel Reisner, April 8, 2022.

[36] Personal interview with Nitzan Nuriel, February 14, 2022.

[37] Personal interview with Ehud Olmert, March 3, 2022.

acts. In other words, spiritual leaders cannot shirk responsibility. The spiritual leader, the organization's political or civilian echelon, and the military echelon [are one and the same]. In Hamas, for example, the commanders' ranks are all active terrorist operatives, with a stratum of political leaders above them, and at the very top, a spiritual leader like Sheikh Yassin. Religious terrorist organizations always have a spiritual leader, under whom is the political leadership, and under them, the military establishment.[38]

Former Air Force Commander and IDF Chief of Staff **Dan Halutz** asserts that the more senior the target, the more effective the targeted killing, "since replacing a senior rank takes time, whereas replacing a field rank takes much less time." Referring to the targeted killing of Hamas leader Ahmed Yassin, Halutz says that the rate of terrorist attacks was directly proportional to the increase in the rate and quality of targeted killing operations. "We felt this most strongly with Yassin's elimination," he says. "We saw the effect very clearly. What is the effect? Firstly, it affects the frequency of attacks. And secondly, it affects how bold they are, because they understood that in terms of intelligence, we had them in the palm of our hand…".[39]

According to **Moshe ("Bogie") Ya'alon**, who was the IDF chief of staff at the time of Yassin's killing:

> I thought it was right to target Sheikh Yassin. Sharon was the prime minister, Dichter was the head of the ISA, and we entered into a discussion about whether it was legitimate or illegitimate. Is he a political leader, and therefore an illegitimate target? I argued that terrorism has no political echelon. I also actually had evidence that the policy of terrorism was dictated by Sheikh Yassin… The person who actually made the decision about the strategy of terrorist attacks was Sheikh Yassin. Sharon was undecided. His hesitancy didn't have to do with the moral question of whether or not he deserved it. He thought that if we opened a front with the political echelon, then it also opens a front with our political echelon. Sharon decided to take the issue to Elyakim Rubinstein, the attorney general, and the military advocate general was also brought in… There had been a case of a female terrorist who had a prosthetic device, and she left Gaza to get treatment at the hospital. She blew herself up at the Erez Crossing.

[38] Personal interview with Shabtai Shavit, February 17, 2022.

[39] Personal interview with Dan Halutz, March 4, 2022.

The person who had approved her suicide was Sheikh Yassin. This information convinced Elyakim Rubinstein, and it also led Sharon to becoming convinced...As far as I'm concerned, whoever determines the policy is a ticking bomb, and should be treated accordingly.[40]

Former senior ISA official **Shalom Ben Hanan** also justifies the targeted killings of terrorist leaders when they are considered ticking bombs. "Targeted killings of top-ranking officials are carried out, in my view, only when it is absolutely clear that it is an official who induces acts of murder; in my experience, I don't know of any targeted killings carried out to convey a message or harm a symbolic figure, and subsequently morale, even if this did occur given the target's status."[41]

Ben Hanan links the leadership of terrorist organizations to the hierarchal chain of ticking bombs:

> The elimination of people like Ahmad Yassin or Salad Shehadeh was most justified; they met the criteria of a 'clear and present danger.' Ahmad Yassin was a ticking bomb even if he was a senior Hamas official. A senior Hamas official who sends terrorists with explosive belts to carry out attacks in the heart of Israel, for example to the Dolphinarium [a suicide bombing that took place in Tel Aviv in June 2001 in which 21 civilians were killed, most of them teenagers], to Sbarro [a suicide bombing in a Jerusalem restaurant in August 2001 in which 15 civilians were killed and about 140 injured, to the Park Hotel [a suicide bombing in a Netanya hotel in March 2002 which killed 30 Israelis and wounded 160] is a ticking bomb for all intents and purposes. There is a race to eliminate such a person before he carries out the next attack. It's impossible for us to define only the perpetrator as a ticking bomb, while the head of the snake continues to recruit, arm and dispatch terrorists to harm hundreds of people. Yahya Ayyash was such a target, as was Mahmoud Mabhouh, and many others. On the other hand, I don't believe that the protocol of targeted killing should be employed against a political or religious leader, even if he engages in severe incitement. The test must be one of actual involvement in terrorist activity.[42]

---

[40] Personal interview with Moshe ("Bogie") Ya'alon, February 17, 2022.

[41] Personal interview with Shalom Ben Hanan, February 21, 2022.

[42] Ibid.

5 THE PRINCIPLE OF DISTINCTION ... 135

This, Ben Hanan believes that a political or religious leader should not be targeted, even if he incites the murder of Jews in the name of Islam. "I have not heard of such a person being targeted. I'm not aware that this has ever happened. In the 26 years I have been in the service, there has never been such a thing... I don't know of an ideological leader having been killed because he delivered extremist sermons in the mosque... same with a political leader. What is a political leader? The question is whether it's a political leader who has turned to terrorism, and therefore he is a terrorist operative, then in that case the definition of political leader no longer applies." Ben Hanan cites the case of Yasser Arafat, a political leader by all accounts. "There was a debate about Yasser Arafat during the al-Aqsa intifada. Should he be targeted or not? And the decision was that he shouldn't be. Even though he was a threat. He ceased to be a political leader as soon as he started the [al-Aqsa] Intifada and provided backing, financially rewarded terrorists, issued directives to carry out attacks, and inflamed the masses...".[43]

Former IDF Chief of Staff **Gadi Eisenkot** believes that senior terrorist operatives and leaders should not be granted immunity: "If he is leading a war or a campaign, I think there is no dilemma. But even then, it has to be done in a well-thought-out way. I'm not sure we should be dropping a bomb on his head." As an example of the set of considerations that must be taken into account in this regard, Eisenkot raises the dilemma surrounding the targeting of Arafat during Operation Defensive Shield, when the IDF Special Forces were a few meters away from Arafat, who was locked up at his headquarters in the Muqata in Ramallah. He says, "It is quite clear that Arafat led the campaign and sent and directed the terrorists. Egoz [an IDF commando unit] could have marched four meters and killed him. Why didn't they? There is also significance here to his being a national symbol, of the struggle of the Palestinian people, which could have repercussions for generations. In addition, what would this do to the man and his image? And how will it impact our effectiveness?".

Eisenkot argues that when it comes to the question of whether or not to carry out targeted killings of leaders of terrorist organizations, the decision-making process must take the overall picture into account. This

---

[43] Ibid.

should be reflected in the defining of the required achievement from the military operation in general, and from the targeted killing in particular.[44]

Brig. Gen. (Res.) **Gal Hirsch** explains that the issue of targeting someone with leadership status is indeed examined from all angles before the decision is made, and that sometimes the discussion even deals with a target's future leadership potential. Hirsch describes a meeting he had with an ISA official on the subject:

> He comes and shows me a potential target – a very well-known leader... and I say that it's possible, it can be done. But I told him, 'Listen, I'm in favor because I think this man is going to kill a lot of Israelis in the future as well. He has already killed, and will kill, many Israelis, but you should know that he is considered someone with leadership potential and he is a leader... [In the end] he was not targeted, and he killed a lot of Israelis. This is a person who to this day is a danger to the State of Israel.[45]

Dan Meridor, who represents the school of thought that seeks to reduce the use of targeted killings, says in this context that he believes that the targeting of the leadership of terrorist organizations can be approved, but only in very exceptional cases. "The word leader is a general one—there are leaders of all kinds," he says. "Stalin was a leader and so is Muhammad Deif [the head of Hamas's military wing]. There are cases in which I would say yes [to a targeted killing] and they are very rare... The question is whether it is effective or not."[46]

Former Deputy Head of the Mossad **Naftali Granot** explains that, in his view, the targeted killing of a terrorist leader may be considered effective only if the removal of that leader results in a substantial change in the terrorist organization's activities, or its decline or disbandment, which would, of course, lead to the prevention of many potential attacks. Granot notes a number of targeted killings carried out against terrorist leaders in the past that he believes led to this desired outcome, such as that of Zuheir Mohsen, the secretary general of the pro-Syrian Palestinian

---

[44] Personal interview with Gadi Eisenkot, March 2, 2022.

[45] Personal interview with Gal Hirsch, February 20, 2022.

[46] Personal interview with Dan Meridor, February 16, 2022.

terrorist organization As-Sa'iqa in 1979, which resulted in its disbandment, as well as that of PIJ leader Fathi Shaqaqi in 1995 in Malta, which significantly impaired the functioning of the organization.[47]

Former senior ISA official **Oz Noy**, on the other hand, once again makes a distinction between a targeted killing of the terrorist leadership in the Gaza Strip and of that in the West Bank. In his view, whereas targeted killings should not be carried out in the West Bank, in Gaza, an individual decision must be made regarding each potential target. In this regard, it must be assessed whether "harming him will have a significant impact... and that it's not just because he annoyed you. There must be a very clear purpose to the operation."[48] Justice **Aharon Barak** links the issue of whether to target terrorist leaders to the question of who constitutes a combatant. He claims there are varying degrees of involvement in terrorism, and the question is where to draw the red line. He notes that in the Supreme Court's ruling on targeted killings, he debated what the court's position should be with regard to terrorist leaders, and ultimately decided to leave the question unanswered. But, he says, "If you asked me today, I would also include the terrorist leader because of his duality, because he is involved in leading the organization's terrorism policy and is at the same time the organization's leader."[49]

In the public opinion poll conducted by ICT, respondents were asked about their position on the targeting of the "political, diplomatic, or ideological leader of a terrorist organization." Here, there was a certain decrease in the Israeli public's level of support for the action (though a clear majority—62%—still supported it). 43% of respondents defined such an action as "very important," and 19% defined it as "important."[50]

8. Supporter of terrorism

This profile depicts a person (not necessarily a terrorist operative who has formally enlisted in the organization) who supports the organization's terrorist activities, whether by way of incitement

---

[47] Personal interview with Naftali Granot, February 17, 2022.

[48] Personal interview with Oz Noy, February 16, 2022.

[49] Personal interview with Aharon Barak, February 20, 2022.

[50] National Public Opinion Poll on Targeted Killings, conducted for the International Institute for Counter-Terrorism (ICT) by *Ma'agar Mochot*, February 21, 2022.

on social networks, oral or written incitement on various platforms, donations to terrorist organizations, etc. In this case, it is not possible to point to the terrorism supporter's direct operational involvement in the organization's terrorist activity, although, as stated, he may openly declare his support for it. On the face of it, the Israeli interviewees, decision-makers at the political or operational-security level, do not believe that people in this category should be targets for targeted killings.

In accordance with the proposed Target Profile Axis, the greater the operative's degree of involvement in carrying out terrorist attacks, or in the military activity of the terrorist organization as a whole, the greater his legitimacy as a target. Thus, the bright green area of the model, indicating a high degree of legitimacy of targeted killings, includes the following three profiles: A ticking bomb—an operative about to carry out an attack; an operative involved in the preparation or planning of a (concrete) attack; and an operative involved in producing capabilities for a (general) attack—"ticking infrastructure." These operatives share a high level of operational involvement in the execution of terrorist attacks (be they concrete or not). The domain of the model marked in dark green includes operatives whose targeting is probably legitimate depending on the concrete circumstances of each person and each case. These include a military commander in a terrorist organization (either senior or junior), a military operative in a terrorist organization, an "administrative" terrorist operative (someone involved in working on the infrastructure that supports the execution of terrorist attacks), and a political leader of a terrorist organization who guides and directs the organization's terrorism strategy. The left side of the model's legitimacy scale, the red-colored area, denotes profiles of figures who are, per se, illegitimate targets for targeted killings. The two profiles in this category are the political or ideological leader of a terrorist organization who is not directly involved in guiding the organization's terrorism policy or in directing the organization's terrorism strategy, and the supporter of terrorism who does not provide operational support for the organization's terrorist activities.

Meir Dagan, former Head of the Mossad and National Security Advisor, addressed the issue of the effectiveness and legitimacy of the targeted killing of terrorist operatives, and stressed the importance of the target's operational involvement and the need to adhere to a systematic policy: "Sporadic eliminations are worth nothing. Eliminations of senior operational personnel, along with striking at the leadership level as a permanent and ongoing policy, are a very good thing. When I say 'leadership,' I mean, of course, in the widest sense. Would I always choose to kill the number one? Not necessarily. I look for the supreme operative echelon, the one that really runs things, that has the most dominant influence on the ground" (Bergman, 2018, p. 582).

The Operational Need Model—Assessing the Need for Targeted Killings

In order to determine the degree of necessity of a targeted killing operation, two axes must be combined—the Target Profile Axis detailed above, and the Operational Opportunity Axis described in Chapter Two. Their combination defines the importance of the operation (identifying the profile of the target and the extent of his involvement in terrorist attacks) and the degree of urgency in carrying out the operation (defining the nature of the intelligence and operational **opportunity** for the targeted killing). The diagram below presents the combination of these two axes (Fig. 5.2).

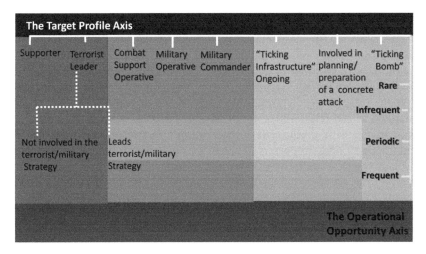

Fig. 5.2 The target profile axis and the operational opportunity axis

The above diagram dictates the degree of legitimacy of the targeted killing operation and defines when it is necessary and legitimate to carry out such an action. As shown in the diagram, targeted killing is always legitimate when it is being executed in order to thwart ticking bombs (regardless of how frequently the target appears on the "intelligence radar" and how seldom the operational **opportunity** arises for the targeted killing operation). This is demarcated by the green-colored area on the right side of the scale. As for the next six types of targets (operatives who are involved in the initiating and planning of attacks, "ticking infrastructure" operatives, military commanders and operatives, combat support operatives, and leaders of terrorist organizations who are involved in guiding the organization's terrorist/military strategy and activity), while their terrorist-military profile lends legitimacy to the targeted killing operation, there is less urgency to carry out the operation, therefore, there is a greater impact on operational opportunity considerations and the implications of the operations, as well as on additional considerations, such as the degree of proportionality. In case of rare or infrequent opportunity, the level of legitimacy to conduct targeted killings against these operatives is high even if the operation will be accompanied by proportionate collateral damage (represented by the green-colored background). In cases of periodic opportunity, there is a lower level of legitimacy to conduct targeted killing operations against these operatives which may be accompanied by collateral damage (represented by the yellow-colored background). In cases of frequent opportunity, there is the lowest level of legitimacy to conduct targeted killings operations that will inflict significant collateral damage (represented by the orange-colored background)). When would it be illegitimate to carry out a targeted killing? The area marked in red refers to the types of political/ideological leaders who are not involved in guiding the organization's terrorism /military strategy and activity, and supporters of terrorism. It is illegitimate to target these operatives even when there is a rare or infrequent operational opportunity.

Case Study: The Targeted Killing of a Political Leader—Sheikh Ahmed Yassin

Background and involvement in terrorism: In 1987, during the First Intifada, Ahmed Yassin founded Hamas, the Islamic Resistance Movement, and became the organization's spiritual leader and guide. In 1989, he ordered the abduction and killing of two Israeli soldiers, Ilan Sa'adon and Avi Sasportas, in order to negotiate the exchange of their bodies with Hamas prisoners serving time in an Israeli jail. He was arrested, and during his interrogation admitted that he had established a military wing within Hamas, approved the recruitment of terrorists, and ordered terrorist attacks. For this he was sentenced to two life sentences in an Israeli prison (*Ahmed Yassin*). In 1997, after the Mossad's failed attempt to carry out a targeted killing of Khaled Mashal, the head of Hamas's political bureau, Israel was forced to release Yassin in accordance with the demands of King Hussein of Jordan.[51] After Yassin's release and return to the Gaza Strip, he resumed his involvement in directing terrorist attacks. In 2003, the United States included Sheikh Yassin, along with five other Hamas leaders, on its terrorist blacklist, and froze their assets.

Targeted killing operation: In September 2003, following the collapse of the ceasefire ("*hudna*") with Hamas, a failed attempt was made to kill Ahmed Yassin when a quarter-ton bomb was dropped on a building where he was staying with Ismail Haniyeh. The two men both survived. About six months later, on March 22, 2004, another attempt was made on Yassin's life, which this time succeeded. He was killed by three Hellfire missiles fired at him from Air Force helicopters as he exited a mosque. Two of his bodyguards and six other people were also killed in the strike (Hess, 2019).

Reactions: Yassin's killing led to global condemnation of Israel, including by friendly countries such as Australia, the United States, and some European states (Levy, 2011). The UN Security Council proposed a resolution to condemn Israel, but it was not passed due to a US veto. The Palestinians, for their part, promised a harsh response. Zakariya al-Zubaidi, commander of the al-Aqsa Martyrs Brigades in the West Bank at the time, said: "Our response to the assassination of Sheikh Yassin will not be like any other. Those who ordered the killing have committed a grave mistake. They will pay very dearly… Yasin was not only a symbol of resistance, but a symbol of Palestinian unity… The resistance shall intensify with the sheikh's death. Our brigades will retaliate and the response this time will be more painful. We shall not yield until the last drop of our blood." Despite these words, the targeted killing actually led to a decrease in terrorist attacks against Israel (Shalev, 2020).

---

[51] For the case study on Khaled Mashal, see Chapter Six.

On the face of it, this case study represents the model's seventh profile, that of the political leader or ideologue who directs the organization's terrorism strategy. Yassin does indeed meet the profile's political characteristics, being the founding leader of Hamas as well as the spiritual leader of the movement and its main ideologue. However, Yassin was involved in initiating and directing terrorist attacks, both before his imprisonment and after his release in 1997. As then-IDF Chief of Staff, Maj. Gen. **Moshe (Bogie) Ya'alon**, noted, "Sheikh Yassin was not a political or a religious leader; he was a terrorist and directly responsible for terrorist acts against soldiers and civilians. He headed a terrorist organization that acted against the State of Israel. He incited and served as a source of inspiration for murderous terrorist attacks." Israeli prime minister at the time, Ariel Sharon, went on to say that "Yassin was the first and foremost murderer among the Palestinians" (Berger, 2004).

REFERENCES

Ahmed Yassin. https://www.jewishvirtuallibrary.org/ahmed-yassin

Annan's strong condemnation of assassination policy (2001, August 7). *Reuters*. https://www.ynet.co.il/articles/1,7340,L-992389,00.html

Berger, Gal. (2004, March 23). In the short term, the motivation for terrorist attacks will increase. *News1*. http://www.news1.co.il/Archive/001-D-42903-00.html?tag=12-39-00

Bergman, R. (2018). *Rise and kill first: The secret history of Israel's targeted assassinations*. Random House.

Customary IHL. IHL database. https://ihl-databases.icrc.org/customary-ihl/eng/docs/v2_rul_rule4

Figel, Yoni. *The suicide bombing at Dizengoff Center, March 4, 1996*. Keren Inbar. https://www.keren-inbar.org.il/----4--1996

Frisch, F., & Bar Gefen, L. (2001, July 3). The kitchenette has decided to expand the targeted killing policy. *Ynet*. https://www.ynet.co.il/articles/1,7340,L-875828,00.html

Ganor, B. (2003). *The Counter-Terrorism Puzzle- A Guide for Decision Makers*. Mifalot.

HCJ 474/02. (2011, January 30). Thabet v. Attorney General Judgment.

HCJ 769/02. (2006). *The public committee against torture in Israel v. The Government of Israel, 62*(1), 507.

Hess, S. (2019, November 13). The founder, the chief of staff, the money changer: The significant assassinations in Gaza. *Ynet*. https://www.ynet.co.il/articles/0,7340,L-5624182,00.html

5 THE PRINCIPLE OF DISTINCTION ... 143

Intelligence and Terrorism Information Center. (2006). *Justice and terrorism: A decision by the Supreme Court of Justice allows Israeli security forces to continue to carry out "targeted killings" against operatives of terrorist organizations while placing restrictions and limitations*. https://www.terrorism-info.org.il/he/18664/

Kremnitzer, M. (2006). *Is everything kosher when dealing with terrorism?* The Israel Democracy Institute.

Landau, N. (2019, November 12). Netanyahu: Abu al-Ata was a ticking bomb, Israel is not interested in escalation. *Ha'aretz*. https://www.haaretz.co.il/news/politics/1.8119144

Levy, E. (2019, November 12). Every bomb should hit the target: Senior Islamic Jihad official eliminated. *Ynet*. https://www.ynet.co.il/articles/0,7340,L-562 4194,00.html

Levy, S. (2011, August 11). Targeted killings: By air, sea and land. *Mako*. https://www.mako.co.il/pzm-magazine/Article-0aadf0d8991f131006.htm

Rosenzweig, I. (2014). Targeted killings during high and low intensity warfare. In P. Sharvit & A. Kurz (Eds.), *Law and National Security: Selected Issues* (pp. 41–52). INSS.

Shalev, C. (2020, January 7). Sikul Memulkad. *Ha'aretz*. https://www.haaretz.co.il/opinions/.premium-1.8367975

Stein, Y. (2003). By any name illegal and immoral. *Ethics and International Affairs, 17*(1), 127.

Walzer, M. (2006). *Just and unjust wars: A moral argument with historical illustrations*. Basic Books.

Waked, A. (2001, January 10). Ehud Barak and the Israeli government—war criminals. *Ynet*. https://www.ynet.co.il/articles/0,7340,L-420468,00.html

CHAPTER 6

The Principle of Proportionality: Are Targeted Killings Really Targeted?

Intrinsically, targeted killings are carried out in the areas in which terrorists live and operate. In most cases, these areas are densely populated cities and villages, in which the terrorists reside either within or in close proximity to civilian structures. When the terrorist belongs to a "skeleton organization," i.e., a hierarchal, underground terrorist group consisting of one or more covert cells, he inherently lives and works in a civilian environment, hiding his terrorist identity and activity (Ganor, 2008). When the terrorist belongs to a "hybrid" terrorist organization, that is, a terrorist organization that controls a population and territory that is not under the effective control of a state (Ganor, 2015), he is usually intentionally assimilated into the civilian population, who, either voluntarily or by force, act as "human shields" for the terrorist operatives. Terrorist organizations deliberately ignore (and even deliberately exploit) the first Additional Protocol to the Geneva Convention, which prohibits the use of the civilian population for the purpose of immunity from military action. The protocol states that: "The presence or movements of the civilian population or individual civilians shall not be used to render certain points or areas immune from military operations, in particular in attempts to shield military objectives from attacks or to shield, favor or impede military operations. The Parties to the conflict shall not direct the movement of the civilian population or individual civilians in order

© The Author(s), under exclusive license to Springer Nature   145
Switzerland AG 2022
B. Ganor and L. Koblentz-Stenzler, *Israel's Targeted Killing Policy*,
https://doi.org/10.1007/978-3-031-13674-0_6

to attempt to shield military objectives from attacks or to shield military operations" (ICRC, 1977).

The fight against terrorist organizations and operatives blurs the boundaries between the battlefront and the home front. Correspondingly, when the State of Israel decides to carry out the targeted killing of a terrorist operative entrenched in a civilian environment, it may unintentionally harm civilians in the target's vicinity. This "side effect" does not, of course, make the military action unlawful, but even when the target is a legitimate one, the knowledge that civilians may be harmed requires the application of the test of proportionality, which effectively limits the use of force (Shaul & Golan, 2004).

Israel, like any other country, has a moral obligation to protect its citizens from the threat posed by terrorist organizations. However, Israel and other democracies have a parallel moral obligation to avoid intentionally harming civilians who are not involved in terrorist activities and who do not pose any danger. The obligation to eliminate a terrorist who is about to carry out an attack may sometimes dictate the use of heavier munitions, which may cause considerable collateral damage among the population in which the terrorist is embedded. On the other hand, the risk of harming uninvolved civilians and the desire to reduce collateral damage as much as possible necessitates the use of munitions that are as light as possible, which may decrease the chances of striking and neutralizing the terrorist. The success of the operation would therefore be at stake, and the terrorist may survive and eventually carry out his plot to execute a terrorist attack against the citizens of the country. The delicate balance between the State of Israel's moral duty to protect its own citizens from danger, on the one hand, and on the other hand to minimize the danger posed to Palestinian civilians not involved in terrorism as much as possible, makes targeted killing operations particularly complex and problematic (Kasher & Yadlin, 2003).

This chapter will explore the issue of proportionality in targeting killings, examining the main dilemmas, challenges, and solutions involved, as well as the procedures that Israel has adopted to ensure that targeted killing operations are as proportionate as possible.

DEFINITION OF THE PRINCIPLE OF PROPORTIONALITY

According to humanitarian law and the principles of just war theory, even when military action is taken against a legitimate target, one of the criteria that must be satisfied in order for the action to be considered legal and ethical is the principle of proportionality. This is a moral test based on a balance between conflicting values and interests (Special Investigatory Commission, 2011). The main issue is that this principle has been subject to very vague interpretations; therefore, there is substantial difficulty in applying it (Guiora, 2012). The basic explanation given for this principle in the Additional Protocol to the Geneva Convention, Article 51 (5) (b) is that there is a prohibition on carrying out attacks "which may be expected to cause incidental loss of civilian life, injury to civilians, damage to civilian objects, or a combination thereof, which would be excessive in relation to the concrete and direct military advantage anticipated" (ICRC, 1977). The prohibition therefore applies not only to death and bodily harm, but also to suffering and destruction. The expected long-term consequences of the attack on the civilian population must therefore also be taken into account. For example, foreseeable damage to electricity networks or communications infrastructure may cause detriment to the well-being of civilians (Dörmann, 2012). In moral and legal terms, therefore, it can be said that an action in which there is a use of force is expected to do more good than harm, and to be important, ethical, and effective in terms of achieving the desired goal (Kasher, 2009; Nathanson, 2010).

An explanation for this test is offered by the New Catholic Encyclopedia, which details the "principle of double effect," defined as "a rule of conduct frequently used in moral theology to determine when a person may lawfully perform an action from which two effects will follow, one bad and the other good." In modern warfare, the principle of double effect is often applicable, and therefore it is claimed that during a (just) war, a nation is allowed to launch airstrikes on an important enemy military target, even when a small number of non-combatants will be killed; this is because the greater good, achieved through the destruction of the target, compensates for the negative effect. However, this is not the case if the number of people killed in the attack is disproportionate to the benefit achieved (Dershowitz, 2004).

Col. Pnina Sharvit-Baruch, former head of the International Law Department in the Military Advocate General's Office, and **Dr. Gabriella Blum**, former strategic advisor to the head of the Israeli National Security Council, argue that the legality of an action should be examined based on the picture that was available to those deciding to carry it out at the time of the decision, and not retrospectively, based on the action's results. In their view, the high level of uncertainty in the context of the war on terror may lead to a gap between anticipated damage and actual damage. Because of the ethical issues involved, including the possible deaths of innocent people, targeted killing missions have often been postponed or called off in circumstances when it turned out to be impossible to carry them out without disproportionately endangering innocent people (see the test case of Salah Shehadeh) (Shaul & Golan, 2004). Former IDF Chief Military Advocate General **Sharon Afek** adds that the responsibility for adhering to the principle of proportionality lies first and foremost with the military commanders, who are required to apply the principle in concrete situations. "This is a decision to be made by the commanders. There are no formulas here either. It's each case on its own merits."[1]

Shimon Peres, former president and prime minister of the State of Israel, highlighted the importance of preserving the lives of civilians on the other side and the need to postpone the operation if uninvolved civilians are in danger of being harmed. According to Peres, when a person is a ticking bomb, there is no doubt that the targeted killing is justified, since it is a case of "if someone comes to kill you, rise up and kill him first," and the state is obligated to protect innocent Israeli citizens; however, the fact that terrorist operatives who know they are "wanted" often surround themselves with innocents in order for them to serve as human shields makes it very difficult to carry out these operations. In his opinion, even in a case in which the terrorist deliberately surrounds himself with human shields, it is necessary to carefully assess how much harm will be caused to innocents, and whether the operation can be postponed to a later date when there is less risk of collateral damage.[2]

In March 2002, Israel suffered the most severe terrorist attacks against its citizens since the Second Intifada began in 2000. That month, 136 Israelis were killed, 81 of them in 15 suicide bombings. As a result, and in order to protect the security of the country's citizens, Israel launched Operation Defensive Shield (Brun, 2022). The operation resulted in casualties among uninvolved civilians on the Palestinian side. In a letter sent by then-IDF Chief of Staff Maj. Gen. Shaul Mofaz to IDF officers and soldiers, he stated that "Our war is not against the Palestinian people. We are fighting terrorism and its perpetrators...We will make sure to maintain our humanity and avoid harm to civilians and innocents, because

---

[1] Personal interview with Sharon Afek, March 13, 2022.

[2] Personal interview with Shimon Peres, 2008.

6 THE PRINCIPLE OF PROPORTIONALITY ... 149

this is our uniqueness and the backbone of our strength in the ongoing struggle that still holds true for us" (Letter from Chief of Staff Lt. Gen. Shaul Mofaz, 2002).

During the operation, then-UN Secretary-General Kofi Annan, who generally opposed Israel's policy of targeted killings, wrote a letter to Prime Minister Ariel Sharon, saying: "Israel is fully entitled to defend itself against terror...It is incumbent on all parties to take urgent steps to de-escalate the level of violence. Israel should contribute to this effort by ensuring that the I.D.F. uses only weapons and methods that minimize the danger to the lives and property of Palestinian civilians, in conformity with its humanitarian obligations" (*Kofi Annan's blunt words criticizing Israeli tactics*, 2002). Annan's words implied that targeted killing is the tool that most effectively reduces damage to the lives and property of the Palestinian civilian population. However, there are those who maintain that when innocent Palestinian civilians are harmed during a targeted killing by Israel, it is a violation of the Geneva Convention and a blurring of the moral distinction between terrorists and the State of Israel—after all, they claim, what is the moral difference between terrorists killing innocent people and Israel doing the same? (Kremnitzer, 2010). To this, Prof. Alan Dershowitz responds that one cannot morally compare the harm caused to innocent people by Israel to that caused by terrorists, because for Israel, it is a case of negligent homicide and not of first-degree premeditated murder, as it is in the case of the terrorist (Dershowitz, 2004), who wants to kill as many innocent people as possible as a means of achieving a goal (Kremnitzer, 2007).

The claim regarding killing out of negligence—and not first-degree murder—is echoed by Prof. Kremnitzer. He, too, says that there is a moral difference between terrorists killing innocent people and Israel doing so in the context of a targeted killing operation. Kremnitzer argues that the terrorist intentionally operates in a civilian environment, and does so for two reasons: Firstly, sometimes this environment provides him with protection from Israel (because a democratic state must respect the rules of international law). Secondly, because any harm caused by Israel to the civilian environment serves terrorist goals (because Israel is then condemned). Thus, the terrorist behaves in a manner contrary to ethics and international law (the Geneva Convention), and therefore can be said to bear the moral responsibility for any harm caused by Israel to innocent Palestinians—although there is no doubt that Israel experiences moral anguish when this occurs (Kasher & Yadlin, 2003).

The importance of proportionality considerations and dilemmas in Israel's targeted killing operations can be learned from the views expressed by decision-makers who have been involved in carrying out these actions. Former IDF Chief of Staff **Gadi Eisenkot** sees proportionality as an ethical matter: "Collateral damage is a very important component," he says. "I was involved in many dilemmas and overall, I think the heart of the Israeli security establishment is in the right place." Eisenkot cites as an example a case in which information was received about the whereabouts of Hezbollah Secretary-General Hassan Nasrallah—a 17- or 18-story building housing 60 or 70 families. It was clear that an early warning to the occupants of the building to evacuate would significantly lower the chances of successfully striking Nasrallah. Moreover, he notes that the decision to spare the lives of 60 or 70 families may lead to the killing of 70 soldiers and the firing of missiles into Israeli territory. He says that this is the essence of the dilemma.[3]

Another former chief of staff, **Gabi Ashkenazi**, also provides an example of the dilemma of proportionality in the decision-making process in targeted killings:

> The question is, where is the line drawn? Suppose [the target] is in the car with his wife and this is your only chance [to perform the operation]. Do you decide to strike him and his wife? Or, for example, you know he lives in a certain place, and you realize that the only way to strike him is from the air, but then it could be that the house next door will collapse and a wall will fall, and there are families there. Do you go through with it or not? These are the kinds of discussions that we would grapple with all the time. And I can tell you that there have been a lot of opportunities in which we stopped the operation because of the 'Plus One.' [The Plus One] could be the driver, an older son, and so on.[4]

Indeed, Brig. Gen. (Res.) **Gal Hirsch** also notes that he witnessed many cancelations of targeted killing operations during his service "due to military ethics, values, moral dilemmas. This is not just a legal dilemma; it has always been a moral dilemma. The possibility of harming uninvolved people."[5]

---

[3] Personal interview with Gadi Eisenkot, March 2, 2022.

[4] Personal interview with Gabi Ashkenazi, February 24, 2014.

[5] Personal interview with Gal Hirsch, February 20, 2022.

Former ISA official **Oz Noy** expands on the dilemmas involved in collateral damage in targeted killings:

> The greatest complexity in these operations is in fact the uninvolved people. The aim is to carry out a clean action and strike only the operative. But sometimes, reality does not allow for this. The question is, if someone is driving a terrorist, he knows he's driving a wanted person. He even knows that he's driving someone who is a target for elimination. But he is not connected to a terrorist attack. He is not the target. So should he also be included in the circle? These are questions that depend on the reality. Reality sometimes forces you to expand the circle.[6]

Former ISA Chief **Avi Dichter** helps illustrates the dilemma with another example: "The operational aspect is very complex. If there is a vehicle traveling on a main road and the target is inside, the Air Force can predict everything, but it cannot know if the vehicle will pass a taxi carrying innocent people and if the missile will hit them. This is a capability that does not exist. So you try to bring him to open areas, but what do you do in a city?... This luxury, of firing at a target that is in an environment with no innocents around, is very rare."[7] According to Dichter, the issue of collateral damage is an ever-present consideration. "Sometimes I see that he's driving towards a crowded area, for example towards the market, and I understand by calculating the times that he will arrive at the market more or less at the same time that the missile will be ready to be launched. So you don't launch the missile. With all the pain and sorrow that comes with that. And there have been many such cases."[8]

Former Director of the Counter-Terrorism Bureau at the Prime Minister's office **Nitzan Nuriel** describes the procedures Israel uses to minimize the collateral damage from targeted killing operations as much as possible: "We always try to find the most suitable and accurate weapon for the target, or we try to distance the [civilian] population using a practice like 'knock on the roof'.[9] We look for the operational position that will

[6] Personal interview with Oz Noy, February 16, 2022.

[7] Personal interview with Avi Dichter, March 11, 2022.

[8] Ibid.

[9] A practice used by the ISA and the IDF in cases in which there is a concern that there are civilians in a building about to be bombed. According to this procedure, the residents are contacted by phone and warned of an imminent attack. After that, a small

cause the least collateral damage. We are world leaders in this. In surgical strikes. In adapting the weapon to the target. In doing everything possible to minimize the collateral damage."[10]

Former Shin Bet official **Shalom Ben Hanan** adds:

> The use of the tool of targeted killing has been made with discretion and under the imposition of significant restraints. In my experience, many times decisions have been made not to carry out a targeted killing, even when it came to ticking bombs and targets who were murderers with blood on their hands, due to fear of collateral damage and similar ethical considerations. I don't want to get into mantras about us being the most moral army or agency in the world, but I certainly believe that our moral standards are extremely high, and have sometimes even cost us human lives. Similarly, I do not know of any cases in which a target could have been arrested or impeded in other ways and in which a targeted killing was carried out nonetheless. Even in the difficult days of the al-Aqsa Intifada, there were long discussions, and sometimes terrorists were not approved for targeted killing even when it was clear that they would continue to harm civilians, but the collateral damage was considered disproportionate or inappropriate.[11]

Ben Hanan says that even at the height of the Second Intifada, when many Israelis were being killed and injured in terrorist attacks, at the stage at which ISA operational plans were presented for approval (before the authorization of the political echelon), there were those who would say, "We can't do this because X number of innocent people will be killed."[12] Ben Hanan emphasizes that "the level of collateral damage you can allow yourself should first and foremost be derived from the threat level of the target. To say he's a ticking bomb is not enough. How much damage is he going to do to us? How 'ticking' is his level of threat, his level of sophistication, his status?"[13]

---

missile is fired near the house or on the roof to inform the inhabitants that they must leave the building; only then is the bomb that destroys the house launched.

[10] Personal interview with Nitzan Nuriel, February 14, 2022.

[11] Personal interview with Shalom Ben Hanan, February 21, 2022.

[12] Ibid.

[13] Ibid.

Shabtai Shavit, former head of the Mossad, highlights the fact that targeted killing operations are more selective than other offensive operations. He explains that "The perpetrators live in the community. It's difficult to identify and isolate them. They make sure that they are in a civilian environment and they use the population as human shields (including the elderly, children, and babies)." According to Shavit, targeted killing makes it possible to "harm someone whom we have judged it necessary to eliminate, but we do not want to harm innocents." Therefore, he explains, Israel has developed a special doctrine (as mentioned above) that begins with a warning that an action is about to be taken that will cause the building to collapse and calls for residents to evacuate. In the second stage, a missile with a minimum amount of explosives is fired at the roof of the building to give a final warning to civilians to leave. Shavit emphasizes that this is done out of moral and humanitarian considerations.[14] He recounts a Mossad operation in a neighboring country in which an important Fatah terrorist operative was supposed to be eliminated. "We booby-trapped the car, and during the night, information came in that he was going to be driving his daughter to school in the morning; we canceled the operation. If I know that we can't strike even the most evil person in the world without harming his family, I won't do it. Abu Jihad was eliminated with his wife and daughter in the room, and they were not touched."[15]

ASSESSING MILITARY EFFECTIVENESS VERSUS HARM TO UNINVOLVED CIVILIANS

According to the Supreme Court's ruling in the petition on targeted killings, if there is a chance that civilians will be harmed during such an operation, then an assessment must be made as to whether the action satisfies the test of proportionality—that is, whether the benefit to be gained from achieving the military objective is proportionate to the harm that may be inflicted on innocent civilians in the vicinity of the attack. If the anticipated harm outweighs the expected benefit, the action should be postponed (HCJ 769/02, 2006).

[14] Personal interview with Shabtai Shavit, February 17, 2022.

[15] Ibid.

Justice **Aharon Barak** states that the principle of proportionality involves four conditions: "The first condition is that the harm is for a worthy purpose...The second condition is a rational connection between the measure of targeted killing and the purpose it is intended to achieve (even if it is not immediate)... the next condition is about whether this measure is necessary, that is, are there alternatives?...and the last question is regarding balance: Does the benefit achieved by the use of targeted killing outweigh the benefit that could be achieved by other means?"[16]

Daniel Reisner, on the other hand, explains the difficulty in calculating the proportionality of counter-terrorism activity in general and targeted killing in particular: "The test of proportionality in international law is the need to balance expected military benefit and expected harm to innocent people. I don't know how to compare them... The chief of staff put together a team, that included Amos Yadlin, to come up with criteria and tests for these things. And the answer was: there is no answer." Reisner suggests distinguishing between three colors—white, black, and gray. "Obviously, if you are going to hit one terrorist and in the process 20 innocent civilians will be killed, it's black. And it's clear to everyone that if you are going to kill 20 terrorists and in the process kill one civilian, it's white... My answer is that you do not do black, and you definitely do white. And when it's gray, a decision has to be made on a case-by-case basis."[17]

Asa Kasher points out in this context that "It is the commander who makes the proportionality calculations according to international law. He knows better than anyone else what the expected achievements of the action are, and on the other side of the scale he puts collateral damage. He has a staff officer who tells him what is happening in the neighborhood in Gaza, who lives there, and what the collateral damage will be." Kasher adds that in his opinion, the decision to refrain from the operation should be made only in extreme situations, for example, the bombing of an arms depot that endangers a bus full of children, and which can also be bombed another day.[18] Kasher explains that the lives of the soldiers must also be taken into consideration, and not only the potential of harm to civilians

---

[16] Personal interview with Aharon Barak, February 20, 2022.

[17] Personal interview with Daniel Reisner, April 8, 2022.

[18] Personal interview with Asa Kasher, February 23, 2022.

on the enemy's side.[19] In their article "Military Ethics of Fighting Terror: An Israeli Perspective," Maj. Gen. (Res.) Amos Yadlin and Asa Kasher state that "A combatant is a citizen in uniform... his blood is as red and thick of citizens who are not in uniform" (Kasher & Yadlin, 2010, p. 17). With this statement, the two in effect distinguish between the obligation to preserve the lives of the civilians on the other side (who are not citizens of the state) and the obligation to protect the lives of soldiers; their claim is that the obligation to the lives of soldiers is greater. Kasher maintains that "the entire military world behaves like this. Only a few people, those who want to please, say that it's wrong. There is no commander who would massively risk the lives of his soldiers just because a civilian might be put in harm's way."[20]

Knut Dörmann, former head of the Legal Division of the International Committee of the Red Cross (ICRC) in Geneva, stresses that although the principle of proportionality has such vague interpretations, in order to determine whether the results of an attack are likely to be proportionate or disproportionate, only those benefits that are "military," "concrete," and "direct" should be taken into account; hypothetical, indirect and long-term political benefits should not be weighed (Dörmann, 2012, p. 16). In the event that prior to the action, it arises that the extent of the expected damage to the other party is greater than the benefit to be had, it is necessary to seek an alternative course of action (Zamir, 2007). Should innocent people be killed as a result of an action that did *not* lead to the achievement of the intended goal, then that action would not be in compliance with the rules of the principle of proportionality (Nathanson, 2010).

IDF Maj. Gen. (Res.) **Eyal Zamir** proposes taking into account a number of parameters to help make the right decision that will comply with the principle of proportionality: 1. The degree of immediacy of the danger posed—the more immediate the danger, the more urgent the action. 2. The value of the action—the more important the target (due to the cumulative damage he causes over time, or even in a single action, being very high), the more willing the state will be to pay a higher price in terms of harm to the civilian environment surrounding the target. 3. The degree of operational opportunity—the more opportunities there are

---

[19] Ibid.
[20] Ibid.

to strike the terrorist, the more one can wait for an opportunity that will result in less damage to the civilian environment; conversely, the harder it is to obtain intelligence on the target and the more elusive he is, the more important it is to act when a good opportunity arises. 4. The extent of the availability of other effective options—if there is more than one possible course of action, the action in which the least damage will be caused to innocent people should be chosen, if it will allow the threat to be thwarted (Zamir, 2007). **David Kretzmer** also suggests three parameters that may help determine whether a targeted killing is proportionate or not: 1. The degree of danger to life that would result from the terrorist's continued activity. 2. The chance of danger to human life that would be realized if the terrorist's actions do not cease immediately. 3. The danger of civilians dying or being wounded as a result of the attack on the suspected terrorist (Kretzmer, 2005).

Other criteria that can be used as a basis for the decision to carry out a targeted killing operation are those proposed by **Amos Guiora**. The parameters he suggests are based on the questions of who the threat is, why he is threatening, and how the threat can be stopped. Namely: 1. Is it possible to accurately identify the threat, and if so, is he a legitimate target for attack? 2. Is the expected threat from this person such that it is necessary to stop him at that moment, or are there possible alternatives for halting his actions? And is the intelligence by which the answer to this is determined reliably? 3. What is the expected collateral damage from the action? (Guiora, 2012).

Asa Kasher and **Maj. Gen. (Res.) Amos Yadlin** (former commander of the Air Force) state that a counter-terrorism action is justified when it is carried out under the following five conditions:

1. Its purpose is to protect civilians from terrorist attacks.
2. It is relatively effective, compared to any other action, or refraining from action, which may expose citizens to a more serious danger.
3. It is designed to minimize collateral damage as much as possible.
4. The action is proportionate in terms of the advantage it provides in protecting citizens compared to the collateral damage it causes.
5. It upholds the principle of universal fairness—similar actions under similar conditions would be justified elsewhere (Kasher & Yadlin, 2010).

Reisner notes that in assessing the proportionality of an operation, additional subtests may be of use, such as the distinction between men, women, and children, which has been applied in practice in "gray" targeted killings, as well as the target's level of seniority.[21] Indeed, Israel seems to have adopted as a basic moral-normative principle that if it turns out that children are within the radius of the expected collateral damage from the military action and they are likely to be harmed, approval for the action will not be granted. Reisner believes that these subtests used in Israel are more relevant than the ones that have been customarily used in the United States, for example. "In the Gulf War, the Americans determined that a sector commander could authorize up to a certain amount of civilians killed, and beyond that, the president's approval was required," he explains. According to Reisner, after September 11, 2001, the Americans began to use targeted killings much more than Israel, and did things that were not done by the Israelis, including targeted killings of U.S. citizens. In contrast, says Reisner, the Israeli military "does the best factual analysis possible. With operations research, it estimates how many people are liable to be harmed and decides on a case-by-case basis whether it is reasonable or not."[22]

Former IDF Chief of Staff **Moshe Ya'alon** points out that beyond the rules of ethics and international law, the response of the Israeli public must also be taken into account. He says in this regard, "For example, in "Operation Anemone Picking" [the operation that was planned to eliminate the Hamas leadership during a meeting in Gaza in September 2003], it was clear to me that if a building with 40 families in it was struck, the Israeli public would be outraged, and justifiably so, to a large extent."[23]

Reisner says that in any case of targeted killing that results in collateral damage (whether it was known about in advance or came as a surprise), a committee is set up to conduct an investigation of the operation.[24] This procedure was also put in place in the Supreme Court's ruling, which stated that following a targeted killing operation, a commission of inquiry should be conducted if uninvolved civilians were harmed. The committee has the authority to investigate targeted killings performed

---

[21] Personal interview with Daniel Reisner, April 8, 2022.

[22] Ibid.

[23] Personal interview with Moshe ("Bogie") Ya'alon, February 17, 2022.

[24] Personal interview with Daniel Reisner, April 8, 2022.

since the publication of the ruling (December 2006), and not retroactively (Rosenzweig, 2014). **Kasher** emphasizes in this context that insofar as errors occur that affect the collateral damage in an operation, they are due mainly to intelligence errors and not errors in calculating the worthwhileness of the operation. These intelligence errors can also be categorized, he says—they do not involve the identification and incrimination of the target ("When the ISA incriminates, there are no mistakes, there is a cross-checking of sources"), but rather usually stem from the question "What do we know about the situation on the ground [that is relevant] to the calculation of collateral damage?" That is, there is a lack of knowledge of what the situation is in nearby buildings. Kasher points out that such errors can also have the reverse impact—a decision to cancel a targeted killing operation may end up having been unnecessary.[25]

Avi Eliyahu concludes, "At the intelligence level, the ambition is to create as much sterility as possible...We live in a moral, ethical world— that is how we educate our soldiers, and quite rightly. That is why we are perceived as a moral army." Eliyahu says that in Operation Protective Edge, the ratio between the number of uninvolved people who were harmed and involved people who were harmed was 1:1, whereas the minimum ratio in similar operations in the world is 7:1. This is especially significant given the fact that the IDF was operating against a terrorist organization that has a policy of using civilians as human shields, in an area that is one of the five most densely-populated in the world. "What I want to say is that moral and ethical considerations play a very significant role in our decision about what collateral damage we are willing to risk. We are committed to by our commanders and decision makers, and rightly so! We really treat every uninvolved person as a significant casualty and we want to keep these to a minimum. It comes from our ethical and moral outlook as a nation, and this is infused in the army and the commanders."[26]

On the face of it, the national public opinion poll conducted by ICT in early 2022, examining Israeli public opinion in the issue of targeted killing, substantiates Eliyahu's claim. The poll showed that Israelis, the vast majority of which support the use of targeted killings in the framework of Israeli counter-terrorism activity, maintain a high degree of

---

[25] Personal interview with Asa Kasher, February 23, 2022.

[26] Personal interview with Avi Eliyahu, April 6, 2022.

balance with regard to the proportionality of the operation. In answer to the question "During the execution of a targeted killing, civilians who are not involved in any terrorist activity may also be harmed. In such a case, is it justified, in your opinion, to carry out the targeted killing?" 21 percent of the respondents answered that the action would be unjustified, while 17 percent considered it "unquestionably" justified. However, half of the respondents—50 percent—believe that the legitimacy of the action depends on the one hand on the identity of the target, and on the other hand on the number of citizens who may be harmed. Most respondents therefore underscored the need to maintain the normative principle of proportionality.[27]

THE PROPORTIONALITY EQUATION IN TARGETED KILLINGS

Boaz Ganor proposes the use of an equation to examine whether a planned targeted killing operation is likely to be proportionate. The equation allows one to quantify the military necessity of the targeted killing on the one hand (the equation's numerator), and the expected collateral damage on the other (the denominator) (Ganor, 2015).

$$P = \frac{\text{MilitaryNecessity(Advantage)}}{\text{ExpectedCollateralDamage}} = \frac{X \times Y \times Z}{N_a^1 + N_b^2 + N_c^3}$$

In the definition of Military Necessity, the variable X is determined by the **urgency of the need** to carry out the targeted killing. The need is determined by numerical values on a scale of 1–10. The more immediate the planned terrorist attack that the operation is intended to thwart, the higher the value, as follows: Minimal Urgency—Minimal danger of a concrete terrorist attack (2); Preliminary Stage—The targeted killing is intended to foil an attack that may occur at some point (4); Early Stage—The terrorist is in the initial stage of planning an attack (6); Advanced Stage—The terrorist is in the advanced stage of carrying out an attack (8); Ticking Bomb—The terrorist has completed preparations for the attack and is about to carry it out (10).

The variable Y reflects the extent to which the planned targeted killing is necessary. This variable indicates the added value of a targeted killing

---

[27] National Public Opinion Poll on Targeted Killings, conducted for the International Institute for Counter-Terrorism (ICT) by *Ma'agar Mochot*, February 21, 2022.

over other alternatives, in terms of the foreseeable damage to the state's combat forces, i.e., the number of troops who may be killed in an alternative operation to targeted killing that would cause minimal collateral damage.

The variable Z calculates an estimate of the number of casualties expected from the terrorist attack that will occur if the targeted killing is not carried out. The calculation of this variable is based on intelligence information and experience accumulated from past attacks.

The equation's denominator assesses the expected collateral damage from the targeted killing operation. Here, the variable N represents the total expected number of casualties, and is divided into letters and numbers $(N_c^1 + N_b^2 + N_3^a)$. The letters a, b, and c denote different categories of expected casualties, and the numbers represent the changing degree of precaution that must be taken not to harm them (by increasing the number of casualties by exponents of one, two or three). The variable $N(a)$ represents the estimate of the number of casualties among uninvolved civilians, whom it is forbidden to harm intentionally (this number is increased by an exponent of three to reflect a maximum obligation to protect their lives). Variable $N(b)$ denotes a moderate obligation to protect the lives of casualties in targeted killings, representing the category of those who are non-operational combat-supportive civilians, militiamen, and human shields who have volunteered for the mission of protecting the terrorists. This number is increased by an exponent of two and reflects, as stated, a moderate obligation to safeguarding the lives of these people. The variable $N(c)$ reflects the number of terrorist casualties in a targeted killing operation (aside from the terrorist who was the planned target in the first place). Because harming them is permitted (whether this was pre-planned or not), this variable reflects a low level of precautionary obligation by the attacking state (with the number raised only by a power of one) (Ganor, 2015).

The proposed formula constitutes an important attempt to quantify the elusive concept of "proportionality," which is subject to various interpretations. The equation recommends a classification of different types of casualties in military activity in general and in targeted killings in particular, and sets different levels of the obligation on the part of the state to avoid casualties among these groups. Because of this, and based on intelligence information, expert assessments, and past experience, the proposed equation makes it possible to evaluate the proportionality of a targeted killing prior to its execution. On the basis of this formula, decision-makers, as well as various international bodies, can determine a threshold for targeted killing actions that are proportionate (legitimate) versus disproportionate (illegitimate), depending on the needs and subjective conditions at the particular time and place.

Israeli Attempts to Minimize Collateral Damage

Israel's attempts to minimize collateral damage from targeted killing operations are carried out by the security and political echelons in a number of ways, from postponing the operation if it is known that the collateral damage is likely to be greater than its effectiveness, to choosing the size of the munition that will yield the expected result and cause the smallest number of casualties (Ganor, 2015), to selecting a method of action and type of weapon that allows for precise "surgical" strikes that carry a relatively small risk to the civilian population (Reich, 2004). Naturally, weapons that are inaccurate or have a large destructive radius are problematic when it comes to targeted killings carried out in an urban environment with civilians or civilian infrastructure in the vicinity. Powerful bombs fired from the air, artillery, and mortars can be problematic due to the difficulty involved in aiming them at specific targets, or due to their large destructive radius. Therefore, if the operation is carried out within a civilian environment, weapons and munitions must be chosen that are more accurate and discriminating (than artillery fire, mortars, or unguided munitions) (Dörmann, 2012).

Since the beginning of the wave of targeted killings during the al-Aqsa Intifada in 2000, attack helicopters have become a key means of carrying out targeted killings of operatives of terrorist organizations. According to a former commander of an Israeli Air Force base, "The desire to strike who you mean to, and not who you don't mean to, made it necessary to use a weapon that allows for a direct hit on the target, but will not cause destruction beyond that. The attack helicopter is such a weapon. If you need to strike a window, or a particular vehicle, with an attack helicopter you can launch a missile and hit only the target, and not its surroundings" (Naom & Winkler, 2001). Former Air Force Commander and IDF Chief of Staff **Dan Halutz** explains that:

> The air force began its targeted killing operations in 2000 with combat helicopters (Apaches and Cobras), because helicopters allow for precision munitions, which cause less collateral damage. With helicopters, you can

fire a missile loaded with ten kilograms of explosives, whereas with a plane, you can also drop a one-ton bomb. Later, we also used fighter jets for these operations, which used very precise laser-guided munitions that could strike with an accuracy of a few meters. The use of fighter jets ensures that the strike on the object will be deadly, and ensures the success of the operation with less risk to the aircraft itself. From the second half of 2001, the air force also began to use UAVs for targeted killings... In addition, a number of types of munitions have been developed for drones, making their level of accuracy as high as possible.[28]

Halutz goes on to explain that in order to maintain proportionality and minimize harm to the uninvolved, in some cases, even after the UAV has launched the missile, in the few seconds before the strike it is possible to divert the missile if a change has taken place and previously unknown information has been received regarding uninvolved civilians in the area. According to Halutz, in such cases, areas are sometimes defined ahead of time to determine "where to drop the weapon in case you need to stop. This is so you don't divert the missile from one street to another, and hit uninvolved people there. If, for example, it's an area with lots of buildings, you will try to find an open lot, so that if there's a problem you can divert it to there." Halutz defines this as a "degree of freedom given to the people guiding the operation. A fighter pilot can't see this. If he the pilot has fired, in 99 percent of cases, it's impossible to stop the missile. With a drone, when it drops a bomb, there is a slightly longer time, so you can divert it because you are dictating the target all the time."[29]

On the other hand, the use of a missile with too small a warhead may prevent the achievement of the required goal of the targeted killing operation. For example, in September 2003, several months after the elimination of Salah Shehadeh, the commander of Hamas's military wing (see the case study later in this chapter), there was a gathering of many senior Hamas figures—including Muhammad Deif, the head of the military wing; Adnan al-Ghoul, the "engineer" in the Gaza Strip who was in charge of the Qassam project; Sheikh Ahmad Yassin, the spiritual leader of Hamas, and Ismail Haniyeh, head of Yassin's office—in one building in Gaza. The Israeli decision-makers who knew about the meeting ahead of time decided to carry out a targeted killing. However, in light of the

---

[28] Personal interview with Dan Halutz, March 4, 2022.

[29] Ibid.

lessons learned following the collateral damage incurred as a result of Shehadeh's elimination, it was decided to use a small quarter-ton bomb (instead of a one-ton bomb as was originally planned) in order to minimize damage to the civilian environment. The bomb did hit the target, but did not do the job, failing to kill any of the Hamas officials—the bomb destroyed only the top floor of the building, and the meeting was being held on the first floor (Shaul & Golan, 2004; Hemo & Lachter, 2021). The participants of that meeting brought Israel a great deal of devastation in the years that followed this failed attempt, causing many casualties in the numerous terrorist attacks that they planned, prepared, and carried out. Just one example is the suicide bombing carried out in January 2004 at the Erez Crossing, which killed four people and injured ten (Shaul & Golan, 2004).

Avi Dichter, former director of the ISA, describes the incident as "the State of Israel's biggest miss. The entire 'dream team,' from Sheikh Yassin and below, were in one house in Gaza."[30] Former Air Force commander **Dan Halutz** explains, "A munition of one ton would have destroyed the building from top to bottom, whereas the quarter-ton bomb destroyed only the second floor of the building."[31] Former IDF Chief of Staff **Moshe Ya'alon** illustrates the dilemma of proportionality by pointing out that "the bomb that could have killed the entire Hamas leadership would have probably also hit about forty apartments in the building next door."[32]

One of the participants in that meeting was Muhammad Deif, the head of Hamas's military wing in the Gaza Strip, who later became one of Israel's most wanted men. Israel attempted to eliminate him five times, but without success (Shaul & Golan, 2004). Deif inherited command of Hamas's military wing from Yahya Ayyash, who was killed in 1996 (Waked & Greenberg, 2006) (see case study in Chapter 7). In one of these attempts, Israel launched two Hellfire missiles at Deif's vehicle. One missile hit the front of his car, and the two people sitting in the front seats were killed. Although Deif was seriously injured, he himself was not killed—the goal of the operation was not attained. **Matan Vilnai**, a minister in the Israeli government at the time, claimed that in this

---

[30] Personal interview with Avi Dichter, March 11, 2002.

[31] Ibid.

[32] Personal interview with Moshe ("Bogie") Ya'alon, February 17, 2022.

case, too, the purpose of the operation was not achieved because "Israel fired missiles rather than dropping a larger bomb in order to avoid harming innocent civilians" (Frisch & Waked, 2002). According to the Palestinians, the operation killed two Hamas members as a result of the explosion, and injured 25 people, including children (Hemo & Lachter, 2021; Ynet reporters, 2002). This goes to show that even when relatively small munitions are used due to concerns about proportionality (to the point that the success of the operation is jeopardized), significant collateral damage may still occur, and uninvolved civilians may be harmed. To this day, Muhammad Deif is one of Israel's most wanted terrorists. He is the commander of the al-Qassam Brigades, leads Hamas's military campaign against Israel, and is involved in the planning of terrorist attacks (Hemo & Lachter, 2021). In this context, Muhammad Deif is responsible, among other things, for the Gaza Strip's "Metro" project— an extensive network of underground tunnels excavated on the outskirts of the eastern part of Gaza City and the northern Gaza Strip. The purpose of the tunnels was to allow terrorist operatives from Hamas and Islamic Jihad to open a battlefront against IDF forces in the event of a ground operation into the Gaza Strip, to install a networked system of underground rocket launchers to facilitate the firing of thousands of rockets at the Israeli home front, and to enable the hiding and movement of terrorist operatives. In many cases, these tunnels are built under protected Palestinian civilian facilities, such as hospitals and schools. Another purpose of the tunnels was for them to be used in the abduction of IDF soldiers, alive or dead, for bargaining purposes (Sirioti, 2021).

Such examples of failed targeted killings, stemming from the use of too small an amount of explosives due to humanitarian concerns about proportionality, illustrate the difficulty decision makers face in approving and planning these operations. **Reisner** maintains that the IDF's failure to eliminate the Hamas leadership convening in the Gaza Strip as a result of it employing too weak a weapon is not necessarily a bad thing, because such failures lead to successes later on. "We learn from them," he says. "In contrast, one does not learn from successes." In his opinion, unsuccessful attacks are a learning tool through which the IDF's military doctrine can be developed.[33] This military doctrine is also based, inter alia, on operations research that calculates the results of the missile's possible hit on the

---

[33] Personal interview with Daniel Reisner, April 8, 2022.

target. According to **Asa Kasher**, the Air Force has an operations research unit that is able to calculate all the parameters, such as which aircraft to use, at what time of day, etc., thereby ensuring that the terrorist is hit and that the collateral damage is minimal.[34]

CASE STUDY: SALAH SHEHADEH (2002)

In the early 2000s, Salah Shehadeh was one of the most senior leaders of Hamas—the second in the hierarchy under Sheikh Yassin, who was considered the spiritual leader of the Hamas movement. Shehadeh was the commander of Hamas's military wing, the Izz ad-Din al-Qassam Brigades (Yadlin, 2004). With the outbreak of the Second Intifada in the territories in 2000, Shehadeh was identified as the person behind Hamas's military actions. Some in Israel even claimed that the damage he caused was more severe than that caused by Muhammad Deif, Israel's "number one most wanted man" (Waked et al., 2002). In a testimony given by then-ISA Director Avi Dichter and then-IDF Chief of Staff Moshe Ya'alon during the commission of inquiry established to investigate the operation and its consequences, they claimed that "During the Intifada, Salah Shehadeh was established as the leading figure in Gaza... the most dominant military figure in Hamas in Gaza, with very close "foreign" ties to Khaled Mashal in Damascus." Ya'alon also claimed that "Salah Shehadeh, for us, is an arch-terrorist" (Special Investigatory Commission, 2011, pp 58–59). **Dichter** adds, "Salah Shehadeh was Sheikh Yassin's right-hand man, but he surpassed Sheikh Yassin. He was the most problematic element in Hamas. The one who established ties with Iran, who started helping Hamas in 2001. And we had our eye on him for a very long time."[35]

Between July 2001 and July 2002, Shehadeh was responsible for dozens of terrorist attacks against Israeli civilians and soldiers. As a result of his involvement in terrorist activities, 474 civilians and soldiers were killed and 2,649 injured. This activity classified him as a legitimate target for elimination, whose threat to Israeli citizens was certain, immediate, and significant. This classification prepared the ground for the targeted killing operation (Special Investigatory Commission, 2011).

---

[34] Personal interview with Asa Kasher, February 23, 2022.

[35] Personal interview with Avi Dichter, March 11, 2022.

Prior to the decision on the operation, and because the state has a duty to consider additional, more moderate, methods to targeted killing, Israel assessed alternative measures to prevent Shehadeh's continued activity, including arrest and trial. Israel tried several times to appeal to the Palestinian Authority to arrest Shehadeh, but they refused (Byman, 2006). The possibility of arresting him in an Israeli ground operation was also determined to be impractical, since Shehadeh had sought refuge in a densely-populated refugee camp, making such an operation likely to endanger both the lives of the soldiers and the lives of uninvolved civilians. It was then decided, as a last resort, to hit Shehadeh directly from the air (Byman, 2006; Special Investigatory Commission, 2011). The IDF carried out the targeted killing of Shehadeh in July 2002, and the collateral damage that was caused as a result is considered to be the most severe of any Israeli operation.

INTELLIGENCE INFORMATION

During the efforts to locate Shehadeh, seven apartments in different areas of Gaza City were identified as places he had resided during this period. Knowing that he was wanted, he would change his place of residence frequently (Special Investigatory Commission, 2011). In July 2002, in the Daraj neighborhood in the northern Gaza Strip, the apartment in which Shehadeh was hiding was discovered. The apartment was located in a two-story building in a densely-populated refugee camp. According to intelligence gathered, the first floor housed a warehouse and the second floor was a residence (ibid.).

The problem was the difficulty of targeting him in a "clean" environment, where it would be possible to ensure that he would be hit without killing other civilians, besides his wife, who was known to have served him as a human shield (Meridor & Fass, 2006). This fear of the presence of uninvolved civilians in Shehadeh's vicinity is the reason that the IDF had already postponed eight operations to target him (Harel, 2002).

Dichter and Ya'alon confirm that there were indeed many attempts to target Shehadeh before the execution of the operation, but each time, the strikes were called off for fear of collateral damage. According to **Dichter**, Shehadeh used to move between houses and buildings. "He would find places that were very difficult to operate in, and it took a while until he finally made a mistake and chose this one house."[36] Ya'alon adds, "I remember that we were looking for Salah Shehadeh for a while. He knew we were very morally conscious; he would go into apartment buildings all the time, a lot of apartments, and we avoided striking him." **Ya'alon** goes on to say that before the operation was carried out, the question arose as to whether his young daughter would be with him. And Dichter explains, "We made it clear that if the little girl was going to be at home, there would be no operation. His wife was a legitimate target, she was collaborating with him. The little girl? We said no. And the intelligence that day said the girl was somewhere else in Gaza, not at home, and unfortunately it turned out that the intelligence was not accurate. He was at home and he was killed, his wife was killed, and innocent people were also killed."[37]

Indeed, on the day of the operation itself, when the plans were presented to then-Israeli Prime Minister Ariel Sharon and then-Defense Minister Fouad Ben-Eliezer, the ISA, which had been tasked with the gathering of intelligence, claimed that there was only a "low probability" of civilians being in the house where he was hiding. According to the information, the people in the house at that time were Shehadeh, one of his assistants, and his wife, who as stated was known to have acted as a human shield for him, so it was decided that the operation should be carried out (Special Investigatory Commission, 2011). Dichter and Ya'alon clarified the reasons for the intelligence error that led to the collateral damage. According to **Dichter**, "We dropped the bomb and did not take into account that the tin shacks that were seen near the building were not café shacks that are only used for drinking coffee and then going home, but that there were also people living there."[38] **Ya'alon** adds:

> There was a house next door that it was clear to us would also be damaged, but according to the intelligence, it was evident that this house was uninhabited at night. The garage at the bottom of the building and the two upper floors were under renovation, and therefore the assessment was that it was vacant. Unfortunately, in retrospect, it turned out that people from the Rafah area, which was a combat zone, had left their homes and settled

[36] Personal interview with Avi Dichter, March 11, 2022.

[37] Ibid.

[38] Ibid.

there for the night. That's why there were 14 casualties among uninvolved civilians, including children. An event that clouded the success of the action.[39]

On top of all the considerations that were taken into account, in order to ensure a greater degree of certainty that there would be no danger to innocent people, it was decided that the action would be taken at midnight, when the streets were expected to be empty of people. It was also assessed that the lying-down position of the people in their sleep would also reduce the probability of large-scale injury (HCJ 5757/04, 2005; Special Investigatory Commission, 2011).

Reisner concludes, "We did not intend to kill so many civilians. I don't know if it was that we made an intelligence error, or that we were mistaken in assessing the damage of the bomb, because these are two things that are done in parallel, but we made a mistake. If we had known that 17 people were going to die, we probably would not have authorized the strike on Salah Shehadeh. He was not worth 17, in terms of the balance."[40]

THE WEAPON SELECTED FOR THE PURPOSE OF THE TARGETED KILLING

The IDF examined which type of munition would make it possible to achieve the purpose of the operation, on the one hand, and reduce the risks involved in carrying it out, on the other. During the discussions, the possibility of dropping two bombs, each weighing half a ton, was considered, but this option was ruled out and it was decided that the operation would be carried out by an F-16 fighter jet that would drop one bomb weighing a ton. The type of bomb that was decided upon is laser-guided and extremely accurate; it was chosen because when dropping a one-ton laser-guided bomb, the risk of missing the target is smaller, and the chance of a more accurate hit is higher (HCJ 5757/04, 2005; Special Investigatory Commission, 2011).

The Israeli Air Force believed that the house that was bombed would be completely destroyed, and that all those living in it would be killed.

---

[39] Personal interview with Moshe ("Bogie") Ya'alon, February 17, 2022.

[40] Personal interview with Daniel Reisner, April 8, 2022.

In contrast, the understanding was that in the nearby houses, the residents would be hit by shrapnel, glass fragments, and blast waves, that would result only in injuries (Prisco, 2011). In addition, the assessment of the IDF's operations research team was that the surrounding buildings would not collapse as a result of the bombing—only the glass would shatter. According to journalist Oren Prisko, "The planners' assumptions about the damage to the houses around Shehadeh's house were incorrect. While the nearby houses were not completely destroyed—as the Air Force predicted—they were damaged, and some of the people in them were killed or injured. The planners apparently did not take into account the dilapidated condition of the buildings [shacks] built near Shehadeh's home" (Prisco, 2011). The considerations and decisions outlined above show that Israel wanted the action to be proportionate, and believed it would be, but was not prepared for what reality had in store.

THE RESULT OF THE OPERATION

Due to inaccurate intelligence (Yadlin, 2004), in addition to Shehadeh and his wife, one of his daughters was killed, as were 11 uninvolved civilians (including 5 children) who were residing in buildings near his home. More than 150 uninvolved civilians were also injured (Special Investigatory Commission, 2011).

Most of the senior officials that were involved in the planning and execution of the operation later appeared before the commission of inquiry set up to investigate the results of the targeted killing, and testified that if they had known the extent of the expected collateral damage, the operation would not have taken place. That is, the intelligence information that was in the decision makers' hands in real time, and on the basis of which they gave the green light to carry out the operation, was at least partially incorrect. Therefore, the collateral damage was unintentional, and not the result of a disregard for human life (Special Investigatory Commission, 2011). After the operation, then-Israeli Prime Minister **Ariel Sharon** said that "This was one of our most successful operations," but added that had he known that there were civilians next to Shehadeh, he would not have approved the operation (Prisco, 2011). Similarly, **Gideon Meir**, then-deputy director-general for media and public affairs at the Israeli Ministry of Foreign Affairs, stated that "the attack was intended to strike a well-known terrorist operative, responsible for hundreds of attacks against Israeli civilians in recent years." He did, however, express regret over the loss of civilian lives during the incident (Waked et al., 2002).

The action, which in retrospect appeared to be disproportionate, had political consequences. Then-UN Secretary-General Kofi Annan, for example, condemned the Israeli attack. His spokesman said, "Israel has the legal and moral responsibility to take all measures to avoid the loss of innocent life; it clearly failed to do so in using a missile against an apartment building" (ibid.).

The questions arising from the dilemma of proportionality in cases of targeted killings are difficult ones, and their answers depend, in many cases, on the respondent's worldview and the nature of his or her involvement and various interests. As long as no guiding principles are agreed upon for determining proportionality in counter-terrorism in general and targeted killing in particular (for example, the assertion that the examination of proportionality be carried out solely on the basis of the information available to the decision-makers before the operation and not on the basis of its retrospective results; the formation of a clear classification of the state's precautionary obligation to prevent harm to various types of involved and uninvolved persons in close proximity to the area of the target; or an attempt to quantify the various variables that must be taken into account in the proportionality equation outlined above), the gaps and disagreements cannot be bridged using objective and impartial tools.

In any case, in the wake of the Shehadeh operation, and prior to the establishment of the commission of inquiry, the IDF decided to reiterate the principles and norms of international and Israeli law and the ethical and moral foundations of the security forces, especially with regards to harm to uninvolved civilians. The IDF also underscored the importance of exercising caution in the selection of the method of striking the terrorist target and the type of weapon to be used in the operation (Special Investigatory Commission, 2011).

REFERENCES

Byman, D. (2006). Do targeted killings work? *Foreign Affairs, 85*(2), 95–112.

Brun, I. (2022). [Hebrew]. *From air superiority to a multidimensional blow: The air force and its place in Israel's military doctrine.* Institute for National Security Studies.

Customary IHL. (1977). Practice relating to rule 14: Proportionality in attack. IHL database. https://ihl-databases.icrc.org/customary-ihl/eng/docindex/v2_rul_rule14

Dershowitz, A. (2004). *The case for Israel.* Wiley.

Dörmann, K. (2012). Obligations of international humanitarian law. *Military and Strategic Affairs, 4*(2).

Frisch, F., & Waked, A. (2022, September 27). Shabak believes that Muhammad Deif was not killed. *Ynet.* https://www.ynet.co.il/articles/0,7340,L-2139673,00.html

Ganor, B. (2015). *Global alert: The rationality of modern Islamist terrorism and the challenge to the liberal democratic world.* Columbia University Press.

Ganor, B. (2008). Terrorist organization typologies and the probability of a boomerang effect. *Studies in Conflict & Terrorism, 31*(4), 269–283.

Glickman, A. (2008, November 17). Mazuz to the prime minister: Accelerate the targeted killings committee. *Ynet.* https://www.ynet.co.il/articles/0,7340,L-3624292,00.html

Guiora, A. (2012). Targeted killing: When proportionality gets all out of proportion. *Case Western Reserve Journal of International Law, 45*(1), 235–258.

Harel, A. (2002, July 23). Israel assassinates the leader of Hamas's military wing in Gaza. *Ha'aretz.* https://www.haaretz.co.il/misc/1.811596

HCJ 5757/04. (2005). *Yesh Gvul v. The Government of Israel.* chrome-extension://efaidnbmnnnibpcajpcglclefindmkaj/https://supremedecisions.court.gov.il/Home/Download?path=HebrewVerdicts/04/570/057/o11&fileName=04057570.o11&type=4

HCJ 769/02. (2006). *The Public Committee Against Torture in Israel v. The Government of Israel, 62*(1), 507.

Hemo, O., & Lachter, E. (2021, May 14). Muhammad Deif and six others: The next Hamas targets. *Mako.* https://www.mako.co.il/news-military/2021_q2/Article-5b74c6a4f0c6971027.htm

Kasher, A. (2009) Operation cast lead and just war theory. *Azure.* https://tchelet.org.il/article.php?id=437

Kasher, A., & Yadlin, A. (2010). Military ethics of fighting terror: An Israeli perspective. *Journal of Military Ethics, 4*(1), 3–32.

Kofi Annan's Blunt Words Criticizing Israeli Tactics. (2002, March 19). *The New York Times.* https://www.nytimes.com/2002/03/19/world/kofi-annan-s-blunt-words-criticizing-israeli-tactics.html

Kremnitzer, M. (2010). Terrorism and democracy and the case of Israel. *Hamishpat, 14*(9).

Kremnitzer, M., Segev, R., Poratt, I., & Enoch, D. (2007). *Collateral damage: The harming of innocents in the war against terror.* Israel Democracy Institute.

Kretzmer, D. (2005). Targeted killing of suspected terrorists: Extra-judicial executions or legitimate means of defense? *European Journal of International Law, 16*(2), 171–212. https://doi.org/10.1093/ejil/chi114

Letter from Chief of Staff Lt. Gen. Shaul Mofaz on Operation Defensive Shield. (2002). https://doi.org/www.idf.il/%d7%a8%d7%90%d7%a9%d7%99-%d7%94%d7%9e%d7%98%d7%94-%d7%94%d7%9b%d7%9c%d7%9c%d7%99/%d7%94%d7%a8%d7%9e%d7%98%d7%9b-%d7%9c-%d7%94-16/%d7%93%d7%91%d7%a8%d7%99-%d7%94%d7%a8%d7%9e%d7%98%d7%9b-%d7%9c/%d7%90%d7%99%d7%92%d7%a8%d7%aa-%d7%94%d7%a8%d7%9e%d7%98%d7%9b-%d7%9c-%d7%a8%d7%90-%d7%9c-%d7%a9%d7%90%d7%95%d7%9c-%d7%9e%d7%95%d7%a4%d7%96-%d7%a2%d7%9c-%d7%9e%d7%91%d7%a6%d7%a2-%d7%97%d7%95%d7%9e%d7%aa-%d7%9e%d7%92%d7%9f/

Nathanson, S. (2010). *Terrorism and the ethics of war.* Cambridge University Press.

Meridor, D., & Fass, H. (Eds.). (2006). *The battle of the 21st century: Democracies fighting terrorism* (pp. 276–277). Israel Institute of Democracy.

Noam, O., & Winkler, R. (2001, October 1). Attack helicopters' window of opportunity. *Air Force Bulletin* (141). https://www.iaf.org.il/601-19685-he/IAF.aspx

Prisco, O. (2011, April 5). Positive information. *The7eye.* http://www.the7eye.org.il/13146

ICRC. (1977). *Protocol additional to the Geneva Conventions of 12 August 1949.* https://ihl-databases.icrc.org/applic/ihl/ihl.nsf/ART/470-750065?OpenDocument

Reich, Y. (2004). The use of technology by terrorist organizations. In O. Kazimirsky, N. Grossman-Aloni, & S. Aludi (Eds.), *Aspects of terrorism and combatting terrorism* (pp. 1–183). Ministry of Defense.

Rosenzweig, I. (2014). Targeted killings during high and low intensity warfare. In P. Sharvit & A. Kurz (Eds.), *Law and National Security: Selected Issues* (pp. 41–52). INSS.

Rosner, T. (2004, December 2). Halutz to Supreme Court: "I am moral and ethical man." *Ynet.* https://www.ynet.co.il/articles/0,7340,L-3012628,00.html

Shaul, S., & Golan, H. (Eds.). (2004). *The limited conflict.* Ma'arachot.

Sirioti, D. (2021, May 15). The demolition of the "Metro"- The destruction of Muhammad Deif's lifetime achievement. *Israel Hayom.* https://www.israelhayom.co.il/news/defense/article/1019453

Special Investigatory Commission on the Targeted Killing of Salah Shehadeh. (2011). https://www.gov.il/BlobFolder/news/spokeshchade270211/he/sitecollectiondocuments_pmo_32communication_spokemes_reportshchade.pdf

Waked, A., Bachor, & Somfalvi. (2002, July 23). Salah Shehadeh killed along with 15 other civilians. *Ynet*. https://www.ynet.co.il/articles/0,7340,L-2015833,00.html

Waked, A., & Greenberg, H. (2006, July 12). Muhammad Deif injured in Gaza airstrike. *Ynet*. https://www.ynet.co.il/articles/0,7340,L-3274196,00.html

Yadlin, A. (2004). Fighting terror from the air. In O. Kazimirsky, N. Grossman-Elhani, & S. Elhadi (Eds.), *Aspects of terrorism and the fight against terrorism* (p. 122). Ministry of Defense.

Yadlin, A., & Kasher, A. (2003). Ethics in fighting terrorism. *National Security* (2–3).

Ynet reporters. (2002, July 23). *Salah Shehadeh killed along 965 with 15 other civilians*. Ynet. https://www.ynet.co.il/articles/0,7340,L-2139673,00.html

Zamir, E. (2007). The moral fight against terrorism. *Ma'arachot* (414), 28–37. Ministry of Defense.

CHAPTER 7

The Boomerang Effect in Targeted Killings—Are Targeted Killings Effective?

Offensive counter-terrorism action in general, and targeted killing operations in particular, may have negative repercussions in the short term (days after the targeted killing), medium term (weeks or months after the operation), or long term (years after the operation). These consequences will be defined here as the "boomerang effect" of targeted killings. This chapter will explore three categories of the boomerang effect: The "tactical boomerang"—retaliatory actions by the terrorist organization consisting mainly of revenge attacks that are generally carried out in the short term following the operation; the "operational boomerang"—military or diplomatic imbroglios caused by the operation, usually transpiring in the medium or short term; and the "strategic boomerang"—developments and processes that result from the targeted killing and have long-term negative impacts with regard to the conflict underlying terrorism, the challenges that terrorism poses to the state, or the state's ability to deal with terrorism. These may include an intensification of hate, the development of a new type of terrorist threat, or the replacement of an organization's leader with a more dangerous or skilled figure.

© The Author(s), under exclusive license to Springer Nature   175
Switzerland AG 2022
B. Ganor and L. Koblentz-Stenzler, *Israel's Targeted Killing Policy*,
https://doi.org/10.1007/978-3-031-13674-0_7

Tactical Boomerang Effect—Revenge Attacks

Terrorist attacks are a function of two variables: the motivation to carry out an attack and the capability to do so. This is referred to as the "terrorism equation" (Ganor, 2021). The higher the motivation and the greater the capability, the higher the probability that terrorist attacks will take place. Any offensive action against a terrorist organization, and certainly an act of targeted killing, will naturally increase the motivation of the organization's operatives and leaders to carry out revenge (boomerang) attacks. Therefore, the consequences of a targeted killing operation, which is intended to prevent attacks and reduce the scope of terrorism, may actually lead to the opposite result and increase motivation for attacks (Ibid).

Targeted killings (especially when carried out against a senior or key terrorist operative, or one of the organization's leaders) are designed to neutralize the target's activity, disrupt the terrorist organization's endeavors, and at the same time deter others from becoming involved in terrorism. The deterrent effect is an outgrowth of the fear and anxiety among other operatives in the terrorist organization, or in other organizations, that they will meet a similar end. In this respect, targeted killings offer a kind of proof of the state's operational capability to reach whomever it wants and make them pay a heavy price for their actions; the action thereby sows fear among terrorist operatives and strengthens deterrence.

However, as Ophir Falk and Amir Hefetz claim, in some cases, targeted killings do not achieve the desired deterrent effect, and may even lead to the opposite result—increased motivation to carry out revenge attacks. The motivation for revenge may be strengthened even further when the operation is accompanied by significant collateral damage—a large number of casualties among uninvolved people in the vicinity of the target (Falk & Hefetz, 2019). For example, in analyzing revenge attacks by suicide bombers after targeted killings carried out by Israel during the Second intifada, Falk and Hefetz found that when the operations resulted in the deaths of uninvolved people, there was an increase in all parameters measured in their study—the number of attacks, the damage they caused, and the number of dead and wounded (Ibid).

Terrorist organizations and their spokespeople tend to accentuate and reinforce the message of the boomerang effect, making direct and implicit threats of revenge attacks following counter-terrorism actions and targeted killings. For example, after the killing of Hezbollah Secretary General Abbas al-Musawi on February 16, 1992, the movement's spiritual leader, Sheikh Muhammad Fadlallah, said, "The jihad battles against the Zionist enemy have begun on all fronts, on the political, security and military levels" (Druckman, 2013). During Musawi's funeral procession, which was attended by some 50,000 Shiite Muslims, participants cried out for revenge on Israel and the United States. Hezbollah's Deputy Secretary Naim Qassem declared, "You have not won. We are waiting for you. The earth will yet tremble under your feet" (Ibid). And indeed, Hezbollah's first retaliation for Musawi's elimination was not long in coming—it was carried out only a few hours after the targeted killing, with the organization firing dozens of rockets at Israeli communities in Israeli's northern border. The artillery fire toward Israel continued over the days that followed, in one instance killing a five-year-old girl (Ibid). The campaign of revenge did not stop there. Not long after Musawi's elimination, a security officer at the Israeli embassy in Ankara was killed by an explosive device that was attached to his car (Ben Yishai, 2003). Then. about a month after the operation, on March 17, 1992, a mass-casualty attack took place at the Israeli embassy in Buenos Aires. A suicide bomber detonated a car bomb carrying between 250 to 340 kg of TNT explosives next to the embassy building. The attack killed 29 people and injured hundreds more (The 20th anniversary of the attack on the Israeli embassy in Buenos Aires, 2012).

Another example of the fallout from a targeted killing, one that illustrates the terrorist organizations' desire and ability to seek retribution in the short term, is that of Abu Ali Mustafa, the leader of the Popular Front for the Liberation of Palestine, in 2001. Mustafa had established military cells throughout the West Bank to carry out terrorist attacks. These cells focused mainly on attacks using booby-trapped cars (Hass, 2001). Following Mustafa's elimination, the PFLP threatened to "harm Israeli leaders and civilians." Rabah Mohana, one of the organization's leaders, declared, "We will seek to target and harm Israeli criminal leaders to respond to the assassination of Abu Ali Mustafa and to block further Israeli attacks on Palestinian leaders...After this crime, every Israeli citizen and every Israeli leader must feel he is a target...The assassination of a Palestinian leader, an Arab leader, will not pass without punishment...We must respond in such a way as to deter Israelis from new attacks on Palestinian leaders" (Waked & Frisch, 2001). Later, the PFLP's military faction announced that the response would be "rapid and painful...The occupation has opened the door to hell and the flames will reach all Zionists everywhere" (Ibid). After Mustafa's death, Ahmad Sa'adat was named as the organization's secretary general. Upon his appointment, he pledged that the State of Israel would pay for the killing of Abu Ali Mustafa. Indeed, on October 17, 2001, the Israeli Minister of Tourism, Rehavam Ze'evi ("Gandhi") was assassinated in a Jerusalem hotel. The PFLP took responsibility for the murder as vengeance for Abu Ali Mustafa (Levy, 2020). According to the Israeli defense establishment, the assassination had been planned for about two weeks by Sa'adat and the commander of the organization's military wing, Ahad Olma (Representing the hard line of the PFLP, 2002).

Revenge attacks, when they occur, can upset the balance of the effectiveness of targeted killing operations, as they lead to claims that the cost of the action outweighs the benefit. Such arguments stem from an understanding of the phenomenon of terrorism as a form of psychological warfare. The terrorists know that they are incapable of defeating the enemy state, and therefore their main goal is to sow fear and anxiety and lower the morale of the public (Israel Democracy Institute, 1997). Targeted killings are intended, among other things, to restore public confidence and strengthen its faith in the state's ability to fight its terrorist enemies effectively and exact a price from them (Ganor, 2017). Revenge attacks can elicit exactly the opposite effect—they can stir anxiety and decrease the public's sense of personal security and morale. This is what former Deputy Director of the ISA **Gideon Ezra** claimed in 1997, when he said that the desire to gratify Israeli society and raise its morale in the wake of terrorist attacks is legitimate, but not always right, as the Israeli public is very unstable. Ezra offered the example of the killing of Musawi in 1992. After the operation, he said, the Israeli public was euphoric. This, however, was soon replaced by depression following the attack on the Israeli embassy in Argentina in response to the elimination (Israel Democracy Institute, 1997).

Former IDF Chief of Staff **Moshe Ya'alon** cites as an example of a tactical boomerang effect the attacks carried out after the elimination of "The Engineer" Yahya Ayyash:

> His killing resulted in four revenge attacks, out of five that were planned. I was then head of Military Intelligence, and I brought the information to Peres and Arafat to warn them of these revenge attacks, which were

planned to be carried out after Eid al-Fitr. It was clear to me that Hamas and Islamic Jihad were going to carry out five revenge attacks. We had information. We knew we had to foil them. It was in the days when Arafat was responsible in Gaza. He was supposed to take care of it. But unfortunately, he brushed us off and allowed them to happen.[1]

Indeed, four retaliatory attacks were carried out following Ayyash's elimination. Shimon Peres, however, who was serving as prime minister at the time, dismisses the claim that these attacks were the result of a boomerang effect in the wake of Ayyash's killing. "It's a journalistic dilemma. There's the story with the 'Engineer.' To me it's nonsense, because we knew the engineer was going to carry out more attacks. Let's say we hadn't eliminated him, and he would have carried out the attacks. What would they say then—'Couldn't you have prevented it?'".[2]

Shimon Peres is not the only one who rejects the tactical boomerang claim. Many Israeli decision-makers, both at the political and the security level, believe that targeted killings should not be linked to the occurrence of revenge attacks in their wake. According to **Meir Dagan**, former head of the Mossad, the "boomerang effect" is nothing but cunning psychological warfare on the part of the terrorist organization, whose purpose is to create a balance of deterrence vis-à-vis Israel. In Dagan's view, large-scale attacks that were attributed to the boomerang effect because they took place after an Israeli action would have been carried out in any case, even if at a later stage (Ganor, 2017). In his words:

> Suppose I didn't do the action [the targeted killing]. Would the organization still have carried out its plans? To the best of my judgement, yes. Perhaps a little differently, perhaps at a different time, on a different schedule, but in general, would the actions have been carried out? The answer is yes. That's why I say that in its true essence, there is no boomerang phenomenon...so the bottom line is that we should act as if it does not exist. I'm talking about the operational aspect. In this aspect, in my opinion, the State of Israel [should define] its military goals without any regard for the boomerang phenomenon.[3]

---

[1] Personal interview with Moshe ("Bogie") Ya'alon, February 17, 2002.

[2] Personal interview with Shimon Peres, February 11, 2000.

[3] Personal interview with Meir Dagan, December 4, 1998.

Referring to academic analyses that point to a supposed boomerang effect, **Asa Kasher** maintains that these involve statistical manipulations that are derived from an examination of a defined period of time following the targeted killing operation. "I believe there is a bluff in articles that claim that this measure does more harm than good. That's not true. It depends on how you cut reality into chunks of time. When you analyze chunks of time in a distorted manner, you create the impression of a boomerang. I think that's not accurate."[4] Former Mossad Chief **Shabtai Shavit** continues this argument, saying that in fact, "There is no empirical tool to test whether targeted killings lead to revenge attacks."[5] Former Defense Minister and IDF Chief of Staff **Shaul Mofaz**, however, proposes examining this issue over a long period of time: "It is true that following targeted killings, for a certain period of time there have been attempts to exact revenge, and there have even been revenge attacks—there's no question about that. But did it raise the level of terrorism? No way."[6] According to Mofaz, when looking at the longer term, the boomerang effect is negligible.

The claim that the tactical boomerang effect of revenge attacks does not actually exist can be explained using the terrorism equation described above. According to proponents of this argument, the main variable in the terrorist equation is the terrorist organization's capability to carry out attacks, whereas the second variable –motivation—is a constant, because terrorist organizations by definition want to carry out attacks. Therefore, even if the targeted killing increases the motivation for revenge attacks, this at most accelerates a terrorist attack that would have taken place anyway, even if the operation hadn't taken place. On the basis of this analysis, it can also be argued that during a period when a terrorist organization is having difficulty carrying out terrorist attacks, and the capability variable is what is limiting the scope of attacks, even if their motivation increases due to a targeted killing, the organization, despite its desire, will be incapable of executing significant attacks.

An example that supports this line of reasoning is the targeted killing of Hamas founder and leader Sheikh Ahmad Yassin in March 2004. Yassin was released from Israeli prison in September 1997, in response

---

[4] Personal interview with Asa Kasher, February 23, 2022.

[5] Personal interview with Shabtai Shavit, February 17, 2022.

[6] Personal interview with Shaul Mofaz, February 23, 2022.

to the demand by Jordan's King Hussein in the wake of the botched Israeli operation to kill Hamas official Khaled Mashal in Amman, and in exchange for the release of the Israeli agents imprisoned in Jordan. Upon his release, Yassin continued to direct Hamas policy from the Gaza Strip, becoming one of the Israeli security services' most wanted men. In the wake of the severe terrorist attacks carried out with the outbreak of the al-Aqsa Intifada in the early 2000s, Israel attempted to eliminate Yassin during a meeting of the leaders of Hamas's military wing in Gaza on September 6, 2003. The attempt failed, according to the heads of the Israeli defense establishment, due to concerns over proportionality and the desire to avoid major collateral damage. On March 22, 2004, another targeted killing attempt was made against Yassin, this time successful; Yassin was struck by Hellfire missiles fired from attack helicopters as he was leaving a mosque. Two of his bodyguards were killed along with him, and other people were wounded, including two of his sons. Following Yassin's elimination, senior Hamas officials declared, "We will respond to any killing of a Palestinian leader. The force of our response will be consistent with the target that was attacked" (Berger, 2004a, 2004b). It is hard to imagine a greater motivation for Hamas to seek revenge than the elimination of their leader and the founder of their movement. And if that did not suffice, about a month after Yassin's death, in April 2004, Israel carried out another targeted killing operation in Gaza against the man appointed as his successor and the new Hamas leader, Abdel Aziz al-Rantissi. Following Sheikh Yassin's death and his appointment as his successor, Rantissi announced that under his leadership, the organization would carry out more terrorist attacks to strike Israelis: "We will chase them everywhere. We will teach them a lesson in confrontation" (*Rantissi: I am the leader of Hamas*, 2004). However, despite the two consecutive targeted killings and repeated Hamas threats, the organization did not carry out any significant retaliatory action; it was only after four months that two suicide bombings were carried out on buses in Be'er Sheva. The attacks killed 16 passengers and injured about 80. Hamas spokesmen declared that these were vengeance attacks for the deaths of their two leaders.

Former Air Force Commander and IDF Chief of Staff **Dan Halutz** believe that in planning and preparing for targeted killing operations, there is no need to take the fear of tactical boomerang attacks into account, because "if you take them into account, you're tying your hands behind your back. We have to fight as if there is no tomorrow and worry about tomorrow as if there is no war."[7]

The public opinion poll conducted by the International Institute for Counter-Terrorism (ICT) at Reichman University in early 2022 shows that 69 percent of the Israeli public support Halutz's position, believing that the potential for revenge attacks by terrorist organizations after targeted killings (i.e., the boomerang effect) should not impact, or should influence only to a small extent, the decision to carry them out. In comparison, 16 percent believe that the boomerang effect should have a major impact on such a decision.

Whether or not a targeted killing leads to retaliatory attacks, former ISA Director **Avi Dichter** believes that "In fighting terrorism, you can't work under the assumption that if you don't carry out targeted killings then you won't have retaliatory actions." In his view, if they are not revenge attacks, "then they will be regular attacks. What's the difference between a revenge attack and a regular attack? Nothing. Apart from the name. Therefore, in combatting terrorism, you must work according to your capabilities, your intelligence, your operational ethics, but you must always continue to act."[8]

Former IDF Chief of Staff **Moshe Ya'alon** concurs with Dichter, saying that even if there is an assessment that the targeted killing will lead to a revenge attack, the operation must sometimes be carried out nonetheless."[9] Another former IDF Chief of Staff, **Amnon Lipkin-Shahak**, also said that the phenomenon of the tactical boomerang does sometimes occur and should be taken into account before carrying out a targeted killing, but the decision, he claimed, should be based on a comprehensive outlook and should find the right balance.[10]

Yigal Pressler, former counter-terrorism adviser to the prime minister, suggests not examining the effectiveness of targeted killings in the short term, but rather over time. Moreover, he believes that if revenge attacks take place, then Israel must continue to escalate its actions against the terrorist organizations so that it will ultimately have the upper hand.[11]

---

[7] Personal interview with Dan Halutz, March 4, 2022.

[8] Personal interview with Avi Dichter, March 11, 2022.

[9] Personal interview with Moshe ("Bogie") Ya'alon, February 17, 2002.

[10] Personal interview with Amnon Lipkin-Shahak, December 23, 1999.

[11] Personal interview with Yigal Pressler, October 31, 1999.

Former Prime Minister **Ariel Sharon** agreed with this approach, saying, "The most dangerous thing is to do something [a targeted killing], and then they do to you what they do [revenge attacks] and you retreat and don't respond any further."[12] Former Defense Minister **Moshe Arens** actually saw revenge attacks carried out by terrorist organizations following targeted killings as conclusive proof that the operation had achieved its goal—hurting terrorists to the extent that they found themselves obligated to respond. "I don't know if they would have blown up our embassy [in Buenos Aires] if we hadn't killed Musawi, and I think this expresses the fact that an event like his elimination causes them strain, and puts them in a position in which they feel obligated to carry out such an action." Arens emphasized in this context that when targeted killings are carried out sporadically, they are, in his words, "counterproductive"—in his view, counter-terrorism policy against terrorist organizations requires such actions to be carried out in a systematic and ongoing manner, which will impair their capability over time and intimidate their operatives.[13]

OPERATIONAL BOOMERANG EFFECT—MILITARY AND/OR DIPLOMATIC IMBROGLIOS

An operational boomerang effect may manifest in military or diplomatic entanglement following targeted killings of terrorist operatives. An operation carried out by special military forces or undercover units may go awry—the forces may be exposed too soon, or be ambushed and find themselves involved in unexpected combat. Such an incident could escalate and end in ground or air rescue with the deployment of substantial military forces. A military entanglement may also result from the absence of an operational intelligence detail, such as the presence of various military forces in the arena, or unknown operational capabilities or special weapons in the possession of the enemy. Alternatively, the entanglement may be the result of a severe operational malfunction (such as a helicopter of the attacking force crashing, a weapons malfunction or failure, the capture of operatives and their being held in captivity or brought to trial, etc.). This type of entanglement can exact a high price, ranging from military escalation to the attacking state being forced to release

---

[12] Personal interview with Ariel Sharon, September 13, 2000.

[13] Personal interview with Moshe Arens, 19 February 1996.

convicted terrorists in a prisoner exchange deal in order to free its captives (see below for the case study of the targeted killing of Khaled Mashal). These released terrorists may rejoin the terrorist organization and carry out further, even more serious, terrorist attacks in the future. The failure of a targeted killing operation and the release of terrorists from prison may also strengthen the terrorist organization's status and help the organization's efforts to recruit more operatives to its ranks (Falk & Hefetz, 2019).

An Israeli military entanglement following a targeted killing may occur in various areas, such as the Gaza Strip, the West Bank, Lebanon, or another enemy state, and may lead to an escalation in violence between the parties. Moreover, even a successful targeted killing operation that did not result in a direct military entanglement, could trigger rocket barrages toward the Israeli home front, which in turn would elicit a powerful response by the Israeli Air Force to stop the rocket fire, potentially resulting a round of violence between the two sides or even a military operation. In this regard, former IDF Chief of Staff **Gadi Eisenkot** says that from the moment the Palestinian retaliatory attacks were added to the equation, the balance of deterrence changed. Eisenkot highlights the fact that targeted killings in the Gaza Strip could lead to rocket fire, so in today's reality, "The decision to carry out a targeted killing must be derived from the intelligence picture, and when the operation is deemed likely to bring about an improvement in Israel's national security, it should be carried out even at the cost of the firing of rockets on Tel Aviv."[14]

Former ISA official **Arik "Harris" Barbing** adds that the danger of escalation, and the possibility of being dragged into a round of fighting— in the past mainly in the West Bank, and today principally in the Gaza Strip—is indeed taken into account in the decision-making process on carrying out targeted killings.[15]

Against this backdrop, former head of the Mossad's Intelligence Directorate **Amnon Sofrin** notes that the fear of a military entanglement necessitates the tightening of cooperation between the various bodies involved in targeted killings, for example between the IDF and the ISA. He says that when the ISA is planning to carry out a targeted killing operation, it must coordinate with the person in the IDF responsible for

---

[14] Personal interview with Gadi Eisenkot, March 2, 2022.

[15] Personal interview with Arik "Harris" Barbing February 21, 2022.

the sector in question—the brigade commander, the division commander, etc., as they should be aware of the matter and take into account its possible implications for the area. According to Sofrin, the military is likely to suffer the "ricochets" of the operation.[16]

Avi Eliyahu maintains that the fear of such an operative boomerang effect leads to paralysis and the decision to refrain from going through with certain targeted killings. He believes that targeted killings are a very important counter-terrorism measure, but that the adversary (Hamas and Islamic Jihad in the Gaza Strip and Hezbollah in Lebanon) now understand that they can impact Israeli decision-making processes in this regard by threatening violence and the launching of rockets at Israel. Eliyahu describes a kind of "mutual deterrence" that has developed between the parties and notes, "I think the main consideration is the concern over escalation...the fact that they have the ability to respond in a way that can disrupt our daily lives and affect Israeli decision making, the balance of deterrence between the parties, and the use of the measure of targeted killing."[17]

The operational boomerang may, as stated, also be manifested in a diplomatic imbroglio and damage to the bilateral or multilateral diplomatic relationship between Israel and other countries. Such harm may be the result of the revealing of the identities of the operatives in a targeted killing operation that took place on the soil of a state that is an Israeli ally, or when it turns out that the operatives were posing as citizens of that country, or were carrying false documentation indicating that they were nationals of a different country. For example, in January 2010, a targeted killing, which was attributed to Israel, was carried out in Dubai against senior Hamas operative Mahmoud al-Mabhouh. Mabhouh was, among other things, a liaison between Hamas and Iran and was engaged in the transfer of weapons to the Gaza Strip. He was personally involved in the abduction and murder of two IDF soldiers, Avi Sasportas and Ilan Saadon, in 1989. Mabhouh was killed in his room at a Dubai hotel by a cell who, according to the chief of the Dubai Police, belonged to the Mossad. Following the investigation of the affair by the local police, photographs and identifying details were released about 33 suspects who were alleged to have taken part in the targeted killing operation. The

[16] Personal interview with Amnon Sofrin, February 22, 2022.

[17] Personal interview with Avi Eliyahu, March 2, 2022.

Dubai police claimed that some of the suspects carried UK, Irish and Australian passports. These allegations brought about a diplomatic crisis and punitive measures against Israel. About two months after the incident, Britain expelled an Israeli diplomat who was claimed by *The Daily Telegraph* to be a Mossad representative in the country, and two months later, Australia did the same. The United Arab Emirates expelled the head of Israel's secret mission that had been operating in the country until then (Ravid, 2022).

Former ISA official **Shalom Ben Hanan** uses this example to illustrate the importance of taking into account the possible diplomatic operational boomerang effect when planning and approving targeted killings. In his words,

> In making a decision on targeted killing, it is also necessary to take into account broader considerations and implications, for example policy, and include them in the decision-making process. A tactical targeted killing may have broad strategic consequences and may not always be the right move. In operations such as the one against Khaled Mashal in Jordan, or the one against Mahmoud Mabhouh which was attributed to Israel, the ramifications must be considered even if the operation is successful, and certainly when the original plan goes awry. There may be far-reaching implications way beyond the consequences of the operation. According to reports in the foreign media, passports of friendly countries were used in the Mahmoud Mabhouh operation; the diplomatic outcry was harsh and threatened our relations with those countries. This type of consideration affects much broader circles and sometimes has strategic implications.[18]

Former Mossad Director **Shabtai Shavit** says in this context that diplomatic considerations become much more central when the targeted killing is carried out in a friendly country, as opposed to the territory of an enemy state. "Diplomatic concerns should be taken into account, in case of a mishap, even when it comes to passports or helpers that are from an allied country... The decision whether to carry out targeted killings in a friendly country goes to the prime minister."[19] **Asa Kasher**, on the other hand, does not give too much weight to international criticism in the context of targeted killings, saying, "The expression 'international legitimacy' seems

---

[18] Personal interview with Shalom Ben Hanan, February 21, 2022.

[19] Personal interview with Shabtai Shavit, February 17, 2022.

to me a vague expression that people use to give themselves power. What exactly is international legitimacy? Who provides it? How does one provide it? Why is it important?" Kasher maintains that the world does not set itself a higher moral standard than Israel does, and is therefore not entitled to criticize its actions. On the contrary, Israel acts out of self-defense, with strict criteria regarding proportionality. Kasher distinguishes between international legitimacy or moral espousal of targeted killings and Israeli diplomatic interests, especially vis-à-vis the US administration and the UN Security Council, which are, in Kasher's opinion, the only two bodies whose position should be taken into consideration in Israel's decision-making process.[20]

In any case, the decision to carry out a targeted killing operation that is "low profile" and leaves "room for denial" for all parties—the attacking state, the country in which the operation takes place, and the terrorist organization to which the target belongs, may reduce the risk of military or diplomatic entanglement. Former Director of the Counter-Terrorism Bureau at the Prime Minister's Office **Nitzan Nuriel** says in this context that sometimes the other side needs a vague and broad enough explanation to avoid attributing the operation to Israel and claim that it may have been carried out by another party. Moreover, if the plan of the operation includes an element according to which the action is exposed only after a long period of time, the time elapsed may also help obscure Israel's responsibility for the action (Nuriel calls this the "cooling off effect").[21]

Strategic Boomerang Effect—long-Term Consequences

The strategic boomerang effect may be seen when there are serious consequences of a targeted killing that persist over time. These may be the result of the elimination of a terrorist leader or senior official and his replacement by another and more dogmatic leader; the increasing of the terrorist organization's motivation to obtain new technological or operational capabilities that will change the balance between the organization and the state and deter the latter from carrying out similar operations in

---

[20] Personal interview with Asa Kasher, February 23, 2022.

[21] Personal interview with Nitzan Nuriel, February 14, 2022.

the future; the acceleration of the organization's armament or its development of new types of threats, or the boosting of the status of the terrorists in the eyes of their public, the deepening of hatred, and the intensification of the entire conflict. **Daniel Reisner** explains this by saying, "Every escalation you undertake leads to escalation on the other side...that is, when you invent something new, you're also creating motivation for the other side to invent something new, to get you back. These are matters that need to be taken into consideration. I can only say that in the system, it's very difficult to factor in such considerations. Everyone is busy with the question of how to prevent tomorrow's terrorist attack. The thinking is very tactical."[22] Former ISA official **Oz Noy** explains how targeted killings can contribute to the bolstering of the status of terrorists, explaining that sometimes these operations were double-edged swords; they gave prominence to people who were known to be on Israel's "most-wanted" list. In his words, "In many cases, these were just criminals, thieves, rapists, human scum who became superheroes on the Palestinian street. They became an object of admiration. And then we saw that there were quite a few activists who did everything they could to become 'wanted,' in order to gain this status. To transform from people who were nothing to the idols of the street, the idols of the youth."[23]

Former Director of the Counter-Terrorism Bureau at the Prime Minister's Office **Nitzan Nuriel** also refers to the erosion in deterrence that may result from targeted killings: "There is a certain point at which these arch-terrorists understand that it will happen to them, come to terms with this fact, and even 'anticipate it' to some extent, and therefore the deterrence fades." Nuriel goes on to explain, "How many times have we eliminated the number one wanted terrorist in Jenin? Probably 10 times. Because when you eliminate the number one wanted terrorist, the number two wanted terrorist then becomes the number one." Nuriel points to the fact that in a large institutionalized organization, such as Hamas, there is no shortage of replacements. The only question is whether the replacement is as dangerous and skilled as his predecessor, falls short of him, or exceeds his capabilities.[24]

---

[22] Personal interview with Daniel Reisner, April 8, 2022.

[23] Personal interview with Oz Noy, February 16, 2022.

[24] Personal interview with Nitzan Nuriel, February 14, 2022.

As mentioned, a clear example of a strategic boomerang effect is when the elimination of an organization's leader or senior official leads to his replacement by another figure who is more militant and influential than his predecessor, or bolder and more skillful, and therefore poses a greater danger to the state and its citizens. (See the discussion on the targeted killing of terrorist leaders in Chapter Four).

The targeted killing of a leader of a terrorist organization is a strategic counter-terrorism operation. Such an action may have geostrategic implications in the local, regional, and even global arena (an example of this is bin Laden's elimination and its impact on global terrorism and the strengthening of al-Qaeda's rival ISIS). The degree of effectiveness of a targeted killing of a terrorist organization's leader should therefore be assessed with regard to certain questions and variables, such as the impact of the leader's elimination on the organization's terrorism policy—will a new leader adopt a policy on terrorist attacks that is more aggressive or more moderate than that of his predecessor? What will the degree of lethality and sophistication of these attacks be? Furthermore, the impact of the targeted killing of the organization's leader should be evaluated in connection to the new leader's worldview, the degree of his pragmatism, dogmatism, and aggressiveness, as well as the implications of the change in leadership on the chances of resolving the conflict peacefully. The personal characteristics of the leader to be targeted must be compared with those of the person who will likely be chosen to take his place; these include their personal status among the organization's members, their charisma and their ability to enrapture their followers, the trust placed in them by the public they claim to represent, their religious or ideological status, their standing and connections with regional and international actors such as state sponsors of terrorism, the nature of their decision-making processes (centralized or decentralized), and more. The answers to these and other questions impact the assessment of the strategic boomerang effect.

The decision to carry out the targeted killing of a leader of a terrorist organization should clearly, therefore, take into account who may be appointed as his replacement. The personal characteristics of the two leaders, as stated above, must be weighed, keeping in mind that the degree of support they receive and the strength of their authority is often a result of their personal charisma (Price, 2019). Their status may also be a function of their religious or ideological authority, their closeness to the "founding generation" and previous leaders of the organization, and so on. Although some believe that terrorist operatives who replace leaders eliminated in targeted killing operations are generally less experienced than their predecessors, and therefore the percentage of failed terrorist attacks following the elimination will increase and the number of casualties will decrease (Ben-Israel, 2006), it must be borne in mind that there is no senior operative or terrorist leader who is irreplaceable. While the replacement may perhaps be less skilled than his predecessor, he may also be more dangerous (Kremnitzer, 2006).

A clear example of this is the change in Hezbollah's leadership in the early 1990s, following Israel's targeted killing of the organization's leader Abbas al-Musawi. In retrospect, the leader who replaced Musawi, Hassan Nasrallah, turned out to be more charismatic, more skilled, and more dangerous than his predecessor. Nasrallah, a captivating Shiite cleric, faithfully represented the most extreme line in Hezbollah, characterized by a hatred of Jews and Israel, and sought to bring about the destruction of the state in every way possible (Druckman, 2013). Indeed, after Nasrallah's appointment as Hezbollah's secretary general, the organization expanded its belligerence against IDF forces stationed in southern Lebanon, and eventually transformed from an uninstitutionalized Shiite militia into an organized military organization armed with tens of thousands of rockets and anti-aircraft, anti-tank, and coastal missiles. Nasrallah led Hezbollah's establishment as a hybrid terrorist organization, controlling territory and population, and in addition to its military wing also advanced its social and political wing, making electoral and other gains in the Lebanese government (already in the first year of his tenure, Hezbollah won 12 seats in the Lebanese parliament). Moreover, under Nasrallah's leadership Hezbollah has carried out major terrorist attacks against Israel, including the abduction of Israeli soldiers (Levy, 2021) and under Iranian orders even joined the defense of the Assad regime in Syria. This example of Musawi's replacement by Nasrallah contradicts the claim made by **Shaul Mofaz**, who served as defense minister and IDF chief of staff, according to which "Whoever takes the eliminated leader's place takes time to integrate, and also lives with a sense of being hunted. He invests in self-defense and shies away from some of the actions that have been planned" (Levy, 2020). Although since taking on the role, and to this day, Nasrallah has been careful to protect himself and tends to avoid public appearances, this does not seem to have harmed his ability to lead the organization and even escalate its military and terrorist activities.

Among the rationales given for the effectiveness of targeted killings of terrorist leaders is the argument that the urgent need to locate a replacement leader may whip up rivalry and competition between senior operatives in the organization's top ranks "contending for the crown." For example, following the elimination of Hamas leader Ahmad Yassin, Abdel Aziz al-Rantissi announced that he was now the leader of the organization, as Sheikh Yassin had appointed him as his deputy while he was alive. However, Said Siam, another senior Hamas official, announced that the new leader would be Khaled Mashal, the head of Hamas's political bureau. Ultimately, at the end of the period of mourning Rantissi was chosen as Yassin's successor (*Rantissi: I am the leader of Hamas*, 2004). Although the internal competition did not appear to prevent an orderly transfer of power to Rantissi, neither he nor his successor, the "domestic" leader of Hamas (inside the Gaza Strip) Ismail Haniyeh, succeeded in approaching the status of Ahmad Yassin, the organization's founding leader, who was regarded as the supreme military, political, religious, and ideological authority of Hamas.

Another rationale for the effectiveness of targeted killings of an organization's leaders and senior operatives is that the act will deter others from serving in senior positions in the organization, which will, in turn, disrupt its activities. This assessment is based on the assumption that, in principle, the leaders of terrorist organizations are not suicide terrorists and are indeed afraid of death (Plotzker, 2004). Regarding the effect of disruption to the organization's activities due to the elimination of a terrorist leader or senior operative, in 2002, a Hamas spokesman even acknowledged this, saying "I cannot help but admit that the killing and arresting of Hamas leaders has an impact on our ability to work" (Ganor, 2017, p. 76) However, it would appear that although this type of disruption does occur, its effect is in most cases temporary and short-term.

On the other hand, the elimination of members of the top echelons of a terrorist organization can have long-term detrimental effects—the removal of the operative can lead to the decentralization of leadership, chaos, and a lack of control over the organization's terrorist activities; it may also remove from the arena a leader whose authority and charisma has the potential to make him a key player in the future in reaching a compromise and perhaps even bringing an end to the conflict. Such criticism has indeed been leveled at Israel after it eliminated senior terrorist operatives (David, 2003). One such example may have been the targeted killing of Khalil al-Wazir, also known as "Abu Jihad," Yasser Arafat's deputy in the

Fatah organization. As head of Fatah's military wing, he was responsible for carrying out numerous terrorist attacks, and was even deemed responsible for the outbreak of the First Intifada in the territories in 1987. The operation targeting Abu Jihad was carried out in Tunis in 1988. Although Israel hoped that his elimination would lead to the subsiding of the uprising in the territories, this did not occur. In retrospect, his death seems to have left a deep void in the Palestinian leadership, leaving Yasser Arafat, then-head of the Palestinian Authority, alone, without the counsel of a talented and pragmatic strategist (Melman, 2004). The Intifada spiraled into a phenomenon that the Palestinian leadership was unable to control and curb. Moreover, it is possible that if Abu Jihad had continued to serve as head of Fatah's military wing, a few years later, with the beginning of the Oslo process between Israel and the Palestinians in 1992, he may have helped rein in the terrorist groups (Hamas and Islamic Jihad) who opposed the agreement and carried out suicide bombings in Israel in order to derail it.

In conclusion, the strategic boomerang effect that can occur due to the elimination of a leader or senior official of a terrorist organization is difficult to measure and assess. In most cases, it is not known who will be chosen as a replacement, and certainly, the familiarity with the replacement will be limited in comparison to that of the target himself. Therefore, these assessments are usually carried out retrospectively, as an historical analysis, long after the targeted killing has taken place.

Case Study of a Targeted Killing with an Operative Boomerang effect—the Attempt on Khaled Mashal

Background: Khaled Mashal was born in 1956 in the West Bank village of Silwad, and moved to Kuwait with his family after the Six Day War in 1967. In 1971, Mashal joined the Muslim Brotherhood, and after the establishment of Hamas, he began to be active within the organization. Mashal later moved to Jordan, where he was responsible for the organization's international fundraising efforts (*Profile: Khaled Meshaal of Hamas*, 2006). In 1996, he was appointed as chairman of Hamas's political bureau, based in Amman (Melman, 2007).

Preparations for operation: In 1997, two major suicide bombings were carried out in Jerusalem within one month of each other. The first took place in the Mahane Yehuda market in Jerusalem. Two Hamas suicide bombers, disguised as ultra-Orthodox Jews, detonated, killing 16 people and wounding 170. The second attack, which took place about a month later, was a triple suicide bombing on the Ben Yehuda pedestrian mall in central Jerusalem; five people were killed and more than 90 were injured in the attack. Then-Prime Minister of Israel Benjamin Netanyahu and the diplomatic-security cabinet decided to carry out targeted killings of senior Hamas leaders. Head of the Mossad at the time, Danny Yatom, deliberated with the heads of the Mossad's departments and operational units, including the commander of "Caesarea," the special operations division; the head of "Tevel," the division responsible for relations with foreign intelligence organizations; the commander of "Tzomet," the division responsible for gathering intelligence through agents; the head of the research division, and others, to decide on the targets. Yatom asked for a list of potential targets, but it emerged that the majority of the Hamas leadership was in the Palestinian territories (and therefore the responsibility of the ISA and not the Mossad). The two senior Hamas officials living outside of the territories were Khaled Mashal and Moussa Abu Marzouk, deputy head of Hamas's political bureau. Marzouk was an American citizen, and so it was decided not to target him in order to avoid damaging Israel's relationship with the United States. Khaled Mashal, however, who was living in Jordan, was easily accessible and the intelligence gathered on him was abundant. It was therefore decided that he would be the target of the operation (Melman, 2007). There was a concern, though, that killing Mashal in the territory of Jordan, which only three years earlier had signed a peace agreement with Israel, could lead to a strategic boomerang in the form of serious damage to the bilateral relations between the two countries. For this reason, a covert and special method was chosen that would not leave an Israeli "fingerprint" (Melman, 2007). Moreover, an instruction was given before the operation that it should not be carried out at any cost, and that if there was not absolute certainty that the operation would succeed, it must be aborted (Dayan, 1997).

Prior to the operation, intelligence material was collected with regard to Mashal's routine conduct in Amman, and detailed plans of the operation were prepared, including an escape route (Melman, 2007). In retrospect, it emerged that during the planning of the operation, in the month of September, King Hussein of Jordan sent a message to Benjamin

Netanyahu saying that Hamas was ready for a ceasefire, but the message did not reach its destination (Dayan, 1997).

The attempt: After the operation was approved by Netanyahu, and following the intelligence gathering process, which lasted about three weeks, the targeted killing attempt was carried out on September 25, 1997. Mossad agents arrived in Jordan on various flights, using forged Canadian passports. The plan was to surreptitiously inject poison into Mashal's body on one of the streets of Amman. One of the Mossad agents, who was the liaison between Mossad headquarters and the operational cell, had an antibody to the chemical with which they planned to poison Mashal. On the day of the operation, Mossad agents followed Mashal in a rental car from the time he left home and until he reached the building where his office was located. As soon as Mashal got out of the car, one of the agents approached him and another held a device to his ear, transmitting the poison. Mashal collapsed, and the Mossad agents fled toward their escape vehicle. The vehicle was supposed to take them tens of kilometers from the scene, but due to some confusion, after only 300 m, the agents claimed the driver told them to get out, which they did. Mashal's bodyguard, who had been following the agents, caught them and they were arrested by the local police (Gal, 2013). The agents claimed to be Canadian tourists, but this was refuted by the Canadian consulate (Operation Cyrus—The failed attempt on Hamas chief Khaled Mashaal in Jordan, 2018).

Consequences of the operation: The botched operation led to complications in Israel's diplomatic relations with other countries; the attempted killing caused severe damage to Israel's relationship with Jordan. Danny Yatom, then-chief of the Mossad, went to Jordan to ask the king for his help in releasing the imprisoned Mossad agents. King Hussein, on his part, announced that the operation threatened to undermine the peace process, and jeopardized the legitimacy of the king and the Hashemite dynasty. He demanded that Yatom bring the antidote that would save Mashal, as well as the formula of the poison that was used, and claimed that if Mashal died, the peace agreement with Israel would be annulled. He also threatened to execute the Mossad agents in the event that Mashal did not survive. In addition, Jordan closed the Mossad office that had been secretly operating in the country (Cowell, 1997; Gal, 2013; Operation Cyrus—The failed attempt on Hamas chief Khaled Mashaal in Jordan, 2018).

The Mossad did hand over the antidote to the Jordanians and Mashal regained consciousness, but the crisis with the Jordanians was deep and long-lasting. The damage from the strategic boomerang did not end there—in order to prevent the peace agreement with Jordan from being made void, Netanyahu agreed to King Hussein's request to release Sheikh Yassin from Israeli prison and transfer him to the Gaza Strip. In exchange, the two Mossad agents who had been arrested in Jordan were released (Gal, 2013). Furthermore, in light of the Mossad agents' use of forged Canadian passports, Israeli-Canadian relations also suffered a blow. Mossad Chief Danny Yatom was forced to resign from his post (Gal, 2013) and the Mossad entered years of operational stagnation. Hamas, on the other hand, gained popular support and prestige, and Khaled Mashal became a revered figure in the organization (Limor, 2017).

Israel's failed attempt to eliminate Khaled Mashal in Jordan thus led to an operational boomerang effect—a serious diplomatic crisis with a neighboring Arab state. Moreover, the operation also jeopardized Israel's strategic peace relations with Jordan, which had been formulated and signed only a few years earlier. Had the unsuccessful operation indeed led to the severance of diplomatic ties between the two countries, the cancelation of the peace agreement between them, and the escalation of the conflict, it would have led to a long-term strategic, and not just an operational, boomerang effect.

References

Ashkenazi, E. (2019, November 13). From "Spring of Youth" to Yassin: A history of targeted killings. *Walla! News*. https://news.walla.co.il/item/332 3605

Ben-Israel, I. (2006). Dealing with suicide terrorism. In H. Golan & S. Shay 1294 (Eds.), *A ticking bomb [Petzatza metakteket]*. Tel Aviv: Maarachot.

Ben Yishai, R. (2003, November 16). Who said it was bin Laden? *Globes*. https://www.globes.co.il/news/article.aspx?did=741898

Bennet, J. (2002, March 12). Mideast turmoil: News analysis; Mideast balance sheet. *The New York Times*. https://www.nytimes.com/2002/03/12/world/mideast-turmoil-news-analysis-mideast-balance-sheet.html

Benziman, U. (2003, June 12). On the road to nowhere. *Ha'aretz*. https://www.haaretz.co.il/misc/1.888289

Berger, G. (2004a, March 23). In the short term, the motivation for terrorist attacks will increase. *News1*. http://www.news1.co.il/Archive/001-D-42903-00.html?tag=12-39-00

Berger, G. (2004b, March 23). Hezbollah threatens: Israel will be attacked if it continues. *News1*. https://www.news1.co.il/MemberLogin.aspx?ContentType=1&docid=42972&subjectid=1

Blau, U. (2008, November 27). License to kill. *Ha'aretz*. https://www.haaretz.com/1.5066136

Breiner, J. (2008, April 2). Life imprisonment for a Palestinian policeman who murdered Israeli. *Walla! News*. https://news.walla.co.il/item/1259364

Collaborator: "The engineer disguised himself as a woman, answered the phone, exploded and 'salamtak'. (2018, April 22). *Ma'ariv*. https://www.maariv.co.il/news/military/Article-633876

Cowell, A. (1997, October 15). The daring attack that blew up in Israel's face. *The New York Times*. https://www.nytimes.com/1997/10/15/world/the-daring-attack-that-blew-up-in-israel-s-face.html

David, S. (2003). Fatal choices: Israel's policy of targeted killing. *Review of International Affairs, 2*(3), 138.

Dayan, I. (Producer & Director). (1997). *Elimination of Khaled Mashal—Uvda Investigation*. [Video/DVD] Channel 2.

Druckman, Y. (2013, February 16). The elimination that gave rise to Nasrallah. *Ynet*. https://www.ynet.co.il/articles/0,7340,L-4345331,00.html

Encyclopedia—Ideologies, terms and political organizations, Musawi Abbas. Ynet. http://www.ynet.co.il/yaan/0,7340,L-799024-Nzk5MDI0XzE2ODNwNTQ2Nl8xNDg2ODNcyMDAeq-FreeYaan,00.html

Falk, O., & Hefetz, A. (2019). Minimizing unintended deaths enhanced the effectiveness of targeted killing in the Israeli-Palestinian conflict. *Studies in Conflict & Terrorism, 42*(6), 600.

Frisch, F. (2004, March 22). A vicious killer in a wheelchair. *Globes*. https://www.globes.co.il/news/article.aspx?did=782608&fid=2

Gal, S. (2013, October 4). Sixteen years later: Mashal file opened. *N12*. https://www.mako.co.il/news-military/security/Article-449a98746848141004.htm

Ganor, B. (2017). *The counter-terrorism puzzle- A guide for decision makers*.

Ganor, B. (2021). Targeted killings: Ethical & operational dilemmas. *Terrorism & Political Violence, 33*(2), 353.

Hass, A. (2001, August 27). Abu-Ali Mustafa—George Habash's right hand man. *Ha'aretz*. https://www.haaretz.co.il/misc/1.729051

Hess, S. (2019, November 13). The founder, the chief of staff, the money changer: The significant assassinations in Gaza. *Ynet*. https://www.ynet.co.il/articles/0,7340,L-5624182,00.html

Israel Democracy Institute. (1997). *Terrorism and the State—Minutes of Discussion*. Unpublished manuscript.

Judea and Samaria District—The first years. (2018). Israel Police. https://www.gov.il/he/departments/general/police_judea_and_samaria_district_history

Kam, E. (2006). The Ayatollah, Hezbollah, and Hassan Nasrallah. *Strategic Assessment*, 9(2), 9.

Kremnitzer, M. (2006). *Is everything Kosher when dealing with terrirism?* The Israel Democracy Institute.

Levy, E., & Zeitun, Y. (2019, November 12). A "ticking bomb:" This is the senior Islamic Jihad member who was killed. *Ynet*. https://www.ynet.co.il/articles/0,7340,L-5623584,00.html

Levy, E. (2020, September 27). 20 years later: The riots, the severe terrorist attacks, the failed talks, and the missed opportunity that could have changed the picture. *Ma'ariv*. https://www.maariv.co.il/news/military/Article-792221

Levy, S. (2021, June 4). He turned Hezbollah into a terrorist monster: A brief history of Nasrallah. *Mako*. https://www.mako.co.il/pzm-magazine/Article-ff45db65936c971026.htm

Limor, Y. (2017, September 24). Twenty years since the attempt on Mashal: The failure and the lessons. *Israel Hayom*. https://www.israelhayom.co.il/article/505963

Melman, Y. (2004, March 23). Assassinations were once a last resort today, today they are carried out wholesale. *Ha'aretz*. https://www.haaretz.co.il/misc/1.954331

Melman, Y. (2007, September 25). Back to the crime scene. *Ha'aretz*. https://www.haaretz.co.il/misc/1.1444172

Operation Cyrus—The failed attempt on Hamas chief Khaled Mashaal in Jordan. (2018, April 26). *NZivnet*. https://www.nziv.net/6678/

Pedhazur, A. (2004). The new terrorism and the Palestinian arena. In Ministry of Defense (Ed.), *Aspects of terrorism and counter-terrorism*, (pp. 1–183). Tel Aviv: Ministry of Defense.

Plotzker, S. (2004, April 18). A familiar script. *Ynet*. https://www.ynet.co.il/articles/1,7340,L-2904087,00.html

Price, B. (2019). *Targeting top terrorists: Understanding leadership removal in counterterrorism strategy*. Columbia University Press.

Profile: Khaled Meshaal of Hamas. (2006, February 8). *BBC News*. http://news.bbc.co.uk/2/hi/middle_east/3563635.stm

Rantissi: I am the leader of Hamas. (2004, March 24). *Reuters*. https://news.walla.co.il/item/522593

Ravid, B. (2022). *Trump's peace: The Abraham Accords and the reshaping of the Middle East*. Miskal by Yedioth Ahronoth and Chemed Books.

Representing the hard line of the PFLP. (2002, January 15). *Ha'aretz*. https://www.haaretz.co.il/misc/1.764520

Tal, N. (2002). Israel and suicide terrorism. *Strategic. Assessment*, 1(5), 25–32.

The 20th anniversary of the attack on the Israeli embassy in Buenos Aires. (2012). Israel Security Agency. https://www.shabak.gov.il/heritage/affairs/Pages/ArgentineBlast1992.aspx

Waked, A. & Frisch, F. (2001, August 28). Abu Ali Mustafa's funeral is being held in Ramallah. *Ynet.* https://www.ynet.co.il/articles/1,7340,L-1058108,00.html

Waked, A., & Greenberg, H. (2004, March 22). Israel eliminated Hamas leader Sheikh Yassin in Gaza. *Ynet.* https://www.ynet.co.il/articles/0,7340,L-2892347,00.html

Yahav, N. (2008, January 20). Reminder: The last elimination crowned Nasrallah. *Walla! News.* https://news.walla.co.il/item/1224144

Yahav, N. (2010, February 28). Dubai: "Mabhouh was poisoned and choked to death." *Walla! News.* https://news.walla.co.il/item/1648094

Zonder, M. (2001, July 27). Shooting and not crying. *Nrg:* http://www.nrg.co.il/online/archive/ART/169/638.html).

CHAPTER 8

A Decision-Making Model for Targeted Killing Operations

Based on the experience Israel has acquired over the years in carrying out targeted killings of terrorists, the following staged model may be proposed as a decision-making tool; it expresses and weighs the moral dilemmas and considerations regarding effectiveness that are analyzed in this book.[1] The combination of the model's components (described at the end of this chapter) should provide answers to the key questions involved in ordering targeted killings. These include: What is the aim of the action? Who is the right and legitimate target? How essential and urgent is it to carry out the targeted killing? Is there another effective course of action that could achieve the necessary goal? What is the extent of the collateral damage expected in the operation and is it proportionate? Is the action likely to be effective or will the cost outweigh the benefit?

NORMATIVE CONSIDERATIONS AND IMPLICATIONS

The first part of the proposed model examines the central moral dilemmas involved in carrying out targeted killings:

---

[1] The proposed model is based on the model published in Boaz Ganor's 2021 article Targeted killings: Ethical & operational dilemmas, in Terrorism and Political Violence, 33(2), 353–366, 10.1080/09546553.2021.1880234: https://doi.org/10.1080/09546553.2021.1880234

© The Author(s), under exclusive license to Springer Nature Switzerland AG 2022
B. Ganor and L. Koblentz-Stenzler, *Israel's Targeted Killing Policy*, https://doi.org/10.1007/978-3-031-13674-0_8

A. The aim of the targeted killing operation—The objectives that have formed the foundation of Israel's policy of targeted killings in its war on terror can be classified into six groups:

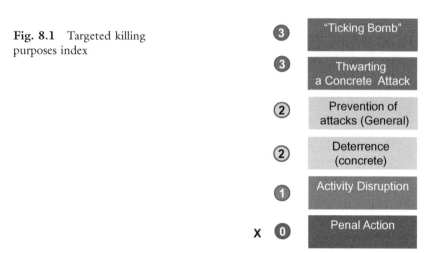

Fig. 8.1 Targeted killing purposes index

1. Targets that are a "ticking bomb"—a ticking bomb, for our purposes, is a terrorist who is at a stage where the necessary preparations for carrying out an attack have already been completed and where the terrorists are either already on their way to executing the attack or are about to embark on it. The thwarting of these terrorists (whether they are the perpetrators themselves or other terrorists in the chain of command and control of the attack, or are a key link in the execution of the attack), will result in the prevention of a concrete terrorist attack.
2. Targets involved in the preparations for a concrete attack (even when it is only in the initial stages of planning) and whose thwarting may prevent the occurrence of a concrete terrorist attack.
3. "Ticking infrastructure" targets—i.e., military commanders in terrorist organizations that play a central role in the execution of terrorist attacks, or terrorist operatives with the unique technical knowledge required to carry out attacks, whose thwarting

is very likely to prevent terrorist attacks, even when there may not be an indication of a concrete one about to take place at the time of the targeted killing.

4. Deterrence—Targeted killings designed to achieve a concrete deterrent effect on terrorist operatives holding similar positions in the same organization or fellow organizations.

5. Disruption of the organization's activities—These targeted killings are intended to thwart a key operative in the terrorist organization in order to disrupt the organization's activities, even when it is not necessarily possible to point to a direct connection between the terrorist and a particular concrete attack.

6. Punitive action—In these cases, the operation is carried out as punishment and retaliation against specific terrorist operatives or their comrades for terrorist acts committed in the past.

In the framework of the proposed model, the first two groups are attributed a high score (3 points per group on a scale of 1 to 3) as they reflect targeted killings intended to neutralize a concrete attack. The third and fourth groups receive a moderate score (2) because they are intended to thwart terrorist attacks in general, when a direct connection to a particular concrete attack cannot be made. The fifth group, reflecting the desire to disrupt the activities of terrorist organizations regardless of the imminence of a concrete attack, is given a low score (1). The sixth and final group reflects a motive that, according to the Supreme Court's rulings, cannot in and of itself constitute grounds for carrying out a targeted killing. Therefore, this group receives a score of 0. Retaliation may be an additional motivation to other legitimate reasons for carrying out a targeted killing, but as the sole motive, it nullifies the legitimacy of a targeted killing. (Fig. 8.1).

B. Identity of the target—One of the main considerations taken into account when carrying out targeted killing operations reflects the principle of "distinction" in international law and deals with the question of the identity of the target. This issue is discussed in detail in Chapter Four in the analysis of the "axis of the profile of the target." The identity of the target can be classified into six groups:

Fig. 8.2 Identity of the target index

1. **Perpetrators of terrorism**—terrorist operatives who carry out the attacks themselves. These can be cells or individual terrorists involved in carrying out various types of attacks, such as shootings, extortion attacks, suicide bombings, and more. (In the above-mentioned profile axis, this category may include both terrorists who are considered a ticking bomb as well as those who are involved in the planning and preparation of concrete terrorist attacks).
2. **Preparers and planners of terrorist attacks**—This group includes terrorist operatives who regularly take part in the planning and preparation of terrorist attacks. Their elimination may therefore prevent the occurrence of future attacks, though not necessarily concrete ones. (In the profile axis, this category may include terrorists defined as "ticking infrastructure").
3. **Military commanders**—Senior terrorist operatives who belong to the military and security wings of the terrorist organizations and who command and manage the organization's military and terrorist activities.
4. **Military operatives**—Terrorist operatives belonging to the military and security wings of the terrorist organizations. These operatives constitute the "fighting force" of the terrorist organization and are involved in its military and terrorist activities.

This category also includes combat support operatives in the terrorist organization.

5. **Political and ideological leaders**—This group comprises the political or ideological leaders of the terrorist organizations.

6. **Supporters of terrorism and accomplices**—This group includes people who are not members of the terrorist organization and are not involved in initiating, planning, or carrying out terrorist attacks, but who are passive supporters of terrorism— they identify with the organization and even openly support it—or active supporters of terrorism—they provide assistance to the terrorist organization by donating money or other means to support its activities.

The first two groups are given a maximum score of (3), as they represent targets involved in the stages of preparation and execution of terrorist attacks. As military commanders or operatives, the third and fourth groups constitute legitimate targets, but because they are not necessarily involved in carrying out attacks, they receive a moderate score (2). The fifth and sixth groups represent people whom it is illegitimate to target in the context of targeted killings, since they are not defined as military operatives and/or those involved in the execution of terrorist attacks. Hence, the score given to these groups is 0. However, it should be emphasized that in many terrorist organizations, the political and ideological leaders are also those who determine the organization's military policy and terrorism strategy, and in many cases even order the execution of concrete attacks. In these cases, the organization's leader may be considered equivalent to its military commander, and may be designated as belonging to the second group (Fig. 8.2).

C. Proportionality—One of the considerations underlying the decision to carry out a targeted killing is the extent of the collateral damage expected in the operation. In this context, one can distinguish between the following five groups that reflect different levels of proportionality:

Fig. 8.3 Proportionality index

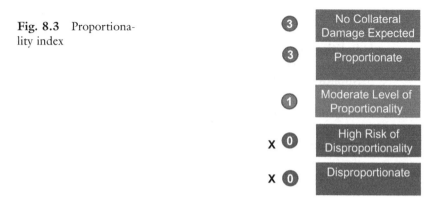

1. **No collateral damage**—Based on the existing intelligence regarding the target and his immediate surroundings at the time of the operation, no collateral damage is expected in the execution of the targeted killing.
2. **Proportionate**—In carrying out the targeted killing, minimal and proportionate collateral damage may be caused in order for the operation to be successful.
3. **Moderate level of proportionality**—The operation may cause moderate collateral damage. The justification and legitimacy of the action may be "borderline" in these cases.
4. **High risk of disproportionality**—The targeted killing may involve a high risk of disproportionate collateral damage.
5. **Disproportionate**—The collateral damage that is liable to be caused due to the targeted killing is disproportionate to the need and benefit of carrying out the operation.

The first two groups represent an assessment that the planned targeted killing operation will either not result in collateral damage, or that the damage will be proportional to the operational need and the benefit derived from the operation. Thus, the score given for such an action in these two groups is the highest (3). The score given to the third group reflects a moderate level of proportionality (2). The last two groups—the fourth and fifth—represent actions that either have a high risk of disproportionality or are absolutely disproportionate. In these cases, the targeted killing is illegitimate, and therefore the score given to these groups is 0. (Fig. 8.3).

D. Possibility of an alternative action—The considerations made at this stage of the decision-making process examine the possibility of taking a different course of action that will lead to the hoped-for result without having to kill the target. These alternatives may include actions such as apprehension and prosecution of the operative, his abduction from a hostile territory, a covert action of one kind or another, etc. In this context, one can distinguish between four possible situations:

Fig. 8.4 Alternative action index

1. The first reflects a situation in which there is no effective alternative to a targeted killing operation that will achieve the desired results.
2. In the second situation, it is possible that such an alternative does exist, though the cost of its execution may be high and severe, for example in terms of the level of risk to the lives of those carrying out the alternative operation.
3. In the third situation, there is an assessment that there may be an alternative to a targeted killing that will lead to the hoped-for results, and the risk involved in carrying it out is acceptable.
4. The fourth situation is one in which there is a good alternative to a targeted killing, and there is little or no risk involved in carrying it out.

In the first situation, there is no choice but to carry out the targeted killing in order to achieve the desired results, and therefore the score given is the highest (3). In the second situation, the expected cost of the alternative action may be high, which supports the preference for the targeted killing; therefore, the score given to this situation is (2). The last two situations—three and four, reflect an assessment that there may be an alternative action that will lead to reasonable or good results, and therefore, the targeted killing should not be carried out. The score given to these situations is 0 (Fig. 8.4).

E. Location of the operation—The following set of considerations relates to the location of the targeted killing operation. These are divided into five groups:

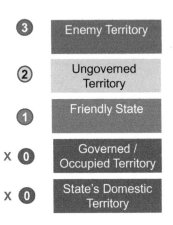

Fig. 8.5 Location of the operation index

1. The first group represents actions carried out in the territory of an enemy state—the targeted killing is required because it is unlikely that the enemy state will agree to extradite the target, it does not prevent him from operating in its territory, and may even sponsor and protect him.
2. The second group comprises actions carried out in areas with no effective governance—in these cases as well, the targeted killing is required because the state has no control and therefore also has no access to the location of the target, which effectively rules out less lethal alternatives.
3. The third group includes actions carried out in the territory of a friendly state and not in the territory of the state carrying out the targeted killing.

4. The fourth group represents targeted killing operations carried out in occupied territory or territory that is controlled by the state planning the operation but not in its sovereign territory.
5. The fifth group comprises targeted killings carried out in the sovereign territory of the state.

The first group reflects conditions in which the state has no choice but to employ the measure of targeted killings, which gives such operations a very high score (3). The second group also reflects a high level of necessity in carrying out the targeted killing, and its score is therefore (2). The third group reflects a situation in which the legitimacy of a targeted killing is questionable, and in which it may also be possible to bring about the neutralization of the threat through coordinated action with that country. However, assuming such neutralization is not possible because the said state is not willing to cooperate or respond to the request or demand to neutralize the target any other way, the score given to this option is low (1). The last two options regarding location reflect a situation where the state is assumed to have effective control, and therefore targeted killings should be avoided and less lethal alternatives preferred. Therefore, the score given to these two groups is 0 (Fig. 8.5).

F. Intelligence Opportunity—These considerations examine the question of whether and to what extent the targeted killing operation in question reflects an intelligence and operational opportunity for its execution. (For a lengthier discussion on this topic, see the analysis of the "operational opportunity axis" in Chapter 2). In this context, four possible situations can be identified:

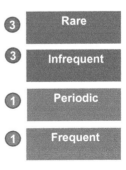

Fig. 8.6 Intelligence operational opportunity index

1. **Rare**—The first situation reflects one in which there is a one-time or rare intelligence and/or operational opportunity, in which a combination of conditions and circumstances required to carry out the operation exists.
2. **Infrequent**—The second situation is an intelligence and operational opportunity that is infrequent.
3. **Periodic**—In the third situation, the operational and intelligence opportunity is one that is likely to occur often.
4. **Frequent**—The fourth situation represents one in which the operational or intelligence opportunity is irrelevant, because the operational intelligence information regarding the target is abundant, so the operational opportunity is one that occurs frequently or is ongoing.

The first and second groups represent a situation in which there is a great need and urgency to carry out the targeted killing at that specific time and place, because if the operation is not carried out, the chances are slim that the rare happenstance of having the up-to-date and detailed intelligence required for this type of operation and the operational capability to carry it out will occur again. Thus, the score allocated to these two groups is high (3). The third and fourth groups reflect a low need to perform the action at that specific time and place, because the intelligence and operational opportunity may recur frequently or be ongoing (Fig. 8.6).

G. Intelligence realibilty—This last set of ethical considerations relates to the quality and degree of reliability of the intelligence information on which the decision to carry out targeted killings is based. This intelligence can be divided into four groups:

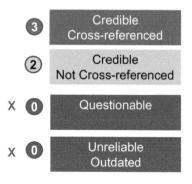

Fig. 8.7 Inteligence realiability index

8 A DECISION-MAKING MODEL FOR TARGETED KILLING OPERATIONS

1. Up-to-date and reliable intelligence information verified by at least two sources.
2. Up-to-date and reliable intelligence information that has not been verified by another source.
3. Intelligence information whose reliability is questionable.
4. Unreliable or outdated intelligence information.

The first type of intelligence information meets the high criteria required to carry out a targeted killing, with regard to the level of reliability of the information, the degree to which it is up-to-date, and in light of the fact that the information is verified by more than one source. Thus, the score attributed to this situation is (3). The second type of information receives a moderate score, because although it is estimated that the information is reliable and up-to-date, it has not verified by another source. The intelligence information in the third and fourth groups does not meet the level of reliability or currentness required to carry out targeted killings, and therefore its score is 0 (Fig. 8.7).

Assessing the Effectiveness of Targeted Killings

After an examination of the major moral dilemmas involved in carrying out a targeted killing, one can then turn to an assessment of the effectiveness of the planned operation. Each of the various measures for assessing effectiveness will be defined on a scale between 3 (very effective and -3 (a high level of counter-effectiveness). The six indices of effectiveness included in the proposed model are:

Fig. 8.8 Tacrical boomerang index

1. **Level of terrorism ("tactical boomerang")**—This index summarizes the assessment of the extent to which a targeted killing may lead to a reduction or, alternatively, an increase in the level of terrorism, both with regard to the number of attacks and the number of casualties. An assessment that the targeted killing will very likely result in a reduction in the level of terrorism will receive

a score of 3, medium probability will receive a 2, and low probability will receive a 1. An assessment that there is a high probability that the targeted assassination will cause an increase in the level of terrorism (in the number of attacks and/or the number of casualties) will receive a score of -3, medium probability will receive a -2, and low probability will receive a -1. (The assessment that the targeted killing is likely to increase the level of terrorism reflects the phenomenon of the "tactical boomerang") (Fig. 8.8).

2. **Level of terrorism ("operational boomerang")**—This index reflects the assessment of the likelihood of military or political entanglement following the targeted killing operation. A military entanglement may be a response of rocket fire toward Israel by the terrorist organization or a deterioration into a round of military combat (in Gaza or Lebanon), or alternatively a military entanglement with a neighboring country. A diplomatic entanglement may include damage to Israel's bilateral or multilateral relations and be expressed by public condemnation of Israel, harm to its diplomatic, trade and cultural relations, sanctions, boycotts, the establishment of an international investigatory commission, or even a deterioration into legal proceedings. The assessment of a high probability of entanglement will receive the score of -3, of medium probability -2, and of low probability 0 (Fig. 8.9).

Fig. 8.9 Operational boomerang index

3. **Level of terrorism ("strategic boomerang")** – This index reflects the assessment that the targeted killing operation may intensify hatred among the terrorist operatives and the public that supports them toward the state that carried out the operation and its citizens, and thus cause the conflict to escalate, deepen and prolong itself. The impact scale of this criterion therefore ranges from 0 (an assessment that there will be no impact) to -3 (an assessment that the targeted killing will have a high negative impact). Another criterion examined in the strategic boomerang index is the assessment of the degree of threat arising from the potential replacement who will

step into the target's shoes. The scale for this assessment ranges from 3 (the target's successor will be much less effective and dangerous than his predecessor, to -3 (an assessment that the target's successor will be much more effective and dangerous than his predecessor) (Fig. 8.10).

Fig. 8.10 Strategic boomerang index

4. **Disruption of the organization's activity**—This index examines the assessment of the degree of disruption to the functioning of the organization in the wake of the targeted killing, divided into three criteria: command and control, building infrastructure capabilities, and gathering resources (money). Each of these three criteria is given a score ranging from 0 to 3, based on whether the targeted killing is expected to result in a major setback to one of the above-mentioned criteria (3), a moderate setback (2), or a minor setback (1) (Fig. 8.11).

Fig. 8.11 Disruption of the organization's activity index

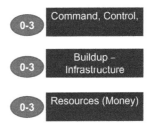

5. **Deterrence Index** – This index addresses three different criteria with regard to deterrence: An assessment of the degree to which other operatives in the terrorist organization or other organizations will be deterred from carrying out attacks due to the planned targeted killing; an assessment of the degree of to which new members will be deterred from enlisting in the terrorist organization due to the operation, and the extent to which the targeted killing

will deter various people from supporting the organization, either passively or actively. The scale for these indices ranges from 3 to -3, and the values represent a high (3), medium (2), or low (1) level of deterrence or alternatively a high (-3), medium (-2), or low (-1) level of motivation to join the organization, be more involved in its activities, or support it (Fig. 8.12).

Fig. 8.12 Deterrence index

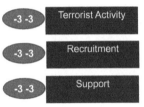

6. **Morale-Psychological Index** – This index measures the degree to which the targeted killing contributes or detracts from the national resilience of the state carrying out the operation, and the degree to which the targeted killing will raise or lower the internal morale of the terrorist organization and/or that of fellow organizations. The scale for these two criteria ranges from 3 to -3 (Fig. 8.13).

Fig. 8.13 Morale—Psychological index

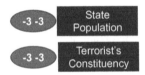

7. **Strategic Impact Index** – The final index examines the strategic impacts that the planned targeted killing may have, divided into three criteria: The first criterion assesses the likelihood that the targeted killing will accelerate the transition process from terrorism to guerrilla warfare (from attacks targeting a civilian population to those against military targets). The second criterion is the assessment of the likelihood that the targeted killing will lead to the organization renouncing its policy of terrorism. The third criterion denotes the likelihood that the targeted killing operation will lead to the eradication of the terrorist organization. These three criteria

comprise a scale ranging from 3, representing a high probability that the process will take place, to 0, representing zero probability that the process will occur (Fig. 8.14).

Fig. 8.14 Strategic impact index

All of the considerations outlined above, both those concerning the moral dilemmas involved in targeted killings and those regarding the effectiveness of these actions, can be weighed in one model that can assist in making decisions as to whether or not to carry out the operation. Thus, based on the existing intelligence prior to the targeted killing operation, and in accordance with the various assessments regarding the characteristics, results, and implications of the planned operation, the values outlined in each of the above indices can be incorporated into the model below, effectively quantifying the various moral and operational considerations.

The values that reflect the operational considerations and the degree of effectiveness of the planned targeted killing are assigned to the relevant indices, and the total score given to each index is then calculated. The values that reflect the moral dilemmas and considerations are also placed in the relevant indices, but are then multiplied; the result is then multiplied by the total effectiveness score. As we can see below, the act of multiplication makes it possible to give greater weight and even veto power to variables whose value is zero, because multiplying them by other variables will make the sum of the entire equation zero, and according to the model, if this is the case, the recommendation is to avoid carrying out the targeted killing. If the result is greater than zero, the action should be considered, and the greater the result, the stronger the recommendation is to carry out the operation.

What are the "veto" values that set the equation to zero? **In the index determining the aim of the targeted killing**, an operation intended solely for the purpose of punishing terrorists is prohibited and will set the equation to zero. **In the distinction index—the identity of the target**, an operation targeting an ideological or political leader (who is not involved in military activity) or alternatively a supporter of the terrorist organization, will set the equation to zero. As for the **index of proportionality**, any collateral damage that involves a high risk of disproportionality in relation to the military purpose that the operation is intended to achieve, or collateral damage that is definitely disproportionate, will result in a sum of zero and a recommendation to refrain from carrying out the operation. **In the index determining the possibility of an alternative action**, an assessment that there is indeed a high probability or certainty that a non-lethal alternative to the targeted killing can bring about the same military-operational achievement will also set the sum of the equation to zero. With regards to the **index indicating the location of the operation**, any action carried out in the territory of the state planning the operation or in territory under its control is unjustified (due to the state's ability to carry out other actions to thwart the planned attacks) and therefore will also set the equation to zero. **The intelligence index** is also given veto power over the execution of the targeted killing; when the quality and reliability of the intelligence information on which the operation is based are questionable or the information is not up-to-date, the sum of the equation will be zero. (Fig. 8.15).

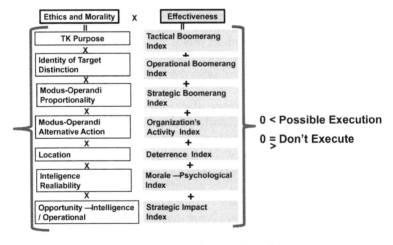

Fig. 8.15 Targeted killing decision making tool model

CHAPTER 9

Summary and Conclusions

In summary, targeted killings are perceived in Israel—by decision-makers at the political level, the operational echelon (the heads of the defense and intelligence establishment), and the general Israeli public—as a central, important, and effective counter-terrorism measure. It can be said that there is a consensus on this issue in Israel, though opinions are divided as to whether this measure should be used frequently, in order to put terrorist organizations on the defensive as much as possible; whether it should be reserved for very special cases, such as the immediate need to impede concrete and imminent attacks; or whether it should be used in order to have an impact on rounds of fighting with the terrorist organizations, for example in the Gaza Strip.

As described throughout the chapters of this book, Israel has used targeted killings since its inception as a response to the ongoing and evolving need to thwart various types of terrorist attacks perpetrated by the Palestinian and Shiite terrorist organizations; the scope of the use of this measure has varied over time. As the challenges have changed over the years, so has Israel's targeted killing policy. This is reflected in the setting of different goals for the targeted killing operations, the adoption of different modi operandi, the selection of different targets, the selection of different types of weapons, and the choice of different operational units to carry out the operations. The evolution that has taken place in Israel's counter-terrorism strategy, and in the role of targeted killings in

© The Author(s), under exclusive license to Springer Nature Switzerland AG 2022
B. Ganor and L. Koblentz-Stenzler, *Israel's Targeted Killing Policy*, https://doi.org/10.1007/978-3-031-13674-0_9

215

this strategy, is also reflected in changes in the decision-making processes prior to the implementation of these operations.

In general, the targeted killings carried out by Israel can be classified into two main groups: The first comprises operations designed to foil terrorist attacks (at different levels of imminency) and carried out against a concrete terrorist enemy—a terrorist operative directly or indirectly involved in the execution of terrorist attacks and whose elimination will most likely lead to the prevention of future attacks. The second category of targeted killings are those carried out against a terrorist-military enemy, that is, military operatives of a terrorist organization at various command levels who take part in the ongoing conflict between Israel and their organizations. These targeted killings are part of the State of Israel's fight against hybrid terrorist organizations—those that control territory and population (such as Hamas in Gaza and Hezbollah, and previously Fatah, in Lebanon) (Ganor, 2015), and who carry out guerrilla warfare and insurgencies (the striking of Israeli military targets) alongside terrorist acts. In either case, whether the targeted killings are directed against terrorist operatives involved in carrying out attacks or against military operatives of the terrorist organization, the justification for carrying them out rests on the laws of war, and not on the country's criminal code. This is due partly to the fact that these terrorist operatives pose an external threat to the state, and may infiltrate Israel from the territories of enemy states, the Gaza Strip, or territories controlled by the Palestinian Authority in the West Bank, for the purpose of carrying out terrorist and guerrilla attacks in Israel; or, they may deploy weapons (such as rocket fire) from these areas toward the territory of the State of Israel, thereby threatening its citizens and its military and security forces.

Targeted killings are not legitimate or justified if they are directed against a citizen of the state, or if they take place in the sovereign territory of the state or in an area controlled by the military or police forces of the state, who are able to reach the terrorist operative and detain him. In these cases, the relevant laws are criminal laws and not the laws of war, and hence the use of targeted killings in these cases would be considered illegal and immoral. This is not the case, however, when a terrorist is arrested in the territory of the state and he and his comrades are armed, shooting, and resisting arrest. Moreover, when there is a particularly severe internal terrorist threat in a country (as there is in Israel), it is certainly possible to pass specific legislation for the crime of terrorism and impose a harsh punishment (even the death penalty) on those convicted of it, though the state will be obligated to arrest and bring the terrorists to trial, and not carry out targeted killings.

All targeted killing operations against those belonging to the second group described above—military operatives involved in hostilities against Israel—were carried out by the IDF. These targeted killings usually took place during rounds of fighting between Israel and the military forces of the various terrorist organizations in the Gaza Strip or other areas. In contrast, targeted killings that were intended to foil concrete or future terrorist attacks (those belonging to first group discussed above), were generally carried out by the ISA and the IDF, in close cooperation and led by one of the two bodies, depending on the circumstances of the case. In instances of targeted killings in the territory of distant or enemy countries, the operations were carried out for the most part by the Mossad, sometimes in cooperation with the IDF. The majority of the targeted killings in the second group (in the framework of the fight against the terrorist organizations) were carried out openly, with the adversary—the terrorist organization—aware that Israel was behind the operation. This was also the case with most of the operations in the context of the first group (those with the aim of foiling terrorist attacks), with the exception of a number of cases in which the targeted killings were carried out under a veil of secrecy, and without Israel taking responsibility for them. Some of these actions took place in the territory of distant lands, enemy states, and territories under the control of terrorist organizations.

This book offers two models for the classification and analysis of targeted killing operations. These models, which are integrated with one another, include the **Operational Need Model**, which combines the **Target Profile Axis**, categorizing the types of operatives against whom the targeted killing is directed (see Chapter 5), with the **Operational Opportunity Axis** (see Chapter 3), and creates a scale of the degree of necessity of carrying out the targeted killing (see Chapter 6); and the **Decision-Making Model for Targeted Killings** (detailed in Chapter 8)—a staged and integral operational model that weighs the moral dilemmas and the questions regarding effectiveness that are analyzed throughout the book.

The proposed classification into two groups of targeted killings in effect creates a distinction between two categories on the **Target Profile Axis**—that of targets associated with the goal of thwarting (concrete or future) terrorist attacks, and that of military terrorist operatives involved in combat against the state. The first category includes four types of targets: "ticking bombs"—terrorists who are about to embark on an attack, having completed all or most of the necessary preparations; terrorist operatives involved in the preparation of a concrete terrorist attack; operatives involved in planning the attack; and terrorist operatives involved in producing the capabilities required to carry out attacks ("ticking infrastructure"). The second category of military terrorist operatives includes three types of targets: military commanders—senior military operatives at the highest levels of command of the terrorist organization; military operatives—lower-ranking combatants and field operatives, and combat supporters—activists who assist in the day-to-day management of the terrorist organization. The **Target Profile Axis** includes two more categories—leaders of terrorist organizations and supporters of the organization. These two categories, however, differ from the others, as the justification, insofar as it exists, to carry out the targeted killing of a leader of a terrorist organization stems from his involvement in shaping the organization's terrorism strategy (therefore belonging to the first group, of thwarting attacks), or his direction of the organization's military activity (therefore belonging to the second group, involvement in military action). As for the supporters of the terrorist organization, who comprise the far end of the scale of the Target Profile Axis, an analysis of the interviews conducted with Israeli decision-makers concludes that they are not legitimate targets for targeted killings.

The first model presented in the book, the **Operational Need Model**, combines the Target Profile Axis with the Operational Opportunity Axis (which is a function of intelligence availability and the operational maturity to carry out the operation) and offers a division into three categories of legitimacy of targeted killings. The first category corresponds with the first group of targeted killings described above, those designed to thwart concrete or future terrorist attacks. In these cases, the action will be considered legitimate in any situation of operational opportunity (subject to its upholding the principle of proportionality). The second category in the model corresponds with the second group, comprising military operatives involved in hostilities. Here, the model states that in principle there is legitimacy to carry out the targeted killing, but there is no urgency to do so, as it is not intended to foil a concrete terrorist attack; therefore, operational opportunity considerations have a greater impact, as do the implications of this opportunity on potential collateral damage. The third category of this model denotes political and ideological leaders of the terrorist organization who are not involved in formulating its terrorism policy or in directing the organization's military activity, as well as supporters of a terrorist organization who are not active members of it. In these cases, according to the model, even when there is a rare operational opportunity to carry out a targeted killing operation against them, it will not be considered legitimate.

The second model presented in this book—the **Decision-Making Model for Targeted Killings**—encapsulates all of the book's insights in an operational model that is staged and integral, making it possible to weigh both the normative issues and the questions related to the effectiveness of targeted killings; it may therefore be used as a tool for prospective decision-making and for retrospective analyses of targeted killings carried out by Israel and by other countries around the world.

The models presented above, which examine the fundamental operational and ethical questions at the core of targeted killings, are modular and integrative. It should be noted that the preliminary calculations of the effectiveness of targeted killing operations are both complex and problematic, especially in light of the fact that these calculations are based on intelligence assessments that are usually incomplete, and not always clear or credible. However, targeted killing operations are by nature a proactive activity. This makes it possible, in most cases, to evaluate the different categories of the aforementioned models and on this basis approve, cancel, or postpone a targeted killing operation; perform it in another location; or use an alternative modus operandi. Furthermore, there is a direct link between the two perspectives—the evaluation of the efficacy of a targeted killing operation and the evaluation of its legality and legitimacy. If the legality and legitimacy of a targeted killing operation are questioned by an international legal tribunal or by the public, this will be detrimental to the efficacy of the operation; it may lead to negative international reactions and dilute the state's deterrent capability.

Moreover, since it is reasonable to assume that a targeted killing operation whose cost outweighs its benefits will not be carried out, the legal and moral considerations become redundant. This insight provides a much-needed link between the two bodies of literature on targeted killings—that on the efficacy of the measure and that on its legality.

With regards to the matter of the effectiveness of Israel's targeted killing operations, the concluding model presented in Chapter 8 proposes calculating their effectiveness by integrating several indices: To what extent is the action expected to reduce the number of attacks or casualties in the future? How likely is the operation to result in a boomerang response? To what extent will it disrupt the functioning of the terrorist organization? To what extent will the action deter other activists from becoming involved in terrorist activities? What will the psychological effects and the impact on morale be? And will the targeted killing lead to a strategic shift in the terrorist organization's activities? In this context, it is worth reiterating the distinction made in the book between the three types of possible boomerang effects in the wake of a targeted killing—the tactical, operational, and strategic boomerangs. The tactical boomerang effect may manifest in revenge attacks; the operational boomerang may involve military entanglement (including the firing of rockets at Israel) or diplomatic imbroglios; and the strategic boomerang effect is expressed in the long-term consequences of a targeted killing. These may include the replacement of the deceased target by a more militant and skilled leader, military and technological build up by the terrorist organization, and an intensification of hatred among the population of the adversary. These calculations of effectiveness may be based on a prospective (forward-looking) assessment carried out as part of the decision-making process on a targeted killing, or may be performed retrospectively to evaluate the effectiveness of a targeted killing operation with hindsight (such an analysis should be performed at different points in time—in the short term [immediately after the operation], in the medium term [several weeks or months after the operation] and in the long term [several years after the operation was carried out].

In any case, it should be borne in mind that the moral considerations and the questions regarding the effectiveness of a targeted killing operation do not reflect the full picture of the considerations facing the decision maker in deliberating whether to carry out such an action. There are also political issues (the state of the political system in the country), geostrategic affairs in the local, regional or global arena, and other considerations that may influence or be affected by the decision to carry out a targeted killing.

In conclusion, the scope of the targeted killings carried out by Israel over the years, the various modi operandi it has employed, and the varied profiles of the targets of these operations make Israel an important case study and a reference for other western democratic countries that use, or are considering using, targeted killings as part of their counter-terrorism arsenal. Although there are differences in the scope, characteristics, and perception of the terrorist threat Israel faces in comparison to other states, the models offered in this book for evaluating the legality, morality, and effectiveness of targeted killings, which rely on the Israeli experience, can assist other countries in establishing a systematic and balanced decision-making process on the subject of targeted killings.

REFERENCE

Ganor, B. (2015). *Global alert: The rationality of modern Islamist terrorism and the challenge to the liberal democratic world*. Columbia University Press.

APPENDICES

Appendix A—Interviewees for this Book

- Maj. Gen. (Res.) Sharon Afek, Former Chief Military Advocate General of the IDF,
- Prof. Aharon Barak, Former Chief of Israel's Supreme Court,
- Yossi Cohen, Former Mossad Director,
- Avi Dichter, Former ISA Director, and Former Minister,
- Col. (Res.) Avi Eliyahu, Former IDF Intelligence Commander of the Southern District,
- Naftali Granot, Former Mossad Deputy Director,
- Lt. Gen. (Res.) Dan Halutz, Former IDF Chief of Staff,
- Shalom Ben Hanan, Former Senior ISA Official,
- Brig. Gen. (Res.) Gal Hirsch, Former 91st Division Commander of the IDF,
- Prof. Asa Kasher, Military Ethics Expert, and Author of the IDF Code of Ethics,
- Col. (Res.) Lior Lotan, Former Prime Minister's Special Envoy for MIA and KIA,
- Dan Meridor, Former Minister,
- Lt. Gen. (Res.) Shaul Mofaz, Former Defense Minister and IDF Chief of Staff,
- Oz Noy, Former Senior ISA Official,

© The Editor(s) (if applicable) and The Author(s), under exclusive license to Springer Nature Switzerland AG 2022
B. Ganor and L. Koblentz-Stenzler, *Israel's Targeted Killing Policy*,
https://doi.org/10.1007/978-3-031-13674-0

224 APPENDICES

- Brig. Gen. (Res.) Nitzan Nuriel, Former Director of Israel's Counter-Terrorism Bureau,
- Ehud Olmert, Former Prime Minister,
- Col. (Res.) Adv. Daniel Reisner, Former Head of the IDF International Law Department,
- Shabtai Shavit, Former Mossad Director,
- Brig. Gen. (Res.) Dr. Amnon Sofrin, Former Head of the Mossad's Intelligence Directorate,
- Lt. Gen. (Res.) Moshe (Bogie) Ya'alon, Former Defense Minister and IDF Chief of Staff.
- Lt. Gen. (Res.) Gadi Eisenkot, Former IDF Chief of Staff.
- Arik (Harris) Barbing, Former Head of the Jerusalem and West Bank Sector of the Shin Bet

Appendix B—Author's Interviewees from the 1990s and 2000s

- Prof. Moshe Arens, Former Minister of Defense
- Lt. Gen. (Res.) Gabi Ashkenazi, Former IDF Chief of Staff and Minister of Foreign Affairs
- Maj. Gen. (Ret.) Meir Dagan, Former Mossad Director
- Rafi Eitan, Former Counter-Terrorism Adviser to the Prime Minister
- Maj. Gen. (Res.) Shlomo Gazit, Former head of the IDF Military Intelligence
- Carmi Gillon, Former ISA Director
- Lt. Gen. (Res.) Amnon Lipkin-Shahak, Former IDF Chief of Staff
- Benjamin Netanyahu, Former Prime Minister
- Ehud Olmert, Former Prime Minister
- Shimon Peres, Former President and Prime Minister of Israel
- Yaakov Perry, Former ISA Director
- Brig. Gen. (Res.) Yigal Pressler, Former Counter-Terrorism Advisor to the Prime Minister
- Yitzhak Shamir, Former Prime Minister
- Ariel Sharon, Former Prime Minister
- Maj. Gen. (Ret.) Rehavam Ze'evi ("Gandhi"), Former Counter-Terrorism Advisor to the Prime Minister and Former Minister

INDEX

A
Abayat, Hussein, 34, 35
Abu Hanoud, Mahmoud, 35
Abu Jihad (Khalil al-Wazir), 21, 22, 191, 192
Abu-Khair, Hussein, 19
Abu Shanab, Ismail, 35
Additional Protocol to the Geneva Convention, Article 51 (5) (b), 147
Adwan, Kamal, 20
Afek, Sharon, 60, 69, 70, 119, 130, 148
Akel, Emed, 25
al-Abed, Hani, 26
al-Aqsa Martyrs Brigades, 89, 125, 141
al-Ata, Abu, 123
Al-Ata, Baha Abu, 38
al-Ghoul, Adnan, 78, 127, 162
Al-Hawajah, Mahmoud, 27
al-Hindi, Amin, 71, 115
al-Kalak, Izz al-Din, 21
Al-Kubaisi, Basil, 18, 19

al-Mabhouh, Mahmoud, 37, 185
al-Musawi, Abbas, 23, 24, 177, 190
al-Najjar, Muhammad Youssef, 20
Alon, Yiga, 14
al-Qassam Brigades, 164
al-Rantissi, Abdel Aziz, 36, 70, 71, 181, 191
Alternative action, 205, 206, 214
al-Wazir, Khalil, 191
al-Zahar, Mahmoud, 29
al-Zubaidi, Zakariya, 141
Amit, Meir, 17
Amman, 29, 181, 192–194
Ankara, 177
Annan, Kofi, 149, 170
Arad, Ron, 24
Arafat, Yasser, 20, 21, 79, 80, 116, 135, 191, 192
Arens, Moshe, 24, 183
Ashkelon, 29
Ashkenazi, Gabi, 34, 72, 104, 150
As-Sa'iqa, 137
Association for Civil Rights, 34
Athens, 19, 21

© The Editor(s) (if applicable) and The Author(s), under exclusive license to Springer Nature Switzerland AG 2022
B. Ganor and L. Koblentz-Stenzler, *Israel's Targeted Killing Policy*, https://doi.org/10.1007/978-3-031-13674-0

225

226 INDEX

Atrash, Muhammad, 26
Atzi, Ali Othman Muhammad, 26
Ayyad, Massoud, 35
Ayyash, Yahya, 28, 29, 71, 126, 163, 178, 179

B
Baader–Meinhof, 19
Barak, Aharon, 61, 121, 137, 154
Barak, Ehud, 25, 26, 35, 103, 114
Barbing, Arik "Harris", 13, 25, 47, 56, 58, 62, 65, 67, 86, 184
Barghouti, Marwan, 116
Basic Law of Israel, 88
Batash, Issam, 125
Begin, Menachem, 104
Beinisch, Dorit, 6, 7
Beirut, 20, 79, 98, 108
Beit Lid junction, 26, 28, 97
Beit Sahur, 34
Belgium, 21
Ben-Eliezer, Fouad, 167
Ben Hanan, Shalom, 47, 48, 62, 68, 86, 117, 118, 134, 135, 152, 186
Biran, Ilan, 27
Black September, 17–20, 79
Blum, Gabriella, 147
Boomerang effect, 2, 11, 64, 175, 176, 179, 180, 182, 183, 185–187, 189, 192, 195, 220
Bouchikhi, Ahmed, 20, 80
Boudia, Mohamed, 19
British Immigration Policy, 15
British Mandate, 13, 15, 79
British Resident Minister, 15
Brussels, 21
Buenos Aires, 24, 177, 183
Bush, George W., 94

C
"Caesarea" (Special Forces Unit), 18, 80, 193
Caesar, Julius, 43
Cairns, Ralph, 15
Canada, 31
Cannes, 21
Ciechanover Commission, 31
Cohen, Noam, 26
Cohen, Yossi, 63, 64, 97, 122
Combatants, 5, 6, 9, 113, 118–120, 137, 218
Combat Support, 131, 140, 203, 218
Committee of Secret Service Chiefs, 18
Committee of Two, 54
Committee X, 18, 97, 108, 109
Communications intelligence (COMINT), 70, 73
Counter-terrorism, 1–3, 9, 10, 13, 15, 17, 22, 25, 27, 43, 52, 58, 66, 70, 73, 88, 91, 92, 102–108, 124, 130, 154, 156, 158, 170, 175, 176, 182, 183, 185, 189, 215, 220
Criminal Investigation Department, 15
Cyprus, 19, 20, 98

D
Dagan, Meir, 49, 103, 105–107, 138, 179
Dahariya Prison, 27
Damascus, 115
Dani, Fadl, 21
Darwish, Ismail, 21
David, Steven, 8, 33, 34
Dayan, 193, 194
Decision-Making Model for Targeted Killings, 11, 12, 217
Deif, Mohammed, 77, 78, 162–165

INDEX 227

Democratic Front for the Liberation of Palestine, 21
Dershowitz, Prof. Alan, 98, 147, 149
Deterrence, 15, 18, 95, 96, 100, 176, 179, 184, 188, 201
Deterrence Index, 211, 212
Dichter, Avi, 46, 47, 64, 65, 68, 69, 128, 151, 163, 165–167, 182
Diskin, Yuval, 34, 72
Distinction Index, 213
Dizengoff Center, 29, 127
Dolphinarium, 36, 100, 134
"Duvdevan" (Special Forces Unit), 27

E
Eilat, 125, 126
Eisenkot, Gadi, 34, 37, 45, 54, 62, 68, 74, 128, 135, 136, 150, 184
Eitan, Rafi, 17, 22, 23, 103
Elazar, David, 98
Eliyahu, Avi, 50, 66, 73, 121, 158, 185
Erez Crossing, 163
Etzel, 14
Europe/European, 15, 19, 37, 79, 141
Expected collateral damage, 157, 159, 160, 169
Ezra, Gideon, 178

F
Fadlallah, Muhammad, 177
Falah, Adel, 27
Falk, Ophir, 8, 176, 184
Fatah, 3, 17, 20, 21, 33, 35, 79, 80, 116, 153, 192, 216
Fatah Hawks, 25
Fatah's Force, 35
Fatah's Tanzim Wing, 34, 116
Fatah's Western Sector, 20
Fedayeen, 16

First Additional Protocol to the Geneva Conventions, 119, 145
First Intifada, 21, 140, 192
Foreign Affairs and Defense Committee, 28
France, 21, 117

G
Galili, 34
Gal-On, Zehava, 89
Gaza City, 164, 166
Gaza Strip, 3, 10, 16, 26, 29, 33, 35–38, 45, 49, 53, 65, 72, 77, 78, 90, 98, 104, 119, 123, 126, 128, 131, 137, 141, 162–164, 166, 181, 184, 185, 191, 195, 215–217
Gazit, Shlomo, 23, 24, 50, 51
General Counsel of the U.S. Air Force, 62
General Counsel of the U.S. Army, 61
Gera, Ehud ben, 43
Ghazala, Munzer Abu, 21
Ghulmeh, Jihad Faiz, 27
Gilad Shalit, 37
Gillon, Carmi, 103, 104
Goldstone Effect, 121
Goldstone, Richard, 121
Granot, Naftali, 67, 124, 125, 136, 137
Great Britain, 21
Gross, Emanuel, 72, 100
Guiora, Amos, 147, 156
Gulf War, 102

H
Habash, George, 108
Haber, Eitan, 108
Hadid, Eyad Abu, 26
Hadri, Hamad, 131
Hafez, Mustafa, 16

228   INDEX

Halutz, Dan, 36, 54, 57, 58, 69, 77, 99, 104, 105, 133, 161–163, 181, 182

Hamas, 3, 24–27, 29, 31–33, 35–37, 45, 53, 70, 71, 76–78, 90, 91, 115, 121, 128, 130, 132, 133, 136, 140–142, 162–165, 180, 181, 185, 188, 191–195, 216

Hamdan of Khan Yunis, Abd al-Rahman, 26

Hammami, Said, 20

Hamshari, Mahmoud, 18, 19

Haniyeh, Ismail, 141, 162, 191

Harari, Mike, 80

Harel, Isser, 16, 17, 35, 78, 90, 166

Hassan, Hatan, 27

Hebron, 26, 27

Hefetz, Amir, 176, 184

Hellfire missiles, 78, 141, 163, 181

Hezbollah, 23, 24, 29, 117, 126, 129, 130, 150, 177, 185, 190, 216

Hirsch, Gal, 33, 55, 100, 136, 150

Hudna, 141

Human intelligence (HUMINT), 70, 73

Human shields, 10, 75, 145, 148, 158, 160, 166, 167

Husain, Kamal, 21

I

Index indicating the location of the operation, 214

Intelligence index, 214

International Committee of the Red Cross (ICRC), 146, 147, 155

1966 International Covenant on Civil and Political Rights (CCPR), 87, 88

International Institute for Counter-Terrorism (ICT), 51,

52, 95, 124, 126, 130, 137, 158, 159, 182

Ishim, Hisul, 85

Israel Defense Forces (IDF), 11, 16, 20, 21, 25, 26, 29, 31, 34–36, 38, 44–46, 49, 50, 54–60, 62, 64–66, 68, 72, 78, 80, 89, 95, 99, 103, 104, 106, 116, 118, 119, 121–123, 128, 133, 135, 148, 150, 151, 155, 157, 158, 161, 163, 164, 166, 168–170, 178, 180–182, 184, 185, 190, 217

Israeli Air Force, 20, 98, 161, 168, 184

Israeli Minister of Tourism Rehavam, 35

Israeli Navy, 20

Israeli Supreme Court, 3, 10, 91, 94, 118

Israel Securities Authority (ISA), 11, 17, 18, 26, 27, 29, 34

Issa, Yusuf, 72

Izz ad-Din al-Qassam Brigades, 71, 76, 128, 165

J

Jabari, Ahmad, 37

Jerusalem, 27–29, 35, 68, 178, 192, 193

Jewish Section, 15

Johnston, Patrick B., 9

Judea and Samaria, 3, 36, 98, 127

K

Kafisha, Taher, 27

Kahil, Kamal, 27

Kanafani, Ghassan, 20, 108, 109

Karmi, Raed, 35, 89

Kasher, Prof. Asa, 85, 86, 88, 93, 96, 99, 101, 115–117, 125–127,

131, 146, 147, 149, 154–156, 158, 165, 180, 186, 187
Katyushas, 80
Kfar Ar-Ram, 26
Khader, Naim, 21
Kidon unit, 79
King Eglon, 43
King Hussein of Jordan, 141, 193
Kiryat Shmona, 80
Kleinwachter, Hans, 17
Knesset, 88, 89
Knut Dörmann, 155
Kremnitzer, Prof. Mordechai, 13, 14, 85, 87, 89, 92, 93, 114, 149, 190
Kretzmer, David, 156
Krug, Heinz, 17
Kuwait, 21, 192

L
Lebanon, 23, 65, 79, 80, 98, 108, 184, 185, 190, 210, 216
Legibility and Speed-of-Exploitation System (L&S), 9
Lehi, 14, 15
Lillehammer, 20, 79, 80
Lipkin-Shahak, Amnon, 103, 106, 182
Lod, 108
London, 21
Lord Moyne, 15
Lotan, Lior, 105, 131

M
Mahane Yehuda market, 193
Makdama, Ibrahim, 35
Malchin, Zvi, 17
Malta, 28, 97, 137
Martyrs, 8
Marzouk, Moussa Abu, 193

Mashal, Khaled, 29, 30, 141, 181, 184, 191–195
Meir, Golda, 17–19, 34, 79, 108
Meir, Goldeon, 169
Meraish, Mamoun, 21
Meretz, 89
Meridor, Dan, 92, 117, 124, 136, 166
"Metro" project, 164
Military Advocate General, 34, 60, 69, 119, 130, 147, 148
Military Commander, 128–130, 138, 140, 148, 200, 202, 203, 218
Military Intelligence, 12, 18, 23, 26, 29, 31, 50, 53, 58, 66, 73, 115
Military Necessity, 159
Military Operative, 129, 130, 138, 202, 203, 216–218
Ministerial Committee on Security Affairs, 18
Mir, Asfandyar, 9
Moafi, Salim, 25
Mofaz, Shaul, 26, 33–35, 37, 44, 45, 57, 123, 124, 148, 149, 180, 190
Mohana, Rabah, 177
Mohsen, Zuheir, 21, 136
Morale-Psychological Index, 212
Mossad, 3, 11, 16–18, 20, 21, 26, 28, 29, 31, 32, 37, 48, 49, 53, 56, 58, 63–65, 67, 79, 80, 96, 97, 99, 103, 108, 122, 124, 132, 136, 141, 153, 179, 180, 185, 186, 193–195, 217
Mubarak, 44
Muchassi, Zaid, 19
Mughniyeh, Imad, 64, 65, 117, 129
Munich, 17, 18, 20, 79, 80, 96, 108
Munich Olympics, 17, 79, 85, 96, 97, 108
Muqata, 135
Muslim Brotherhood, 192

230 INDEX

Mustafa, Abu Ali, 35, 177, 178

N
Nablus, 26, 35
Nasrallah, Hassan, 150, 190
Nassar, Akram, 71
Nasser, Kammal, 20
Natche, Tarek, 27
Nazal, Khalen, 21
Netanyahu, Benjamin, 29, 31, 38,
103, 105, 131, 193–195
Netzarim, 26
Nicosia, 19–21
Noy, Oz, 14, 19, 47, 55–57, 69, 86,
97, 106, 127, 128, 137, 151,
188
Nuriel, Nitzan, 64, 65, 97, 132, 151,
152, 187, 188

O
Offensive Retaliatory Actions, 15
Olma, Ahad, 178
Olmert, Ehud, 44, 52, 53, 94–96,
117, 127, 129, 132
Operational boomerang, 11, 175,
183, 185, 186, 195, 220
Operational Need Model, 12, 139,
217, 218
Operational Opportunity Axis, 74,
139, 207, 217, 218
Operation Anemone Picking, 157
Operation Damocles, 17
Operation Defensive Shield, 36, 135,
148
Operation Guardian of the Walls, 78,
132
Operation Pillar of Defense, 37, 38
Operation Protective Edge, 78, 158
Operation Spring of Youth, 20, 98
Operation Wrath of God, 18–20, 79,
97

OSINT, 73
Oslo Accords, 15, 24, 29, 33
Oslo process, 8, 32, 192

P
Palestinian Authority (PA), 3, 25, 36,
71, 89, 90, 116, 166, 192, 216
Palestinian Islamic Jihad (PIJ), 24, 26,
27, 32, 33, 97, 137
Palestinian Liberation Organization
(PLO), 15, 18–22, 24, 80, 98
Paris, 19–21
Park Hotel (attack), 36, 99, 134
Peace process, 13, 15, 24, 25, 32, 33
Peres, Shimon, 22, 28, 29, 44, 148,
179
Pgiah Monaat, 86
Plaw, Avery, 9
Political and Ideological Leader
(Target Profile Axis), 203, 218
Popular Front for the Liberation of
Palestine (PFLP), 17, 20, 21, 35,
108, 109, 177, 178
Pressler, Yigal, 182
Price, Bryan, 7, 8, 189
Principle of double effect, 147
Principle of proportionality, 6, 129,
147, 148, 154, 155, 159, 218
Prisko, Oren, 169
Punitive action, 90, 113, 201

Q
Qassam project, 162
Qassem, Naim, 177
Qawasmi, Ibrahim, 27
Qibya, 16
Quasi-judicial, 18, 97, 98, 109

R
Rabin, Yitzhak, 24, 26, 28, 72, 97

INDEX 231

Rafah, 25
Ramallah, 35, 135
Ramat Eshkol, 27
Ramila, Marwan Abu, 26
Raziel, David, 15
Red Brigades, 19
Red Prince, 79
Reisner, Daniel, 59–61, 77, 100, 101, 120, 121, 131, 132, 154, 157, 164, 168, 188
Rivlin, Eliezer, 5
Rome, 19, 21
Rousseau, Jean-Jacques, 93
Rubinstein, Elyakim, 14, 90

S
Sa'adat, Ahmad, 178
Sa'adon, Ilan, 140
Salameh, Ali Hassan, 20, 79, 80, 99
Salameh, Hassan, 79
Salim, Jamal, 35
Sarbah, Anoop K., 9
Sasportas, Avi, 141, 185
Sderot, 104
Second Intifada/Al-Aqsa Intifada, 2, 8, 13, 15, 33, 34, 37, 44, 59, 71, 72, 85, 90, 114, 124, 127, 148, 152, 161, 165, 176, 181
Security Cabinet, 23, 26, 52, 53, 62
September 11, 157
Shamir, Yitzhak, 16, 22, 102, 103, 106
Shaqaqi, Fathi, 28, 97, 137
Sharon, Ariel, 37, 45, 60, 105, 142, 149, 167, 169, 183
Sharon, Arik, 22
Sharvit-Baruch, Pnina, 147
Shavit, Shabtai, 16, 48, 49, 63, 96, 97, 132, 133, 153, 180, 186
Shehadeh, Nader, 27
Shehadeh, Salah, 36, 76, 77, 128, 129, 148, 162, 163, 165–170

Sheikh Radwan, 26, 78
Sheikh Yassin, 31, 64, 141, 165, 180, 181, 191, 195
Shiite, 3, 38, 177, 190, 215
Shin Bet/Israel's Internal Security Agency (ISA), 11, 14, 46, 47, 49, 53–56, 58, 62, 65, 68, 69, 71–73, 76, 86, 90, 97, 103, 106, 122, 127, 128, 134, 136, 137, 151, 152, 163, 165, 167, 178, 182, 184, 186, 188, 193, 217
Shuja'iyya, 25
Siam, Said, 191
Sikul memukad, 14, 85, 86
Silwad, 192
Six Day War, 192
Sofrin, Amnon Sofrin, 55, 56, 97, 184, 185
Special Investigatory Commission, 76, 77, 147, 165–170
Special Negotiator on Hostages and Missing Persons, 105, 131
Stein, Yael, 72, 114
Stern Gang, 14
Strategic boomerang, 11, 175, 187, 189, 192, 193, 195, 210, 220
Strategic Decision Index, 213
Strategic Impact Index, 212
Suleiman, Omar, 44, 45
Supporter of terrorism, 137, 138

T
Tactical boomerang effect, 178, 180, 220
Tanzim, 35
Tapuah Junction, 127
Target bank, 53, 66, 67
Targeted assassination, 13, 210
Targeted prevention, 14, 85
Target Profile Axis, 122, 138, 139, 217, 218
Tel Aviv, 26, 28, 29

232 INDEX

Terrorism equation, 176
Tevel, 193
Thabet, Thabet, 35, 116
Ticking bomb, 44, 53–56, 86, 92,
117, 122–125, 127, 134, 138,
140, 148, 159, 200, 202, 218
Ticking infrastructure, 127, 138, 140,
200, 202, 218
Timor, Chaim, 20
Tominaga, Yasutaka, 9
Tulkarem, 35, 89, 116
Tunis, 21, 22, 192
Tuqan, Samir, 21
Tzomet, 193

U
UN Human Rights Committee, 87
1948 United Nations General
Assembly's Resolution on the
Universal Declaration of Human
Rights (UDHR), 87
United States (US), 117, 141, 157,
177, 193

V
Vilnai, Matan, 163
Visual intelligence (VISINT), 73

W
Walzer, Michael, 93, 114
War of Independence, 16

Weizmann, Ezer, 22
West Bank, 25, 26, 33, 35, 38, 49,
65, 90, 116, 122, 127, 137, 141,
177, 184, 192, 216

Y
Ya'alon, Moshe (Bogie), 66, 95, 106,
118, 133, 134, 157, 163, 168,
179, 182
Yadlin, Amos, 85, 91, 146, 149, 155,
156, 165, 169
Yamur, Hamed, 27
Yariv, Aharon, 17, 19
Yaron, Ruth, 36
Yassin, Ahmed, 36, 70, 133,
140–142, 191
Yassin, Ali, 21
Yatom, Danny, 29, 193–195
Yehud, 16
Yehuda, Mahane, 193
Yusuf Naj, Abd al-Manam
Muhammad, 26
Yusuf, Nasser, 27

Z
Zamir, Zvi, 18, 99, 155, 156
Zayd, Mussa Abu, 19
Ze'evi Rehavam ("Gandhi"), 35, 107,
178
Zussman, Asaf, 2, 9
Zussman, Noam, 2, 9
Zwaiter, Abdel Wael, 19